Re-defining Feminisms

Re-defining Feminisms

EDITED BY

RANJANA HARISH

V. BHARATHI HARISHANKAR

RAWAT PUBLICATIONS

Jaipur • New Delhi • Bangalore • Hyderabad • Guwahati • Kolkata

ISBN 81-316-0123-4

Reprinted, 2014

Published by
Prem Rawat for **Rawat Publications**
Satyam Apts, Sector 3, Jawahar Nagar, Jaipur 302 004 (India)
Phone: 0141 265 1748 / 7006 Fax: 0141 265 1748
E-mail: info@rawatbooks.com
Website: www.rawatbooks.com

New Delhi Office
4858/24, Ansari Road, Daryaganj, New Delhi 110 002
Phone: 011 2326 3290

Also at *Bangalore, Hyderabad, Guwahati* and *Kolkata*

Typeset by Rawat Computers, Jaipur
Printed at Thomson Press (India) Ltd., New Delhi

Dedicated to the loving memory of

RITA NAGAR DESAI

who braved through the re-definitions that life held out.

Contents

II
Re-think

III
Re-view

IV
Re-mark

Foreword

PUSHPA BHAVE

Former Head, Department of Marathi, SNDT University, Mumbai
Drama Critic, Peace Activist & Feminist

The word 'feminisms', used in the plural, is a conceptual strategy. The philosophy of feminism does not limit itself to gender difference or to difference experienced only by women. Feminisms look at the human world with fresh perceptions. Women have learned from the patriarchal logic of using the category 'human' for a restricted, non-inclusive usage. So feminisms accept that it cannot be a monolith, it looks at the human predicament from various angles. Moreover, the feminist theory of creating knowledge as they go along in activism, keeps knowledge fluid as an ongoing process. They do not want to crystallize knowledge systems to exclude the other's perception. As such, though we have various feminisms, the process of rethinking, revaluation does not stop.

As academician we do look at the established schools of thought historically. Liberal, Radical, French, Anglo-American, Existentialist, Psychoanalytic, Marxist, Postcolonial, Post-modern, Eco-feminism; one look at this list would speak of the cultural history, multidisciplinary outlook. One might cynically question the above feminisms as originating from patriarchal knowledge. Feminism has crossed the barrier long back. Various feminisms have critically examined the various disciplines, and their hypotheses, from their own perspective. In fact, a strong argument like the Marxists was first questioned by feminists. The subtle use of linguistics and psychology by feminism has added to the discipline.

We reject the claim that it all began with the Women's Year in 1975. In India, when one is re-defining feminism, one is situated in a postcolonial, postmodern situation. The social structure calls for a careful study of the caste and gender inter-connection. As the western feminist thought and its expression was challenged by our Afro-American sisters, it was called white, middle class, Eurocentric. Now, in India we have our Dalit sisters who question the mainstream (?) feminism as 'Brahmani'. Women's autobiographies, especially by Dalit women, challenge the norms of traditional autobiography. Indian feminism, the consciousness of 'me' and the 'other', is very much present in the poetry of women saints. We interpret myths by the tools of feminism.

Dr. Babasaheb Ambedkar had experienced the intersection of caste and class himself. But, apart from that, he pronounced that "women are the gateway to the caste system". He was not holding women responsible but the system which used the concept of chastity to ensure caste purity. Jotirao Phule, Ishwarchand Vidyasagar, Mahatma Gandhi, Vinoba Bhave and Rammanohar Lohia were others on the Indian scene who interpreted the culture of chastity. The Gandhian thought stressed upon the concept of inner strength.

Now to come to the National Conference hosted by the English Department of the Gujarat University in October 2005, the theme of the conference was "Re-defining Feminism/s". The theme of the conference was looked at in the context of the Indian situation, global contemporaneity and the micro-level cultural reality.

Various presentations in the conference used the new methodology of myth, reinterpretation, interpretation of styles of representation in visual and performing arts. Some used lived experiences to elaborate consciousness-raising. Having been held at the university, there were academic presentations which looked at feminisms as philosophy. During the course of the conference the dynamics of caste and politics was also looked at. The problem of violence – domestic and caste violence – was also looked into. The possibility of penetrating the problem of Asian masculinity was also discussed. It was a genuine interconnectivity between academics and the ground level reality.

It is significant that this refereed volume, being brought out as an end-result of the National Conference, is divided into sections such as *Re-design, Re-think, Re-view* and *Re-mark*. I appreciate the thoughtful initiative of the editors Dr. Ranjana Harish and Dr. V. Bharathi Harishankar to take the deliberations beyond the enclosure of the conference and make them accessible to a wide readership. I hope the readers will find this publication meaningful.

Pushpa Bhave

Preface

Feminisms across the globe have taken different *avatars*, based on their original premises. Liberal, Radical, French, Anglo-American, Existentialist, Psychoanalytic, Marxist, Postcolonial, Postmodern, Ecofeminism – the list goes on. The Indian brands of feminism have worked out their varieties across contexts and disciplines. Whether imitative, resistant or assimilative, Indian feminisms provide multifaceted trajectories to both Western and postcolonial feminist models. And, Indian feminisms are now at a crucial juncture when they need to pause and proceed. It is in this context that the whole notion of re-definition assumes importance.

What do we mean by re-definition? The prefix 're-' implies an act of looking back again. The need for a re-definition is either due to gaping lacuna in the existing paradigms or changing situations forcing corresponding changes in perceptions. Re-definition, as we all know, is not a singular act (if it is to be meaningful) but a process involving different stages. Our attempt at re-definition has led us to **four** broad stages in the process, which incidentally forms the focus of each of the sections in this book. This book is divided into four sections, viz., **Re-design**, **Re-think**, **Re-view** and **Re-mark.** For us, each of the verbs informing the section titles provided the route map for the process of re-definition. We are aware of many other possibilities but these four parameters have provided us with frames of reference across disciplines and acted as meaningful vantage points for re-defining a single instance, text or context.

Making a slight deviation from the existing formats of a preface, we would like to comment on the rationale for these sections and our highlights in each section at the beginning of the concerned sections. For now, we look forward to our travel through this book and look back to the little events that made possible this publication.

Some of the papers included in this volume were originally presented at the Ministry of HRD sponsored National Conference on Re-defining Feminisms in India held at the Department of English, Gujarat University, Ahmedabad, in October 2005. When we reviewed the papers for publication, we had to make our choices based on the quality of each contribution and the overall focus of the collection. We also invited certain contributions, which we thought would add value to our endeavour.

We take this opportunity to thank

- Ministry of HRD, New Delhi and CIIL, Mysore.
- The present and former Vice Chancellors of Gujarat University.
- Smt. Pushpa Bhave for the Foreword.
- Ms. Lakshmi Kannan, Prof. Sachidananda Mohanty, Dr. Jayashree, Dr. Mangai and Mr. Aniruddhan for sharing their work with us.
- Dr. Anil K. Khandelwal, CMD, Bank of Baroda for his encouragement and support.
- All our valued contributors for putting up with our punishing deadlines
- Our reviewers for this refereed volume.
- Rawat Publications, Jaipur for making the task of publication easy.

- Our parents, who have mastered the art of keeping their values intact even while willingly engaging in our discussions and revisions of those values.
- Hari, Harish, Omkar and Minu for providing the emotional space for re-definitions to happen.

Thank you all, again and again.

RANJANA HARISH
Gujarat University, Ahmedabad

V. BHARATHI HARISHANKAR
Madras University, Chennai

I

Re-design

Re-design – the first step in our process of re-definition – involves an interrogation and a meaningful re-statement of the basic positions. The importance of such an activity is to objectively re-assess the existing parameters by way of transforming it to the changing contexts. The notion of transformation is important because it is a positive enabler of actions and not merely an interrogation or resistance. It activates perceptions of the world through the self. In our collection, re-design has taken place in **four** different ways. In her article, **Vidya Bal** attempts a re-definition by studying the design map of her own personal experiences as a feminist to the changing faces of feminism in India. The trajectory ranges from the earlier feminist view of the "personal is political" through the view that "women's rights are human rights" and culminating in the belief that "feminism is a way of life". **Shilpa Das** maps the personal-political convergences through an interrogation of existing perspectives on disabilities, especially of women. This article interrogates the social construction of normalcy and disability as well as the culture of silence that exists in Indian feminist discourses on this topic. **Ila Pathak** extends the academic-activist conjunction attempted by Shilpa Das to an activist-socio-political discussion. In her article, Ila Pathak assesses the impact of Gandhism and feminism on the activities of Ahmedabad Women's Action Group (AWAG). Expanding on the feminist activist contribution, **Vibhuti Patel**'s discourse on sexual harassment at workplace explodes the popular myths that veil the harassment of women in public. Her discussion on the role and function of WDCs (Women's Development Cells) provides a neat conclusion to this collection's framework of re-design by looking ahead in the concept of affirmative action. Incidentally, Gujarat University's WDC was inaugurated on the first day of our National Conference on Re-defining Feminisms, where this paper was presented as the keynote.

1

Re-defining Feminism: A Personal Note

VIDYA BAL

Women's Activist and Journalist, Pune

I have been an activist and a feminist for the last 25-30 years. It all started from looking at my personal problems. I was confused, quarrelling and in conflict with myself. It was quite an individualistic perception with of course some knots tied with the reality that surrounded me. When I think today of re-defining feminism, it becomes more meaningful to me to have a glance at my journey in feminist activity.

In the first stage, I was not aware of patriarchy as a system that has been ruling almost the whole of the world for more than 5,000 years. Hence, the conflict and quarrels I was going through were looked upon as personal problems. It was not easy to unburden the traditional conditioning and upbringing as a woman! Hence, everything that I related towards myself and many other women going through was perceived as if it was just because of our womanhood! And this reality is beyond change, was the verdict of the conditioning.

Days passed by. Some reading, some discussions, some waves of feminism slashing from the West – made me think more. Our own history of Maharashtra where many great thinkers and activists like Mahatma Phule, Maharshi Karve, Gopal Ganesh Agarkar, Lokhitwadi, Dr. Ambedkar and many others came to me as a new dawn in my life. This helped me understand the famous slogan – *Personal is Political*.

The first thing on our feminist agenda was awareness raising and action against violence against women. We, a group of about 10 men and women, started working as *Nari Samata Manch* in 1981. In the beginning, people would always try to convince us that there was no violence in urban middle class families, and that slums and rural life have all the problems of violence. The two unnatural deaths of young married girls in Poona in 1982 gave a big blow to this wishful middle class thinking. It led us a step ahead to say that violence against women is a very secular, egalitarian phenomenon that exists cutting across all sections, castes, classes and religions in the society!

My next revelation about feminism was that violence is not just physical, it is psychological as well. In fact, psychological violence is not seen and cannot be shown or proved easily. Not only is it invisible, it has its wounds far deeper and at times beyond healing!

Hence, women have to come out first by themselves, and admit that this unseen way of verbal torture and humiliation is also violence and should not be tolerated. It is as grave violence as beating and battering and burning. Women must speak out and come out with this violence before they die or go mad!

Another important eye-opener was that all educational and consciousness-raising efforts were focussed on women only. Women and young girls started asking about educating men regarding equality of status and opportunity for both men and women. This opened up another area of work. This made us think about programmes focussing on youth. Yet another step further was not just youth but boys at the puberty level are also to be addressed. This is because manhood and concepts of masculine man start shaping the psyche of the boys around that phase of life. All this helped us build the line of appeal to men. Women's questions and problems are not just problems of their own, they are also social problems and men should come forward to eradicate the inequality and gender-blindness in patriarchal system. In the beginning men were at times looked at as enemies by some women and feminism also was taken as a war against men's world. This stage was to be crossed over with a lot of hard work.

All through this journey, violence – both physical and psychological – has been the main focus. But, today, many more dimensions are added to it. The concept of violence against women is broadened and widened. Deprivation of opportunity for education and job, deprivation of health services, deprivation of food – all this is violence. But, the violence of female foeticide is the limit of violence, which is reflected in the male-female ratio, consistently throughout the census reports since 1901 to 2001! The Beijing conference came up with the slogan that *Women's Rights Are Human Rights*! Women have not been considered as human beings and hence have to demand and assert that they are human beings as men are. Women are different but equal to men. The commercial, market-oriented men treat women as commodities and sex objects. They fail to understand that by doing so they not only de-humanize women but they de-humanize themselves as well.

After going through this long journey with experiences in action and education-oriented work, I would say that feminism is a way of life. It aims at both men and women to get rid of shackles of manly man and womanly woman syndrome to become human beings that value equality, freedom, peace, love and friendship for all human beings. Feminism has also to hold hands with all other efforts connected with environment, alternative development, peace, and minority movements. Feminism re-defined would come far away from the position that feminists are away from politics to be apolitical or non-political. Feminism implies that it is a politically conscious way of life. If we have to change the patriarchal system, we cannot be away from politics. I would also underline the fact that by changing patriarchal society we do not want to bring in matriarchal society at all. We dream to bring about a change wherein we go beyond the male/female politics. Men and women should come together as human beings, keeping away the traditionally glorified and ingrained male and female sexuality norms. We also have to be aware, especially in the Indian context, that women in India are not a homogeneous phenomenon as many other countries have. We have to deal with heterogeneity of women and put lot more efforts to build a well-knit feminist movement, so that it would be more meaningful.

2

Invisible Women: Disability, Gender and Feminism

SHILPA DAS

Faculty, National Institute of Design, Ahmedabad

Fact Sheet

- UN: 600 million people globally have disabilities and the day-to-day life of 25 per cent of the world's population is touched in some way by the condition.
- In India, as per the National Census Data of 2001, persons with disabilities constitute about 22 million, or 2.2 per cent of total population.[1]
- But, going by the UN's 5 per cent worldwide prevalence rate, there are an estimated 60 million people with disabilities in India and it directly impacts the lives of about 600 million Indians.[2]
- India has more persons with disabilities than the total population of UK, Canada or Australia.
- National statistics reveal that 55 per cent of persons with disabilities in India are illiterate (about 20% more than the national average), and only 9 per cent of them go on to complete a secondary education or higher.

- Only one-fourth of all persons with disabilities find employment.
- UN: There are 300 million women and girls worldwide with disabilities, most of whom live in developing or resource-poor countries.
- Only 16 per cent of all women with disabilities globally are likely to have any college education compared to 38 per cent women without disabilities and 28 per cent men with disabilities.
- About 50 per cent of persons with disabilities in India are women.
- Only 38 per cent of India's women go to school.
- Only 0.5 per cent women with disabilities get college education.
- In India, women form only 28.45 per cent of the entire strength of the decision-making bodies, with women with disabilities comprising a mere 3.71 per cent.
- 47 per cent of persons with disabilities remain unmarried in India.
- 40 per cent of men with disabilities do not get married.
- 60 per cent of women with disabilities do not get married.
- 90 per cent of women with disabilities in Gujarat (about 47,000) live in rural areas, of which only 1 per cent go to school. As against this, 67 per cent men with disabilities go to school.
- There is no NGO exclusively working for women with disabilities.
- Only one NGO in Gujarat is run by a woman with disability.
- 50 NGOs in Gujarat are run by men with disabilities.
- 0.2 per cent of women with disabilities earn more than Rs. 2,000 per month.

> The problem, unstated till now, is how to live in a damaged body in a world where pain is meant to be gagged uncured, un-grieved over. The problem is to connect, without hysteria, the pain of anyone's body with the pain of the body's world.
>
> — Adrienne Rich, "Cartographies of Silence"

The *raison de etre* for this paper is to provide an overview of the linkages between disability, gender and feminism, and to examine the nature of oppression experienced by women with disabilities. As an Indian woman with a disability doing ethnographic research for a project related to disability (along with an NGO working on disability), talking to various women with disabilities,[3] and writing on other women with disabilities, I am both 'inside' the culture and participating in that which I am observing. We are the sum total of our experience, and we each have the right to interpret our existence in our own ways. Thus, this paper is as much about my own experiences as it is about those of others. I lay no claim to objectivity because to me, it is a word used to impose our way of seeing the world on others while suppressing their way of seeing the world. But, at the same time, the decision to work from the 'inside' and make our experience known ('coming out' as it is termed) is, in itself, a form of self-empowerment.

The number of girls and young women with disabilities in this country or anywhere depends on how 'disability' is defined. A number of diverse definitions exist that are underwritten by different kinds of cultural and historical determinants and often controversial.[4]

Two earlier models of disability need explication here. The first, the Morality Model, suggests that disability is caused by a moral lapse and brings shame to the individual and to the family. Disability is seen as a stigma; the outward manifestation of inner evil or depravity, and the disabled person is a blemished person, to be punished, segregated and isolated at worst, and avoided or pitied at best. Historically, depicting someone disabled as punishment for a crime was standard practice[5] and in many cultures, including our own, this practice has continued till today. I am not saying that the non-disabled community has systematically designed the kind of system we have for its own benefit; the oppressive structures may be the result of a historical process whose originators are long gone, for instance, in the West, the ideas of Charles Darwin and of his contemporary Herbert Spencer who coined the term "survival of the fittest", the Eugenic Theory, as a specific form of Social

Darwinism which posited the view that "the existing social hierarchy resulted from the differences in the innate qualities and capacities of individuals" (Evans, 136). If we look at the social attitude towards disability in India, which is otherwise inclusive in accepting and valuing diversity in so many ways, there is a negative and exclusionary social construct of disability. Research indicates that families see having a disabled child as a question of *karma*, a result of deeds in an earlier birth and as divine retribution (Alur, 7). So people with disabilities and their families must accept their fate with courage and fortitude (Mani, 31). Or, it is more a matter of charity than a human rights issue. Such an approach ensures care and tolerance, but encourages dependency among the disabled. Here, decisions regarding the nature, amount and recipient of charity are the prerogative of the donor.

The second model is the Medical Model, rooted in pathology, and historically adopted by rehabilitation service providers and policy makers. It is less damning than the Morality Model, but the focus is still on the disability, not on the person with disability or the experience of disability. Its chief aim is to correct and cure. Disability is seen as a disaster, as something to fix. Even psychological writing on disability is often reductive, treating disability not as a complex life experience which needs to be understood in the context of relationships, but as a personal tragedy which the disabled person needs to come to terms with.[6] Mainstream therapy that follows the Medical Model has led to traumatic experiences for many persons with disabilities who talk about being objectified, and pathologized, and as suffering loss of body image and self-esteem by public stripping in front of doctors, without regard to modesty or privacy. Although we must admit that the Medical Model, and its accompanying rehabilitation, has significantly alleviated many discomforts with regard to the impairments, and led to greater life opportunities for many people with disabilities, it still conceptualizes them as "being acted upon" and lacking the capacity to transform their lives without the help of professional bodies. This further promotes segregation. Thus, each model offers its own explanation of what the problem is, who holds the problem, who should address the problem, and how.

There is also confusion regarding the terms 'impairment', 'disability' and 'handicap' and the appropriate use of each of these terms that needs clarification at the outset. Disability is broadly understood in a continuum as: disease/accident/ impairment/handicap.

Broadly defined, *impairment* is an individual limitation in the structure and function of an organ. Disability is a lack of ability earlier thought to be a result of impairment (Goffman, 7). Today, disability is conceived as going beyond just the inability to perform a function. Called the Social Model of disability,[7] this is a profound paradigm shift in the conceptualization of disability. It states that the complex human experience of disability is not a function of an individual's material impairment and his/her supposed 'lack' of a normal body, but is instead viewed through the lens of the person with disability as socially and politically constructed. Jenny Morris, in *Pride against Prejudice,* examines such a perspective of the disabled person: "Our grief is not a 'failure to come to terms with disability'. Our dissatisfaction with our lives is not a personality defect but a sane response to the oppression we experience" (Morris, 1996).

So disablement is embedded in ableist environments, which are not accommodating enough and not in the body with disability per se. The burden of disability shifts from the individual to society; the centre of analysis shifts from focusing on an individual's medical conditions to social structures, cultural values, institutions, the built environment and technology; and, the view of the environment as static and the person with disability as alterable, is reversed.

Being disabled is also not equal to experiencing a *handicap*. Disability, in combination with restricting factors in the environment, results in a situation of handicap. While personal factors such as functional ability play a crucial part in overcoming them, handicaps are usually a product of external factors such as social attitudes, extreme poverty, a lack of information and access to quality services. Handicaps perpetuate the exclusion of people with disabilities from mainstream society by preventing them from achieving their full potential. When people are forced to live with handicaps in addition to their disabilities, they experience a loss of freedom and a violation of their human right to a life of dignity and equal opportunity.

However, the Social Model is limited by its predominant socio-political and economic tenets, as it zeroes in only on structural barriers and does not look at other complex layers of a multi-layered picture. It looks at persons with disabilities as a homogenous group, rather than as people with differences and multiple identities, largely ignores gender and other diverse cross-cutting social divisions. Some disability activists such as Susan Wendell advocate a need to include the issues of impairment, the body and experience of the disabled community into the model (Wendell, 1996). They emphasize that disablism makes people constantly aware of their somatic selves (Paterson and Hughes, 597-610). Similarly, Crow suggests that bodily experiences are an inherent part of disabled people's lives (Crow, 59) and that although impairment may not cause disability, it is a precondition for this form of oppression (Crow, 69). She also implies that the Social Model has failed some individuals by making it hard for them to talk about the difficulty and discomfort arising from impairment itself. It is, thus, also important to examine how disability and impairment shape the way people act and think about themselves, and how these too are barriers to their 'being'.

We also need to look at the Minority Model that informs Disability Studies. It is the study, not of disability but of the shared experience of disability. The shared experience, according to Rhoda Olkin, a psychotherapist and a woman with a disability, is one experienced by all minority groups: "prejudice, discrimination and stigma". According to the stigma theory, "when a person with a physical disability meets a stranger, the stranger immediately becomes aware of the person's 'discrediting attribute', in this case, the physical impairment. The impairment results in 'stigma', and the stranger makes many other attributions about the person based on this one attribute such as s/he is unattractive, impotent, or unworthy. The person may be immediately discounted as a possible lover or friend. Hence, the disability becomes an all-permeating, overwhelming classification that eclipses all other personal characteristics, skills and abilities."[8] People who are not part of mainstream population, then, are traditionally seen as inferior and psychologically disempowered. They have "few positive role models and few positive images within the arts and media; they are under-represented politically in terms of issues and office holders; they have significantly limited access to economic resources; they have little or no political power; and they are summarily excluded from the mainstream of life's opportunities" (Olkin, 1999).

In *The Disability Studies Reader*, Davis states that "we live in a world of norms". The problem with disability is not the disability or the person with disability, but rather "the way that normalcy is constructed to create the 'problem' of the disabled person" (Davis, 1997). Ulrike Schildsman says, "the marking on the gauge of normality indicates what society considers acceptable and tolerable; it is supposed to serve as a guide. If people follow that guide, they are assured that they remain within safe parameters" (Schildsman, 7). In defining disability, we always juxtapose it with concepts of normality, which exist within a society. It is the flip side of normalcy, a form of deviance, and persons with disabilities are often conferred with totalizing labels such as 'abnormal', and hence, often undesirable. As Thomson says, disability is "a collection of embodiments whose only commonality is being considered abnormal" (Thomson, 1997). Schildsman redefines handicap using the lens of normalcy: "Handicap is a coin with two sides: that of becoming handicapped and that of being handicapped. This means that society implements special measures, controls, and sanctions to regulate the status of the deviant person at the margins of or outside of normality. That process results in a disciplining of the disabled person and a possible restriction of personal latitude. The disabled person has to accept these given societal norms and adapt himself/herself to the prescribed life"

(Schildsman, 5).[9] This is why, according to Tom Shakespeare, people with disabilities are "Dustbins of Disavowal" (Shakespeare, 1994).

Definitions are important and need to be considered at the outset because "the action that is taken and even social policies that are framed are made on the bases of these. For instance, if disability is seen as a personal tragedy, people with disabilities will be seen as victims of tragic circumstances and social policies will aim at compensating the victims. If disability is seen as social oppression, people with disabilities will be seen as collective victims of an unknowing or uncaring society, and so, social policies will focus on alleviating oppression" (Oliver, 62). All definitions thus explored are also powerful ideologies; informing and colouring the way people think and feel they are or ever can be. However, most versions of disability are not mutually exclusive and the general idea of 'disability' as a homogenizing label is always implicated in this paper.

If disability is a social construct, then, it is related to other social constructs such as gender, age, class and ethnicity, which help us to analyze diversity and avoid unfounded universalization. When 'gender' enters the matrix of disability it constitutes a deep matrix of gendered disability, and plays a significant part in influencing people's experience of a disabling society. The interrelationship between gender and disability is not solely about women and girls. Both are social constructs affecting both men and women and any account of the lives of persons with disabilities has to incorporate accounts of both; however, we look at women here.

The category of 'woman', as informed by particular and essential qualities (both biological and cultural in nature), is intertwined with concepts about disability. This is not an arbitrary combination, but reflects particular social and political interests. While 'woman' is a socially established and stable category, disability, as we shall see, is a flexible category marked by less stability. But, a brief look at their recent historical conceptualizations indicates that feminism and disablism are not different 'isms'. One common thread between the two is that both terms 'women' and 'disabled' have some stereotypes and prejudices heaped upon them most commonly. We do not need to stretch our imagination too much to list a few of these: passive, weak, burdensome, hyper sensitive, unassertive or overly aggressive, dominating, irrational, untruthful, crafty, cunning, mean, deceitful, greedy, difficult, demanding, dependent, deficient and defective, lack of moral, mental and physical control, incompetence, unreliable, emotional, temperamental, morally depraved, imbecile, lazy, unpredictable, requiring protection, untrustworthy, timid, self-centered, unstable, undersexed or oversexed, perverted, likely to be dangerous, the life not worth living and the list goes on.[10] As we can see, most of these characteristics express a too much or too little of something as though it were impossible to strike a healthy balance.

The body, then, becomes an important marker for identity for both women and persons with disabilities. In *Body and Power,* Michel Foucault establishes the interrelationship between body and power and says that in the so-called training of bodies, the formation of the body reveals itself as an essential instrument in the development of human beings. In *Discipline and Punish,* Foucault talks about how the bodies of both women and people with impairments are relentlessly subjected to 'disciplining' – social practices that shape and regulate them. This is mainly done through the politics of medicalization, (clitoridectomies, ovariotomies, drugs to regulate supposedly overly sexed women; surgeries for the congenitally disabled, conjoined twins, hermaphrodites, etc., the Human Genome Project) already discussed earlier, and the politics of appearance (Foucault, 1979). The medicalization of women's and the physically impaired bodies is often employed for the benefit of the politics of appearance; for instance, cosmetic surgery aims at aesthetization and standardization of women's bodies while reconstructive surgery seeks to do the same to the body with impairments. Both are commoditized in the name of enhancement. Both categories of women and persons with disabilities involve a reduction to some aspect of their physical presence: while woman is subjected to the gaze, persons with disabilities are to the stare. While the male gaze makes the normative female a sexual spectacle, the stare reduces the impaired body to a grotesque object, and is the definitive gesture that constructs disability as an oppressive social relationship. In the case of both men and women with disabilities, a visible physical deformity is often taken as evidence of other limitations. Both are dehumanized, express a disempowering notion of human beings as having unworthy and immutable biological destinies outside of a social, cultural and historical context; both are objectified as *things* to be controlled, as lacking the power or choice to alter their lives, and as parts of the vast 'Other'. Disturbingly, both categories acquire the garb of *natural* truths; both occupy a certain rung in the social ladder of hierarchy, and both indicate societal situations of inequality.

On examining the ladder of hierarchy, we find that society always equates human or general normality with male normality; the *libermensch* or alpha male is the essential gender. Female normality is defined on the basis of this norm, and is thus a first level of deviance, the female being subordinate, and the 'Other' to the male. People with disabilities are, then, constructed as the Other of the 'Other'. Disability is understood to be a deviation from the norm of 'able-bodied'. Being a man with disability then is a rung below the norm of the able woman, and women with disabilities are at the fourth level down. It can then be safely said that men and women experience disability differently. Women with disabilities face a double discrimination, because both the female gender and disability are defined by incompleteness in terms of the body in varying degrees. The scenario is further complicated if we are looking at say an Indian woman with a disability who is a Dalit, from a lower economic stratum of society, or the rural sector. Woman herself is traditionally perceived as weak, thus a woman with a disability is considered weaker still. Physical impairments themselves are hierarchically structured: some categories considered weaker and less acceptable than others. For example, people and especially women with mental retardation and/or mental illness come at the bottom of the hierarchy of impairments, below those with physical and learning disabilities, because they are constructed as deviant and dangerous. Thus, women with disabilities form a heterogeneous group, and as a group, experience many different forms of injustice, which interact in complex ways with other systems of oppression. In contemporary terms, this is known as the "theory of intersectionality" and is similar to the way some feminist theorists have resisted the label 'feminism', have shown it to be a flexible and diffuse term, and adopted different names such as Alice Walker's portmanteau word 'womanism' that better addresses the needs of black women and women of colour, Diane Price Herndel and Robyn Warhol's 'feminisms' (Herndl and Warhol, 1997) and Judith Grant's 'hyphenated feminism' (Grant, 3).

For many women in India, their most punishing disability is the attitude taken to them by society.[11] Women are 'hidden' or undisclosed members of many families, especially in our rural areas, even today, and women with disabilities are kept out of sight because of social taboos and stigma (Onial, 12; Ghosh, 13). After years of struggle, men with disabilities have succeeded to some extent in making their voices heard. But, the issues of women with disabilities are same as other women in India plus more [complex] as they lack access to education, resulting in all the problems linked with illiteracy such as poverty, lack of decision-making power and lack of available options. Some national studies say that girls with disabilities are not sent to school, get significantly fewer services than boys and men with disabilities, including rehabilitation and health care, education, assistive technology, vocational training and employment; as adults they often do not marry and rarely inherit or own property; consequently, they are disproportionately represented among the poorest of the poor. Parents of young girls with disabilities may be doubly overprotective, assuming that their daughters by dint of being both female and disabled are doubly vulnerable. Or, they are likely to be far more neglected and victims of taboos and superstitions. They are not considered to be able enough to fulfil the traditional roles of an Indian woman – of wife, homemaker, and mother – and as not conforming to the stereotypes of beauty and femininity in terms of appearance just as disabled men may be considered to be less 'masculine'. However, while therapies for men with disabilities often assert traditional masculine identities, e.g., encouraging them to play wheel-chair sports, therapies for women with disabilities are likely to be about hyper-feminine self presentation, e.g., make up and grooming classes. Thus, traditional roles are imposed on both, they are called upon to perform these roles in order to reduce their visibility as stigmatized others. Also, our society looks at men as 'breadwinners'. So, men with disabilities who have financial autonomy pass the litmus test to qualify to be a good husband and father (the 'supercrip' phenomenon). Our system of arranged marriages, whereby the parents find a boy, and a certain dowry accompanies the girl is oppressive because in the case of girls with disabilities, it means that they would have to give extra dowry, if the girl were to marry a non-disabled boy. Men and boys with disabilities would rather marry a girl without disability than a girl with a disability. So, there is oppression from both parties – the non-disabled boys and men, and men with disabilities.[12] Studies reveal that women with disabilities are two to three times more likely to be victims of physical and sexual abuse than women without disabilities. Also, where reproductive health care needs are concerned, they are not seen as in need of information about birth control or what is possible in terms of having a sex life and children, and so are more vulnerable to reproductive health problems. In many cases, they are not targeted because a 'gender blind approach' is adopted and they are perceived as being unfeminine and asexual (Elwan, 1999). Michelle Fine and Adrienne Asch term this as 'rolelessness', a social invisibility and cancellation of femininity foisted by culture (Fine and Asch, 1988). Our patriarchal society subjects women to experience both institutional and individual discrimination – something men rarely experience. Even policies and practices in the field are not designed to meet their specific needs.

There are many parallels between the principles of feminism and the disability rights movement typified by historic power imbalances between men and women. Yet, women with disabilities across the world, and glaringly in India, have remained almost invisible in both the disability movement and the women's movement – a double bind, because both overlook their specific issues and concerns. The academic high ground of disability studies and the disability movement here in India are as patriarchal as any other cultural context, and as Dr. Anita Ghai points out, usually dominated by elite, middle class men who have focussed on the structural aspects of disability such as employment, income, housing, etc., and who do not share leadership with women. As a result, their concerns are more for things, which affect them the most. Also, most research to capture the experience of women with disabilities is actually 'added on' to masculine viewpoints and thereby subsumed.

There is also a conspicuous absence of feminist scholarly writing related to disability in India and mainstream Western thought by both women with and without disabilities indicating perhaps a lack of power and confidence on the part of the former and apathy of the latter. Paulo Freire describes a 'culture of silence' amongst the dispossessed, which perpetuates their oppression. Such oppression saps them of both the vitality and the critical awareness to respond to their situation, and they "lack even the vocabulary to expose it" (Freire, 12). On the other hand, the lack of integration of disability perspectives into feminism has been viewed by feminist writer with disability, Jenny Morris, as a difficulty for "non-disabled feminists to incorporate our reality into their research and theories..." (Morris, 1991) and by Susan Wendell as there being "no recognition of how people with disabilities understand their social reality" (Wendell, 1996). If current academic feminism, by recognizing that all women have multiple identities, can generate a range of critical areas of study, e.g., Black Feminist Studies, Lesbian Feminist Studies, Latina Studies, and so on, why is there an oversight in the case of Feminist Disability Studies?

In the West, in most earlier work on disability – be it the Marxist, modernist or British version of the Social Model, or the more post-modernist American version, it was assumed that people with disabilities were a homogenous group without any gender or other social distinction. Only recently, women scholars with disabilities in the West, such as Susan Wendell, Jenny Morris and Anita Silvers, have begun to draw on conceptual insights from second-wave feminism, black feminist thought and especially post-modernism and to critique increasingly the hegemony and homogeneity of disability. Disability poses stimulating questions to feminism about issues such as power relations among women, the status of the lived body, the privileges of being able-bodied or what is termed 'normal,' the social construction of the able-bodied, and the uses of identity politics. The overarching concerns of the body of Feminist Disability Studies, that exists, are representation, the body, identity, and activism.

Rosemarie Garland-Thomson writes that feminism's often conflicting and always complex aims of politicizing the materiality of bodies and rewriting the category of woman combine exactly the methods that should be used to examine disability in general and female disability in particular (Garland-Thomson, 4). In other words, within feminist framework, the currently prevalent myths, stereotypes, assumptions, and perceptions of women/people with disabilities need to be challenged and to be examined in the contexts of culture and history, and a view of persons with disabilities needs to be constructed that reflects and honours their collective voice. Feminist writing needs to express the right of women with disabilities to depict their own identity, to discuss and re-define impairment from a cross-disability perspective to enrich the disability debate. For instance, Jenny Morris says that the little analysis that there has been of the lives of women with disabilities has tended to appear as a 'special' area of study that seems to centre on the view of the so-called 'double disadvantage' experienced due to gender and disability and to assess which is 'worse' (Morris, 1998, 4). Such an emphasis is disempowering because it portrays women as passive victims and as lacking agency; it is like an optional added-on extra to the concerns of both feminist analyses and disability studies. In fact, feminist writing, although it is about the difficulties women face in their lives, does not usually victimize the (non-disabled) women whose lives are the subject of research and analysis. Feminist analyses of women's oppression are themselves a way of asserting resistance.

Feminist writing also needs to put the body with disability in the "personal is the political" context. This way, women with disabilities will not be forced into situations of denying their own bodies, and of conforming to the able-bodied world's view of what it is to be a 'normal' person. Morris, in citing Liz Crow from *Encounters with Strangers,* urges on the need to

> put back the experience of impairment into our politics. We need to write about, research and analyse the personal experience of our bodies and our minds for if we don't impose our own definitions and perspectives then the non-disabled world will continue to do it for us in ways which alienate and disempower us. Some people have reacted to this position by saying that there is nothing political to be said about impairment – impairment belongs to the personal world where everyone is different and there are such variations in individual experiences that there are few generalizations to be made. This is a bit like saying that women's experiences of, for example childbirth, are merely personal and individual; that there are no political demands to be made based on the personal experiences of our unequal relationship with doctors, the lack of recognition of the role and expertise of midwives, the denial of autonomy in how we give birth, the professional highjacking of the recognition of pain and the administration of pain control, and so on. The problem is that if we don't express the experience of our bodies, others will do it for us (Morris, 1998, 15).

Some social modellists critique such accounts by saying that they feed into non-disabled people's pity of the disabled. Others (usually male theorists) say that it draws away attention from the fight to change society (Wendell, 73). Such dualistic mode of thinking separates the public/political from the private/personal. But Morris counters that the personal realm has been undermined because it is seen as 'feminine', and strives to reverse this division by arguing that individual voices need to be heard to assign value to individual lives, that "the personal is political" based on the notion that "public policies can be crafted on private experience".[13] Morris insists that Disability Studies must also incorporate such accounts. Susan Wendell echoes Morris when she states that although people with disabilities are diverse, and that there are some who do not "identify with all others who have disabilities or share a single perspective on disability" yet living with disability provides social experiences that are different from persons without disabilities. The significant body of knowledge that has been generated by women with disabilities and that has been ignored and repressed in non-disabled culture should be further developed and articulated" (Morris, 1991, 183; Peters, 227). The standpoints of people with disabilities can illuminate as well as be illuminated by familiar philosophical views; such a feminist epistemology of disability will be encouraging, enlightening, and most of all empowering.

Further, Wendell shows that those theories of embodiment that are skewed by their assumption of non-disabled bodies – i.e., most theories of the body – would be enriched by the inclusion of the experiences of persons with disabilities. She takes issue with the dominant notion that a person's disability is 'purely' physical or biological and thus fully 'there' prior to a society's consideration of it. Such notions do not lead people to ask why norms have been set up as they are and why resources have been distributed in the ways they are to create these particular disabilities. She asserts that the biological and the social are interactive in creating disability. In contrast, people's ability depends upon resources from their various environments that help them function and develop opportunities for themselves. Her alignment, then, is with some of the signature themes of the emerging field of Disability Studies, particularly, that lives lived with disability nevertheless are worth living. Her most provocative and illuminating insight is about "transcending the body", a step up from merely "overcoming limits" of the body. She analyzes thoroughly how and why people with physical disabilities refuse to be circumscribed by their restricting bodies; how they "assess their lives according to how replete their options are, rather than by the satisfactoriness of whatever options they have available" (Wendell, 1996). According to her, feminism is unrealistic and misleading in wanting women to think that they can wrest control of their bodies from men (and patriarchal culture), experience their bodies as pleasant, and thus be in sync with their corporeal selves. Anita Silvers points out how such a "conceptualization disregards physical suffering, which cannot be deconstructed; more egregiously, it is inadequate against the pervasive appeal that dualism exercises in accounting for the relationship of consciousness to body" (Silvers, www, 7). This consideration of disability would require feminists to rethink their rejection of all notions of transcending the body. To this, one may counter that feminism essentially begins with the notion of transcendence, for instance, in Mary Wollstonecraft and others.

The feminist ethic of caring has also come in for considerable flak by feminist disability scholars who oppose its suggestion that care is the sole responsibility of women. They believe that this view, which aims at celebrating nurturing as a virtuous feminine trait, not only undercuts balanced reciprocal relations among women with disabilities and women without disabilities but also portrays women with disabilities as passive and helpless. Silvers explains that "far from vanquishing patriarchal systems substituting the ethic of caring for the ethic of equality, it threatens an even more oppressive paternalism" (Silvers, Ibid). We may contend, however, that care is a responsibility of humankind. The danger is there that she is restricting the feminist ethic of care to the care of persons with disabilities. Another feminist principle to be censured is the liberal ideology that equates autonomy and independence with empowerment. The angst expressed is that it leaves no margin for the needs and accommodation of disabled women's bodies. However, both these issues are debatable.

In terms of activism, feminism needs to advocate from within academia on integrating Disability Studies into education – in sociology, economics, history, law, political science, literature, the fine arts, design studies, international studies, culture and media studies, communication studies, and literary theory, for instance. Doing so will deepen our curricula to include diverse issues, for instance, the history of the disability rights movement, women's history, the lives and artistic products of women with disabilities, books written by them, intellectual property rights matters, product design, digital design and software user interfaces for persons with disabilities, films dealing with and made by persons with disabilities, and so on and so forth.

It is also important for women with disabilities themselves to 'come out' that allows for identification with others so that feelings of isolation are reduced. A fundamental aspect of 'coming out' is saying, "This is who I am and I align myself with this group of people". Thereby, we refute that anatomy is destiny, develop an independent voice, a positive identity encompassing the gendered nature and experience of disability.

Labels like 'Us' and 'Them' can dissolve only by reflecting on the dichotomy of *able and disabled* and realizing that they only serve to force descriptions of experiences into either/or categories, instead of allowing sensitivity to a complex range of responses and attitudes. What is required to get out of the conundrum is the awareness and understanding of our *necessary* human interrelationships. Feminist philosopher Caroline Whitbeck suggests that such a perspective

> has at its core a conception of *self-other* relation that is significantly different than the self-other opposition that underlines (as we have discussed), much of so-called western thought...Since an other is not taken to be the opposite to the self, the character of the self does not uniquely define the character of the other by opposition to it: others may be similar or dissimilar in an unlimited variety of ways. The relation (then) is not fundamentally dyadic at all, and is better expressed as self others relation, because relationships, past and present, realized and sought, are constitutive of the self.[14]

Jennifer Nedelsky reflects: "If we ask ourselves what actually enables people to be autonomous, the answer is not isolation but relationships... that provide the support and guidance necessary for the development and experience of autonomy." [15]

End Notes

1. With 1.6 per cent urban population and 0.6 per cent rural population (as per National Data Census, 2001 and the National Sample Survey Organization Report, 2002-2003.) This is a likely underestimation of the prevalence rate in India because data sources are not easily comparable due to differences in methodology, and the use of inadequately trained surveyors (as per *Country Strategy: India, 2004-2008*, published by Handicap International, India).
2. Note that India's total population is taken at 1 billion plus and the average number of people per family is taken at 5 (as per *Country Strategy: India, 2004-2008,* published by Handicap International, India).
3. What do we mean by women with disabilities? Women with physical, mental, hearing and visual impairments, visible or otherwise, including women with mental illness and mental health problems, learning disabilities, and various chronic conditions such as diabetes, heart or kidney disorders, epilepsy, HIV/AIDS, diseases predominantly including women such as breast cancer, arthritis, Lupus, fibromyalgia and osteoporosis. It includes girls and women with disabilities of all ages, in rural and urban areas, regardless of the severity of the disability, regardless of sexual preference and regardless of cultural background, or whether they live in the community or in an institution.

   As per "Manifesto by Disabled Women in Europe" adopted in Brussels on 22 February 1997 by the European Disability Forum Working Group on Women and Disability, launched in the European Parliament on December 4, 1999. This was a revision of recommendations from the United Nation's Experts Seminar on Disabled Women in Vienna 1990, and a manifestation of the UN Standard Rules on the Equalisation of Opportunities for Persons with Disabilities.

But as per Indian law, under the Persons with Disabilities (Equal Opportunities, Protection of Rights and Full Participation) Act, 1995, disability includes only those who are blind, of low vision, leprosy cured, hearing impaired or having a locomotor disability, mental retardation or mental illness. The definition of disability used to arrive at this data excludes many types of disabilities recognized as such in many countries as haemophilia, autism and AIDS.

4. For instance, World Health Organization or International Classification of Impairments, Disabilities and Handicaps, WHO-ICIDH, Geneva, 1980 on page 20, defines disability as "it refers to restrictions on or prevention of carrying out an activity because of an impairment in the manner or within the range considered normal for a human being, e.g., difficulty in walking, seeing, speaking, hearing, counting, lifting, reading, writing, etc. A disability may last for a long time or a short time, be permanent or reversible, progressive or regressive and may vary in its impact from one situation to another."

It defines impairment as "a permanent or transitory psychological, physiological or anatomical loss or abnormality of structure or function (e.g., an amputated limb, paralysis after polio, diabetes, mental retardation, impaired hearing, nearsightedness etc." Handicap is defined as "a disability that interferes with what is expected at a particular time in one's life (e.g., inability to care for oneself, communicate one's thoughts or concerns, develop a capacity for independent economic activity)."

These definitions, however, have not received universal acceptance, particularly among disabled people and their organizations. Writes Mike Oliver in "Redefining Disability: A Challenge to Research", *Disabling Barriers and Enabling Environments* (1993) by John Swain, Vic Finkelstein, Sally French and Mike Oliver (eds.) (London, California and New Delhi: Sage Publications, 2003), p. 61: "A major criticism is that they have been based upon able-bodied assumptions of disability, and as a consequence, they do not accord with the personal realities of disabled people. This 'lack of fit' between able-bodied and disabled people's definitions is more than just a semantic quibble for it has important implications both for the provision of services and the ability to control one's life."

5. Read J. Evans, "Infantalism, Projection and Naturalism in the Construction of Mental Disablement", in *The Creatures Time Forgot: Photography and Disability Imagery*, by David Hevey et al. (eds.), (London: Routledge) for an interesting perspective on the issue.
6. However, from Freud's work on *Civilisation and its Discontents* through to the work of the Frankfurt school and feminist writers such as Juliet Mitchell and Suzie Orbach in the UK and Nancy Chodorow and Jessica Benjamin in the USA, there have been a few radicals within the school of psychoanalysis who have argued that many psychological ills derive from social oppression.
7. Brainchild of Michael Oliver. Read Mike Oliver, *Social Work with Disabled People* (London: Macmillan, 1983).
8. K. Dovey and J. Graffam, "The Experience of Disability: Social Construction and Imposed Limitation", quoted by George Talporos in "An Essay on Body Image" written for the exhibition *Intimate Encounters.*
9. In *The Rejected Body: Feminist Philosophical Reflections on Disability* (88), Susan Wendell writes of the "the disciplines of normality" – those disciplines "which require us to meet physical standards, to objectify our bodies, and to control them." The less closely our bodies conform to this norm, the more uncomfortable is our position within society. These norms become attached to our value judgements of worth – our own and each others value. We pass judgements accordingly."

   Gramsci used the concept of hegemony to describe a situation where the values of an elite group stand dominant within a society who, through the construction of an all pervasive ethos, maintain their own interests while subordinating those of others.
10. Della Perry and Ruth Keszia Whiteside in an interesting essay "Women, Gender and Disability: Historical and Contemporary Intersections of Otherness", at *www.academyanalyticarts.org/perrywhiteside.htm*, 6, observe how many of these stereotypes were listed in "A Practical Manual of Insanity for the Medical

Student and General Practitioner" of 1902, an academic medical publication, whose authors were doctors Daniel Brower and Henry Bannister (p. 379 and p. 381).

11. Read the 16 points of the Resolution of women with disabilities, men with disabilities, parents, and professionals from all parts of India gathered at the National Conference on Empowerment and Mainstreaming of Women with Disabilities, organized by DPI-India in association with NCPEDP and the Rajasthan Government.
12. Read Laura Hershey, *An Interview with Dr. Anita Ghai, one of India's Advocates for Rights of Disabled Women, www.LauraHershey@compuserve.com.*
13. Finkelstein also asserts that "finding insight in the experiences of discrimination is just a return to the old case file approach to oppression, dressed up in the social model jargon." Read V. Finkelstein, "The Disability Movement Has Run out of Steam", *Disability Now,* February 1996, p. 11.
14. Quoted in "Women, Gender and Disability: Historical and Contemporary Intersections of 'Otherness'", by Della Perry and Ruth Keszia Whiteside, *www.academyanalyticarts.org/perrywhiteside.htm*, 8.
15. Quoted in "Bioethics, Disability and Death: Uncovering Cultural Bias in the Euthanasia Debate" by Jennifer Fitzgerald, *www.metafuture.org/articlesbycolleagues/JenniferFitzgerald/Bioethics*, 11.

Works Cited

Alur, Mithu, "Inclusion in the Indian Context". *Humanscape,* July 2001.

Crow, L. (1996) "Including All of Our Lives: Renewing the Social Model of Disability". In C. Barnes and G. Mercer (eds.), *Exploring the Divide: Illness and Disability*. Leeds: The Disability Press.

Davis, L.J., *The Disability Studies Reader.* New York: Routledge, 1997.

Dovey, K. and Graffam, J., "The Experience of Disability: Social Construction and Imposed Limitation". Quoted by George Talporos in "An Essay on Body Image" written for the exhibition *Intimate Encounters*.

Elwan, Anne, "Poverty and Disability: Background Paper for the World Development Report, World Bank". New York: World Bank, 1999.

Evans, J., "Infantalism, Projection and Naturalism in the Construction of Mental Disablement". In David Hevey et al. (eds.), *The Creatures Time Forgot: Photography and Disability Imagery*. London: Routledge.

Fine, Michelle and Adrienne Asch (eds.), *Women with Disabilities: Essays in Psychology, Culture and Politics*. Philadelphia: Temple University Press, 1988.

Finkelstein, V., "The Disability Movement Has Run out of Steam". *Disability Now*, February 1996.

Fitzgerald, Jennifer. "Bioethics, Disability and Death: Uncovering Cultural Bias in the Euthanasia Debate". ww.metafuture.org/articlesbycolleagues/JenniferFitzgerald/Bioethics.

Foucault, Michel, *Discipline and Punish: The Birth of the Prison*. Trans. Alan M. Sheridan-Smith. New York: Vintage Books, 1979.

Freire, Paulo, *Pedagogy of the Oppressed*. London: Penguin, 1993.

Garland-Thomson, RoseMarie, "Re-shaping, Re-thinking, Re-defining: Feminist Disability Studies". *Barbara Waxman Fiduccia Papers on Women and Girls with Disabilities: Center for Women Policy Studies*. Washington: Women Policy Studies, 2001.

Ghosh, Deepshikha, "'Disability' Muddle Disables Census Staff". *Equity*, Vol. 3, Issue 4, January 2001.

Goffman, Erving, *Stigma*. New York: Simon & Schuster, 1963.

Government of India, Planning Commission's *Encyclopaedia of Social Work*, Vol. II. New Delhi: Government of India, 1968.

Grant, Judith, *Fundamental Feminism: Contesting the Core Concepts of Feminist Theory*. New York: Routledge, 1993.

Handicap International, *Country Strategy: India*. New Delhi: Handicap International, 2004-2008.

Herndl, Diane Price and Robyn Warhol, *Feminisms,* 2nd ed. New Brunswick: Rutgers University Press, 1997.

Hershey, Laura, "An Interview with Dr. Anita Ghai, One of India's Advocates for Rights of Disabled Women". LauraHershey@compuserve.com

Mani, Rama, *Physically Handicapped in India.* New Delhi: Ashish Publishing House, 1988.

"Manifesto by Disabled Women in Europe": *Recommendations from the United Nation's Experts Seminar on Disabled Women in Vienna 1990, and a Manifestation of the UN Standard Rules on the Equalisation of Opportunities for Persons with Disabilities.* Brussels: European Disability Forum Working Group on Women and Disability, February 1997.

Morris, Jenny, *Pride against Prejudice: Transforming Attitudes to Disability.* London: The Women's Press, 1991.

—, "Feminism, Gender and Disability." paper at a seminar in Sydney, February, 1998. http://www.leeds.ac.uk/disability-studies/archiveuk/morris/gender

Oliver, Michael, *Social Work with Disabled People.* London: Macmillan, 1983.

—, "Redefining Disability: A Challenge to Research". In John Swain, Vic Finkelstein, Sally French and Mike Oliver (eds.), *Disabling Barriers and Enabling Environments.* London, California and New Delhi: Sage Publications, 2003.

Olkin, Rhoda, *What Psychotherapists should Know about Disability.* New York: The Guilford Press, 1999.

Onial, Devyani, "Census Miracle: How the Disabled have Disappeared". *Equity,* Vol. 3, Issue 4, January 2001.

Paterson, K. and Hughes B., "Disability Studies and Phenomenology: The Carnal Politics of Everyday Life". *Disability and Society,* Vol. 14 (5): 597-610.

Perry, Della and Ruth Keszia Whiteside, "Women, Gender and Disability: Historical and Contemporary Intersections of Otherness". www.academyanalyticarts.org/perrywhiteside.htm

Peters, S., "The Politics of Disabled Identity". In L. Barton (ed.), *Disability and Society: Emerging Issues and Insights.* London: Longman, 1996.

Schildmann, Ulrike, Lecture: "What is Normal? Normality, Disability-Gender". Women's World 1999: The 7th International Interdisciplinary Congress on Women. Tromso, Norway: June 20-26, 1999.

Shakespeare, Tom, "Cultural Representations of Disabled People: Dustbins for Disavowal?" *Disability and Society.* London: Cassell, 1994.

Silvers, Anita, Review. Susan Wendell's *The Rejected Body: Feminist Philosophical Reflections on Disability,* http://www.apa.udel.edu/apa/archive/newsletters/v97n2/medicine/

—, "Reconciling Equality to Difference: Caring (f)or Justice for People with Disabilities". *Hypatia* 10, no. 1, Winter, 1995.

Thomson, R.G., "Feminist Theory, the Body and the Disabled Figure". In L.J. Davis (ed.), *The Disability Studies Reader.* New York; London: Routledge, 1997.

Wendell, Susan, *The Rejected Body: Feminist Philosophical Reflections on Disability.* New York: Routledge, 1996.

World Health Organization, *World Health Organisation or International Classification of Impairments, Disabilities and Handicaps.* Geneva: WHO-ICIDH, 1980.

3

Need to Re-define Women's Activities in Gujarat: A Case Study of AWAG

ILA PATHAK

Secretary, Ahmedabad Women's Action Group (AWAG), Ahmedabad

It is not given to a women's action group to theorize about 'isms'. But an 'ism' could be a guiding principle for its activities like Gandhism for Gandhians. Ahmedabad Women's Action Group (AWAG) derived its approaches to action through both feminism and Gandhism. As AWAG emerged with a fresh set of ideals and goals for women in Gujarat, the scenario changed little by little.

AWAG's activities covered a large range of issues, from exploitation of woman's body by media to oppression of woman's being within family. AWAG has advocated changes in state's policies and systems or demanded social justice from Panchas of different castes. AWAG has continuously explored ways of asserting women's individuality, their equality, human rights, right to live and enjoy life.

One such exploration is in the direction of assisting women oppressed and exploited within their families. The established system in Family Counselling Centres in Gujarat in early eighties of the previous century was to ask the complainant woman to make up with husband and his family to allow their child to get nurturing from both the parents.

The rationale behind such system was that the "family was an important unit," therefore

(1) a married woman should live with her husband and marital family;
(2) a woman is a mother who should look after her child and the child should not be deprived of father's guardianship;
(3) a woman ought to sink differences, hoping that situation would improve; and
(4) a woman ought not to break the family but should continuously strive towards better relationship.

The feminist groups looked at such problems differently. To them the woman was important. They believed that (1) a married woman may not continue to live in subordination with husband and his family; and (2) a woman can look after her child alone if she so wishes or allow the child to stay back with father. In so doing the woman would have freed herself from oppressive surroundings and started her journey towards freedom. More important, she could survive.

It is easy to theorize thus and appreciate 'new' or 'feminist' approach. But life offers differently. A woman does not always come to an NGO with her problem. Parents come as in the following case:

> An elderly couple said to AWAG's Counsellor: 'We want to file a complaint against our daughter-in-law. She died of burns last night at her marital home.' 'How long was she there?' When was she married?' were the questions asked. 'We had sent her to her marital home yesterday in the morning. She had come back to us fourteen times after her marriage ...'

Or, a neighbour relates the death of a woman thus:

'Jasoda was in a hospital after she had received heavy burns injuries.' Samuben was narrating how Jasoda died of burns injuries. 'I asked her, Why she had to tell a lie to the police. They said that you tried to put up a kerosene lamp at a height, it fell and your clothes caught fire. Tell me the truth. A falling lamp would not burn anything. Who burned you? Well, Jasoda made me take an oath that I would not tell the truth to the police. Then, she said, 'He (Jasoda's husband) came home heavily drunk and I reprimanded him. He was very drunk, he suddenly became angry and threw kerosene at me and before I could stop him, he threw a lighted match at me. The saree of synthetic material immediately caught fire'. Samuben asked Jasoda again why she did not tell all that to the police. Jasoda's reply was, 'When I am dying how could I say that about my husband? Heaven won't forgive me. How would I carry that load of sin?'

Samuben narrated this real-life incident in a public meeting when domestic violence and so-called accidental deaths were being spoken of. Both the above-cited incidents sum up the reasons why women commit suicide or why women do not name any other person, particularly husband, as responsible for their unnatural death.

So, we in AWAG understood that parents did not want to support their daughters after marriage. A woman, whose life at her marital home becomes unbearable, loses will to live and eventually succumbs to death. Women also carry lots of religio-cultural baggage within them, having imbibed the same from family, neighbours, friends etc. Husband is seen as surrogate of god within home and a 'good' wife would say nothing to implicate him. That is how, whichever way one tries to get at the details of circumstances of death, one can find nothing, everyone, including the victim, is tight-lipped about it. But the causes of such deaths are obvious. One is that the woman could not survive at the marital home and the other is that she could not get any support from her natal home.

AWAG was led into studying unnatural deaths of women and to stem increase in the number of such deaths. This led us to do a study. We learned that when women die unnatural deaths, police record them as accidental deaths (ADs). So, the AWAG studied the phenomenon of ADs in detail. The study was undertaken primarily to assess the impact of section 498-A of Indian Penal Code (IPC) in helping women suffering from domestic violence. As the AWAG started the study it became clear that section 498-A, indicating torture by husband and/or his relatives, was hardly ever used by police exclusively; it was clubbed with other sections. In the sample too that we studied more than 60 per cent cases were of unnatural deaths of women and section 498-A was clubbed with other sections in most of these.

From 1984 onwards AWAG has been studying police records of women's unnatural deaths. From 1984 to 1995 we had noticed that number of deaths were increasing. The following table shows the same:

Table 1

Unnatural Deaths of Women in Gujarat, 1984 to 1995

Year	*1984*	*1985*	*1986*	*1987*	*1988*	*1989*	*1990*	*1991*	*1992*	*1993*	*1994*	*1995*
No. of deaths per year	1418	1024	2132	2220	4116	4254	3986	3862	4016	4521	4838	5112
Average no. of deaths per day	3.88	2.8	5.84	6.0	11.27	11.65	10.92	10.58	11.0	12.38	13.25	14.0

Total number of deaths noted here are found in police records under five different heads: (i) murder, section 302 (IPC); (ii) dowry death, section 304-B (IPC); (iii) abetment of suicide, section 306 (IPC); and (iv) accidental deaths as suicides or accidents, section 174 (Cr.PC).

So, in 1995, AWAG decided to study the manner in which these deaths were reported. AWAG has been studying police records from then onwards. A study was undertaken and was published in 1999, entitled 'Aftermath of Domestic Violence Against Women: A Systematic Exploration of AWAG's

Experience with Reference to the Operation of Criminal Justice System in Gujarat (India)'. The figures quoted here are from that study. In all, 1,652 cases were studied. Of these, 1001 were registered as ADs. Of these, many were reported as dying of catching fire in their kitchens. To think that hundreds of women were dying of such negligence! How could they unlearn the lessons of safety learned from the age of eight? Or, did they learn the lessons of submission and sacrifice well? Or, were they victimized because they were not 'submissive'? Did only young women sacrifice their lives? The following table shows the age of women who died ADs:

Table 2

Age in Years of Women Who Died ADs

Years	*0-10*	*11-20*	*21+30*	*31-40*	*41+*	*Not known*	*Total*
No. of women	36	259	363	124	116	103	1001
%	3.6	25.9	36.3	12.4	11.6	10.3	100

Women appear to be most vulnerable between the ages of 11 to 30, their vulnerability appears to extend upto and even beyond the age of 40 years. More than 62 per cent die young. In more than 10 per cent cases, ages were not recorded. We tried to find out more about them: the religion they practised, the castes they belonged to. The following table shows the religion of women victims:

Table 3

Women Whose ADs were Registered as per their Religion

Religion	*Hindu*	*Muslim*	*Christian*	*ST*	*Not known*	*Total*
No. of women	781	84	10	14	112	1001
%	78.1	8.4	1.0	1.4	11.2	100

The numbers almost follow those in population in Gujarat. Women of all religions seem to suffer equally. The number of

Hindu women was further distributed as per caste and shown in the following table:

Table 4

Hindu Women Whose ADs were Recorded as per Caste

Caste	*SCs*	*OBCs*	*Upper Castes*	*Total*
No. of women	200	352	229	781
%	25.6	45.0	29.3	100

Obviously, the women of other backward castes (OBCs) are most vulnerable. So are SC women. The OBC and SC women fall in the poorer class. They go out to earn in addition to looking after their homes and children. The data shows that a very large number of these women were battered. This shatters two very well circulated myths among the upper castes and upper classes of society. One is that these women are very well off monetarily as they themselves go out to earn and so do their husbands and sons. Their incomes are therefore large, only they do not know how to use their incomes in a planned manner. Second is that these women can abuse their husbands, use foul language for all around, so they are free from oppression within the family. One Police Inspector, who had served long years at Meghaninagar and Madhupura police stations, said that these OBC women suffer a lot because their husbands take to alcohol and stop working. Women have to work hard as unskilled labourers. Husbands waking from their alcoholic stupor look for the women as they need food. A husband may notice his wife taking money from or talking to a man (under whom she got her work). So, when she returns home he picks up a quarrel alleging her of bad character and of having sexual relations with that man. The woman retaliates in the beginning but later ends her life, in the face of such frequent quarrels.

Police have their own method of registering causes of ADs. Causes of deaths as recorded in police registers are classified and shown in the following table:

Table 5

Women Whose ADs were Recorded as per the Reasons of Death Assigned

Reason	*Proper accidents*	*Kitchen-based accidents*	*Poison*	*Long illness*	*Not known*	*Total*
No. of women	152	573	176	59	41	1001
%	15.2	57.3	17.6	5.9	4.1	100

By 'proper accidents' here is meant such accidents as when a woman dies of a fall while alighting from a bus, or because a wall collapses under which she was sleeping, etc. The following table shows causes of deaths distributed as per age of the victims:

Table 6

Age of Women Whose ADs were Recorded as per the Reasons of Death Assigned

Reason	*Age (in years)*							
	0-10	*11-20*	*21-30*	*31-40*	*41+*	*NK*	*Total*	*%*
Proper accidents	25	17	32	25	45	08	152	15.2
Kitchen-based accidents	09	168	241	72	42	41	573	57.3
Poison	01	62	72	17	04	20	176	17.6
Long illness	01	05	14	10	22	07	59	5.9
Not known	-	07	04	-	03	27	41	4.1
Total	36	259	363	124	116	103	1001	100

Of more than 57 per cent women who caught fire in their kitchens, more than 70 per cent (168+241) died quite young. More than 12 per cent (72) were senior to them by a few years only. So, more than 82 per cent of the women seem to die in the prime of their lives in their kitchens. This number is so overwhelmingly large that every other means of taking away life (e.g., poison taken by young women of 11-30 age group is reported at 76 per cent (62+72) of all who took poison) appears to fade into insignificance. It is also surprising that even among women dying of long illness young women outnumber older women. The proportion of deaths in the age group over 40 is less than 11-40 years age group. Twenty-nine younger women died of becoming tired of long illness while 22 older women died of similar cause. So, one wonders if the younger women really died of being tired of long illness!

However, what is equally shocking is that the reasons of deaths of older women also point to an equally hideous reality. A 63/70 year old woman dies of catching fire/while heating water/making tea or placing a kerosene lamp. A woman, more than 50/60 years old, consumes poison/acid following quarrels at home.

On perusing these records one gets the feeling that many women suffer silently, more than those who go to police stations, and give up their life when suffering becomes unbearable. Age becomes redundant then, the years of marriage could be more than seven or ten or even twenty. Unfortunately, their deaths are noted in such a way that they seem to die of negligence or because of 'small nothings'. The opaqueness of society is very much evident here in keeping the sufferings of these invisible women.

This study gave AWAG the profile of women victims and reasons stated in police records. But, while studying the women victims, the team developed insight into the plight of women victims. It became clear to AWAG that a woman in distress needed a friendly atmosphere to unburden herself and to get an assurance of support in any option that she may choose for her future life. We thought that this was the minimum necessary service that must be provided to women in distress.

AWAG is an action group. The insight gained from the study was followed up. In fact, AWAG had started advocating woman-friendly approach by the counsellors of Family Counselling Centres (FCCs) or Legal Aid Centres (LACs) run by NGOs. AWAG named this approach as woman-centred/

pro-woman approach. It was also necessary to provide social and legal support to the women in distress. AWAG took up the task of sensitizing the counsellors working in FCCs and social workers of LACs in Gujarat to a woman-friendly approach during 1995 to 1999. To arrest the unnatural deaths of more than fourteen women per day, such pro-woman counselling was necessary, so we discussed that in workshop after workshop with counsellors working in FCCs and social workers of LACs in Gujarat. We also spoke to them of the pro-woman legislations. The procedures to be followed at police stations and the legal procedures at courts were explained to them. Most of them responded positively and started practising the pro-woman approach.

But this did not make any difference to the number of unnatural deaths being recorded. One problem that was stated time and again was the complaint that the police resisted registration of complaints under section 498-A (IPC). If they did not resist, many women could escape being victimized and that would give them a reason to survive.

So, AWAG sought the permission of the Director General of Police, Gujarat to sensitize the police force of the state to women's issues so that they would register complaints of women victims of domestic violence. From January 1998 to the end of 2000 AWAG sensitized 80 per cent of the police in Gujarat to register women's complaints of domestic violence, of mental and physical torture, under section 498-A (IPC). Police records show the following results:

Table 7

Complaints Registered by Police under Section 498-A (IPC), 1993 to 2004

Year	*1993*	*1994*	*1995*	*1996*	*1997*	*1998*	*1999*	*2000*	*2001*	*2002*	*2003*	*2004*
No.of women's complaints	1540	1596	1950	2545	2415	2989	3276	3563	3191	2866	3185	3781
% of women's average complaints per day	4.22	4.37	5.34	6.97	6.62	8.19	8.97	9.76	8.74	7.85	8.72	10.35

It is obvious that registration under section 498-A has increased from 1998.

Looking at the following table, it will be clear that the number of unnatural deaths registered was increasing upto 1998. From 1998 onwards, as registration under section 498-A increased, number of women dying unnatural deaths decreased from 1999.

Table 8

Women Dying Unnatural Deaths of Women Registered in Gujarat, 1993 to 2004

Year	*1993*	*1994*	*1995*	*1996*	*1997*	*1998*	*1999*	*2000*	*2001*	*2002*	*2003*	*2004*
No. of deaths per year	4521	4838	5112	5164	5525	6349	6135	5583	4924	4672	4749	4631
No. of average deaths per day	12.38	13.25	14.0	14.15	15.14	17.39	16.08	15.03	13.49	12.80	13.01	12.68

So, it turned out that when complaints were registered by police under section 498-A (IPC), fewer women died unnatural deaths. The section was added to the Indian Penal Code in December 1983. Since then, it is said that the section is useless. The findings of this study shows that the section is very useful, as it has lessened the number of unnatural deaths of women registered as ADs in police records.

To support the argument that section 498-A is useless, more arguments are advanced. It is said that it adds to the burden of litigation only because women compromise and the time of the courts is wasted. In addition, husbands are put to unnecessary trouble.

Our study looked at these aspects also. One could agree that women do compromise. Reasons of such compromises were looked into. The finding of the study was that social pressure mounts on the woman. Till she agrees to withdraw her complaint, the courts do not bring their complaints on board. Ordinarily, it is said that any case would take years to come upon the board of any court. Our study indicates that cases were brought up in courts within 3/4/5/6 months or ½/3 years. Each of these was compromised, including one of suicide. In the terminology of courts if parties agree to end litigation, that is a compromise, so compromise in the complaint of section 498-A could also be for divorce/separation. Under this section complaints cannot be withdrawn, the woman complainant has to tell a lie in the court to show that she never complained and the court, in its order, states that the respondent was innocent!

In fact, the woman complainant waits and waits to be heard to get justice. But then she capitulates as social pressure mounts. She then compromises on condition that she would not be battered. AWAG's research assistants visited these women and asked whether they were battered any longer. The answer was that battering was there but it was much less. This indicates that litigation was useful. Section 498-A has given a breathing space to the woman and taught a lesson to the husband. We tend to believe that it teaches a lesson to many more who know the couple. Friends, relatives and neighbours learn that the man who was battering his wife was taken into police custody and had to spend some money to get released on bail. He would have spent more had he not compromised with her. Battering a wife appears to them to be an expensive experience. That stops them from being cruel to their wives.

From Table 8 it can be seen that during 1999 and 2004 1,817 lives of women are saved. Their survival is due to registering of complaints at police stations under section 498-A. Questions have been raised about the usefulness of section 498-A. It is stated that domestic violence had not lessened at all so what was the use of the legislation. AWAG's submission is that the legislation has been useful. It has helped many women to survive. Violence against them within their homes has lessened. Thanks to the implementation of section 498-A by Police Sub-Inspectors and Police Inspectors in Gujarat.

The lesson that feminists learned is that as far as possible every woman wants to continue in her married life. When it becomes absolutely unbearable, she tries to get help. It could come to her through a friend, a neighbour, an NGO or directly through police station. Then, once she has registered her protest loudly and clearly in her social milieu, she would return to her husband on condition that she would be respected as a human being and would not be treated as chattel.

What the feminists consider very necessary is certainly that, whether she lives on her terms separately or within family. The legal processes bring the erring husband to toe her line. And that is where the struggle ends.

4

Discourse on Sexual Harassment-Free Workplace for Women

VIBHUTI PATEL

Professor & Head, Department of Economics, SNDT University; Director, Centre for Dr. Ambedkar Studies; and Founder Secretary, WDC, Bombay University

Sexual harassment at workplace (SHW) has remained one of the central concerns of the women's movement in India since early eighties (Patel, 2002). During the 1980s, stringent actions by Forum Against Oppression of Women (Mumbai) against sexual harassment of nurses in the public and private hospitals by the patients and their male relatives, ward boys and other hospital staff; of air hostesses by their colleagues and passengers; of teachers by their colleagues, principals and management representatives; of Ph.D students by their guides; and so on and so forth received lukewarm response from the trade unions and adverse media publicity (FAOW, 1991). But this type of trivialization did not deter the women's rights activists. More and more working women started taking systematic action against SHW. *Baailancho Saad* (i.e., Women's

Voice) in Goa mobilized public opinion, against the Chief Minister, who allegedly harassed his secretary, through demonstrations, rallies, sit-ins till the Chief Minister did not resign. In 1990, the same organization filed a public interest litigation (PIL) to bring amendments in the antiquated Rape Law that defined rape in a narrow sense of "penile penetration into the vagina". Several women's groups came forward in support of new concern that encompassed variety of sexual violence against women including SHW (Chorine et al., 1999).

During the 1990s the most controversial survivor of brutal gang rape at workplace involved an employee of Rajasthan state government who tried to prevent child marriage as a part of her duty as a worker of Women Development Programme. The feudal patriarchs who were enraged by her (in their words, "a lowly woman from a poor and potter community") decided to teach her a lesson and repeatedly raped her (Samhita, 2001). After an extremely humiliating legal battle in the Rajasthan High Court the rape survivor did not get justice and the rapists were allowed to go scot-free. This enraged a women's rights group called *Vishakha* that filed a PIL in the Supreme Court of India (*Combat Law*, 2003).

Some of the noteworthy complaints of SHW that acquired national level limelight were filed by

- An IAS officer in Chandigarh Rupan Deo Bajaj against the super cop K.P.S. Gill
- An activist of All India Democratic Women's Association against Environment Minister in Dehradun
- An air hostess against her colleague Mahesh Kumar Lala in Mumbai
- An IAS officer in Thiruvanathpuram against the State Minister

Before 1997, women experiencing SHW had to lodge complaint under the Section 354 of Indian Penal Code that deals with "criminal assault of women to outrage women's modesty" and Section 509 that punishes an individual/ individuals for using "word, gesture or act intended to insult the modesty of a woman". These sections have left interpretation of 'outraging women's modesty' to the discretion of the police officer.

In 1997 the Supreme Court passed the landmark judgment in the *Vishakha* case laying down guidelines to be followed by establishments in dealing with complaints of sexual harassment. The Court stated that these guidelines were to be implemented until legislation is passed to deal with the issue (Mathew, 2002).

Persuant to this, the Government of India requested the National Commission for Women (NCW) to draft the legislation. A number of issues were raised, and ultimately a Drafting Committee was set up to make a fresh draft. A number of women's organizations were part of this committee, including, from Mumbai, Majlis. Majlis was asked to make the draft. Some women's organizations and women lawyers associated with trade unions in Mumbai have collectively worked on the draft with Majlis. Particular concerns while drafting have been to include the unorganized sector and to incorporate provisions of labour law. The Bill introduced in the parliament and known as 'The Sexual Harassment of Women at the Workplace (Prevention and Redressal) Bill, 2004' provides for the prevention and redressal of sexual harassment of women at workplaces, or arising during and out of the course of their employment and matters connected thereto, in keeping with the principles of equality, freedom, life and liberty as enshrined in the Constitution of India and as upheld by the Supreme Court in *Vishakha vs State of Rajasthan* [1997(7) SCC 323] and as reflected in the Convention on the Elimination of All Forms of Discrimination Against Women (CEDAW), which has been ratified by the Government of India.

Scenario in the Post-Vishakha Guidelines Period

Several organizations have conducted survey research on SHW that were widely disseminated. Survey by Sakshi (Delhi) throws up some worrying data where 80 per cent of respondents revealed that SHW exists, 49 per cent had encountered SHW, 41 per cent had experienced SHW, 53 per cent women and men did not have equal opportunities, 53 per cent were treated unfairly by supervisors, employers and co-workers, 58 per cent had not heard of the Supreme Court's directive of 1997 and only 20 per cent of organizations had implemented Vishakha guidelines (Dalal, 2003). Controversy over SHW by the senior manager of Infosys (Nair, 2003), by the chairman and managing director of NALCO (Ramanujan, 2004), Medha Kotwal petition on SHW of Ph. D student by her guide in M.S. University, Vadodara, complaint against senior professor of Lucknow University (ToI, 2003), and complaint of SHW by the film star Sushmita Sen against CEO of Coca Cola have made employers alert about the economic burden and efficiency loss due to SHW. Still, "most private companies refrain from investing funds in such committees".

Sophia Centre for Women's Studies and Development Study shows that awareness and implementation of the Supreme Court's guidelines is very low and there is need to spread awareness on the same. Study of *Samhita* (Kolkata) throwing light on the processual dimensions of Bhanvari Devi case has alarmed the state and civil society of the enormity and gravity of the menace called SHW (SCWSD & ICHRL, 2003).

Recently, The Times Foundation organized a workshop for the corporate world on SHW. Testimonies of several participants of the workshop revealed that SHW is prevalent even in the companies where the victims are highly educated and have considerable economic leverage. Similar views have been expressed in the business journals (*Business Today*, 1 September 2002).

On 20th October, 2004 the students thrashed anatomy professor from Versova, Andheri for alleged sexual misconduct (*The Indian Express-Mumbai Newsline*, 21 October 2004).

Definition of Sexual Harassment at Work

The Supreme Court directive, 1997 clearly and unambiguously provides an answer to the question, 'What is sexual harassment?'

As defined in the Supreme Court guidelines (Vishakha vs the State of Rajasthan, August 1997) sexual harassment includes such *unwelcome* sexually determined behaviour as:

- Physical contact
- A demand or request for sexual favours

- Sexually coloured remarks
- Showing pornography
- Any other unwelcome physical, verbal or non-verbal conduct of a sexual nature, e.g., leering, dirty jokes, sexual remark about a person's body etc.

The Supreme Court directive has provided a legitimate space for surfacing of hidden realities of SHW in which earlier only victim-blaming, witch-hunting and black-mailing flourished. Now, women are fighting back tooth and nail. Electronic and print media have become extremely responsive to the issue of SHW. My firsthand experience of providing support to women survivors of SHW has convinced me that we need to counter the myths about SHW with concrete facts, case studies and data base.

Myths and Facts

Myth 1: Women enjoy eve-teasing/sexual harassment.

Fact: Eve-teasing/sexual harassment is humiliating, intimidating, painful and frightening.

Myth 2: Eve-teasing is harmless flirtation. Women who object have no sense of humour.

Fact: Behaviour that is unwelcome cannot be considered harmless, or funny. Sexual harassment is defined by its impact on the woman rather than the intent of the perpetrator.

Myth 3: Women ask for SHW. Only women who are provocatively dressed are sexually harassed.

Fact: This is the classic way of shifting the blame from the harasser to the woman. Women have the right to act, dress and move around freely without the threat of attack or harassment.

The most popular slogan of the women's rights movement of last three decades has been:

However we dress, wherever we go.

'Yes' means 'Yes' and 'No' means 'No'.

Myth 4: Women who say NO actually mean YES.

Fact: This is a common myth used by men to justify sexual aggression and one-sided sexual advances.

Myth 5: Sexual harassment is not really an issue. It doesn't hurt anyone.

Fact: Persons subjected to sexual harassment experience a wide range of physical and psychological ailments. There are economic consequences for the victim's physical and mental well-being and the organization's productivity, efficiency and work ethics.

Myth 6: Sexual harassment! It's only natural male behaviour. Men is a hunter and woman is a prey.

Fact: Men are not born knowing how to sexually harass others. It is learned within the context of a sexist and patriarchal environment that perpetuates control over women's sexuality, fertility and labour.

Myth 7: Women keep quiet: that means they like it.

Fact: Women keep quiet to avoid the stigma attached and retaliation from the harasser. Women are afraid that they will be accused of provoking it, of being victimized, of being called liars and made the subject of gossip.

Myth 8: If women go to places where they are not welcome, they should expect sexual harassment.

Fact: Discriminatory behaviour and abuse is unlawful. Women have equal access to all work facilities. Safe workplace is women's legal right.

The Vishakha Guidelines

The Vishakha guidelines categorically state that it is the duty of the employer or other responsible persons in the workplaces or other institutions

- to prevent sexual harassment, and
- to provide mechanisms for resolution of complaints.

All women, who draw a regular salary receive an honorarium, or work in a voluntary capacity in the government, private sector or unorganized sector, come under the purview of these guidelines.

Complaints Mechanism

- All workplaces should have an appropriate complaints mechanism with a complaints committee, special counsellor or other support services.
- A woman must head the complaints committee and not less than half its members should be women.
- The committee should include an NGO/individual familiar with the issue of sexual harassment.
- The complaint procedure must be time-bound.
- Confidentiality must be maintained.
- Complainants/witnesses should not experience victimization/discrimination during the process.

Preventive Steps

- Sexual harassment should be affirmatively discussed at workers' meetings, employer-employee meetings, etc.
- Guidelines should be prominently displayed to create awareness of the rights of female employees.
- The employer should assist persons affected in cases of sexual harassment by outsiders.
- Central and state governments must adopt measures including legislation to ensure that private employers also observe guidelines.
- Names and contact numbers of members of the complaints committee must be prominently displayed.

Employers' Responsibilities

- Recognize sexual harassment as a serious offence.
- Recognize the responsibility of the company/factory/workplace to prevent and deal with sexual harassment at the workplace.
- Recognize the liability of the company etc. for sexual harassment by the employees or management. Employers are not necessarily insulated from that liability because they were not aware of sexual harassment by the staff.

- Formulate an anti-sexual harassment policy. This should include:
  - A clear statement of the employer's commitment to a workplace free of unlawful discrimination and harassment.
  - Clear definition of sexual harassment (using examples), and prohibition of such behaviour as an offence.
  - Constitution of a complaints committee to investigate, mediate, counsel and resolve cases of sexual harassment. The Supreme Court guidelines envisage a pro-active role for the complaints committee and prevention of sexual harassment at work is a crucial role. It is thus imperative that the committee must consist of persons who are sensitive and open to the issues faced by women.
  - A statement that anyone found guilty of harassment after investigation will be subject to disciplinary action.
  - The range of penalties that the complaints committee can levy against the offender.
  - Explicit protection of the confidentiality of the victim of harassment and of witnesses.
  - A guarantee that neither complainant nor witnesses will be subjected to retaliation.
- Publish the policy and make copies available at the workplace. Discuss the policy with all new recruits and existing employees. Third party suppliers and clients should also be aware of the policy.
- Conduct periodic training for all employees, with active involvement of the complaints committee.

Employers' Duty

Freedom from sexual harassment is a condition of work that an employee is entitled to expect. Women's rights at workplace are human rights.

There are four perspectives on SHW as explained below:

Feminists	*Legal*	*Organizational*	
		View A	*View B*
1. Power-relation, male over woman. 2. Constitutes economic coercion. 3. Threatens women's livelihood. 4. Reflects women's subordinate status in society. 5. Asserts women's sex roles over her work role. 6. Parallels rape.	1. Exploitative. 2. Involves both implicit and explicit terms of employment. 3. Used as a basis of employment decisions. 4. Produces consequences from submission to/or refusal of advances. 5. Promotes intimidating, hostile or offensive work environment.	1. Interpersonal. 2. Consists of misinter-pretation or misunderstand ing of person's intentions. 3. "Love affair gone sour". 4. Personal matter. Why should organization get involved? 5. Can hurt reputation of the accused.	1. Interpersonal. 2. Improper use of power to extort gratification. 3. Treats women as sex objects. 4. Coercive, exploitative, improper. 5. Asserts the woman's sex roles over work roles. 6. Aberrant behaviour.

Recommendations of National Commission for Women (NCW) on Safety of Women in and around College and University Campuses

In response to barbaric sexual violence against three women students in three different places within a week in the Delhi University campuses, in 2002, the NCW called an emergency meeting to discuss safety of women in the educational institutions.

Recommendations that emerged out of the meeting convened by NCW with Principal Secretary (Home), Delhi Police Commissioner and heads of educational institutions regarding strategies to prevent occurrence of rape and sexual harassment in and around campus are as follows:

Police

(1) More PCR vans should be deployed for patrolling around the educational institutions.

(2) On the pattern of women help-line, college help-lines should also be provided and its number should be prominently displayed.
(3) Police patrolling should be there around educational institutions at least for two hours before and after the college is over.
(4) There is a need to increase interrelationship between police and educational institutions.
(5) Every case of rape to be handled by a woman police officer.
(6) Attitude of the police needs to be made more positive towards the victim.

Educational Institutions

(1) Educational institutions must ensure proper lighting arrangement in and around their premises, as darkness is conducive to crime. Height hedges should be reduced in the campus for proper visibility.
(2) Internal security committee should be constituted by all the educational institutions headed by the head of the institution, police officer and student representatives should be invited for its meeting to review the security arrangement. If the need arises, other government departments like PWD, MCD or any other may be invited to review the security arrangements.
(3) Internal security committee should have monthly or bimonthly meeting and minutes of the meeting must be maintained.
(4) The experts should be invited for the inspection of the college area to assess the security needs and arrangements in the campus.
(5) Educational institutions must perform their administrative role for the security of the students.
(6) Student must be given proper training in self-defence.
(7) Telephone numbers of college help-lines for women should be displayed at proper places.
(8) Entry into educational institutions should be restricted. It should be through Identity Cards.

(9) Construction workers should not be allowed to stay in the premises of the institutions overnight.
(10) Safety gadgets should be provided in the hostels.
(11) Educational institutions can engage retired police officers on their security committees/boards.
(12) De-politicization of the campus is must and institutions must ensure it.
(13) Awareness programmes on safety and security of students to be conducted on regular basis.

Administration

(1) Arrangements should be made to provide shuttle bus services for colleges.
(2) Residential areas should be separated from educational institutions.
(3) Administration should ensure that there are no dark areas with high hedges.

Media

(1) There is need to sensitize media regarding the repeated telecast of incidents relating to violence against women, which has negative repercussions on the society, especially children.
(2) National Commission for Women directs the media that there should be no intrusion on the privacy of the victim.

Delhi University has passed an ordinance based on its policy against SHW with clearly defined rules and procedures. It has mentioned range of disciplinary action to punish the culprit (employee) of SHW including warning, written apology, bond of good behaviour, adverse remarks in the confidential report, debarring from supervisory duty, denial of membership of statutory bodies, denial of re-employment, stopping of increments/promotion, reverting, demotion, suspension and dismissal. For student culprit the penalties could be in the form of warning, written apology, bond of good behaviour, debarring entry into hostel/campus, suspension for a specific period of time, withholding results, debarring from examinations, debarring from contesting elections, debarring from holding posts such as member of committee of courses, membership of college union, expulsion, denial of admission, declaring the harasser as *persona non grata* for a stipulated period of time and any other relevant mechanism (Court Meeting, 2003).

Crusade of University of Mumbai Against Sexual Harassment at Place of Work

In response to the Supreme Court of India's directive in response to the public interest litigation filed by *Vishakha*, a women's rights group in Rajasthan concerning sexual harassment at workplace, the University of Mumbai established Women Development Cell with twin objectives (Report, 1999): to prevent sexual harassment at workplace, and to promote women's empowerment. The University of Mumbai has 377 affiliated colleges and institutions in its jurisdiction. After successfully completing the institutional support mechanisms of the university level WDC, now, the colleges are starting college level WDCs (Patel, 2004). The management council of the university passed Women Development Policy on 22 December 2002 (WDC, 2003).

The Women Development Cell (WDC) of University of Mumbai has taken lead in encouraging the colleges to start Gender Issues Cells or college level WDC throughout the academic years 2002-03 and 2003-04. Members of the newly developed cells (either Gender Issues Cell or Women Development Cell) in some of the colleges had many queries to be answered. Moreover, it was necessary to motivate those colleges that had not started such cell, to come forward to form one.

Faced with these twin problems, at the beginning of the academic year 2002-03, it was decided to hold seven orientation workshops per year on the basis of geographical area of the colleges and institutions, for dissemination of information concerning policy and formation of Women Development Cell at college/institution level (WDC, 2002).

Report of Orientation Workshops (June 2002-April 2004)

After thorough research, seven colleges were identified for zone-wise orientation workshop for awareness generation regarding goals, objectives, scope and structure of WDC and explanation of modalities of starting WDC at college level. Within two years 14 workshop for teachers, students and employees were organized. The sessions in each workshop focused on the following subject matters:

1. Introduction: Aims and objectives of WDC by chairperson.
2. Sexual Harassment Bill as introduced by the Supreme Court judgment and National Commission for Women Draft Bill.
3. Group discussion on participants' proposal for building awareness in their respective colleges.
4. Reports of the group discussions and final recommendations.

1. The first orientation workshop was inaugurated on 31 August 2002 at the Sophia Centre for Women's Studies and Development and was attended by teachers drawn from South Mumbai Colleges. Mrs. Mrinal Gore, President of *Swadhar*, an NGO dedicated to women's welfare and justice, inaugurated the workshop. For over three decades, *Swadhar* has taken lead in handling of sexual harassment cases in the city of Mumbai. Prof. Rohini Gawankar, Chairperson of the WDC, gave a profile of formation and functioning of WDC. Dr. Anila Verghese, Principal of Sophia College gave assurance regarding support for the activities of WDC. Dr. Vibhuti Patel explained the goals, objectives, structure, function and jurisdiction of WDC as per University Draft Policy for Women Development Cell. Dr. Naina Athalye focussed on the directive of the Supreme Court of India on sexual harassment and highlighted the concerns of women's rights organizations. The second session involved group discussion. Some of the important recommendations emerging out of the discussion were:
   - Mental health of women should be given priority in cases of sexual harassment at workplace.

- There should be more working mother-friendly atmosphere in the colleges.
- We should make our girl students more confident, assertive and self-reliant.
- Women employees, teachers and students must be given proper training in self-defence.

2. The second orientation workshop of WDC for the colleges of the North Zone was conducted at D.G. Ruparel College on 21 September 2002. Prof. P.M. Sule, Principal of D. G. Ruparel College, in his welcome speech, informed that Ruparel College had also inaugurated its WDC Unit in the college on 22 August 2002. Prof. Rohini Gawankar explained the objectives of the cell. The chief guest, Prof. Neera Desai, said that it was necessary to build up the atmosphere of confidence, faith, fearlessness and hope in the college as well as in the university campus for girl students and women employees, who must be aware of their rights.

   Finally, during the group discussion, the participants raised a number of points:

   - Why LMC member must be the convenor of the WDC.
   - If boys make a complaint about harassment by girl students, will it be attended to by WDC?
   - Development measures like arranging informative lectures, self-defence activities to make students fearless and secure were discussed. Some colleges are already doing these activities under NSS.
   - There was a suggestion that even boys must be involved to create healthy atmosphere.
   - It was suggested that a complaint against sexual harassment must be written one and it should be kept secret.
   - One participant raised a point about girls wearing provocative dresses and affecting the atmosphere.
   - Finally, most of them agreed that WDC must take preventive measure against sexual harassment just to

control such attitude, though few such cases take place on our campus.

3. The workshop for the colleges situated in Ratnagiri district was organized at Chiplun College. Its report is available in Marathi.
4. Sant Rawol Maharaj College, Kudal hosted a workshop for colleges of University of Mumbai in Sindhudurg district. Its report in Marathi gives details of the proceedings.
5. Bhausaheb Nene College of Pen organized the orientation workshop for colleges situated in Raigarh district on 7 January 2003. Enthusiasm of the male participants in this workshop was noteworthy. Men constituted 50 per cent of the participants and took active part in the deliberations that aimed at creation of a gender-just society.
6. Dnyanvardhini College, Thane was the venue for the orientation workshop for college teachers of Thane district and it was held on 10 January 2003. WDC has a copy of its report in Marathi.
7. Ghanshyam Das Saraf College, Malad organized the last orientation workshop of WDC that was attended by more than 70 representatives comprising both the teaching and non-teaching staff of different colleges between Bandra to Borivali. Dr. Sunanda Kar, Principal of the college and a member of University's WDC was the organizer of the workshop.

These seven workshops were aimed at providing guidelines for the WDC to colleges and the university departments to solve and investigate gender issues faced not only by the students but also by the teaching and non-teaching staff of the colleges.

In these seven workshops, total number of participants – including women and men – was 218. Only in Pen, out of total number of 36 participants, there were 18 men and 18 women participants. It should be noted that in the remaining six workshops, the total number of male participants was less than 10.

It was suggested that without cooperation of men, WDC would not be able to function effectively. Male members of the university system should get it out of their minds that WDC is meant only for women.

Nature of Issues Faced by WDC

1. Complaints by women teachers concerning use of cyber-porn in the computer rooms of colleges and university departments.
2. Complaints by women students of harassment through SMS messages.
3. Complaints of sexual harassment by authority.
4. Complaints by women students of incestuous sexual assault.
5. Complaints regarding nominal cell where the members of college WDC are treated as dummies/puppets by the principal/management.
6. Complaints regarding cigarette smoking, spitting and alcohol consumption during office hours.
7. Those who have already started Gender Issues Cell, are expected to rename it as Women Development Cell?

WDC has tried to implement some of them. For example, telephone numbers of important women's organizations providing support to women in distress are displayed at our office. The list of special cells for women and children at police stations in Maharashtra is displayed. All those colleges that have given their e-mail IDs to WDC are sent this information through internet/PDF file.

WDC also disseminates literature on the subject and distributes/circulates among colleges.

All important documents, judgments, studies and government directives of the state and central governments as well as UGC are kept in WDC library, which can be photo-copied.

WDC receives several letters and reminders from the state and central government demanding report of WDC activities.

In its letter dated 29 March 2003, the University Grants Commission (UGC) has demanded action plan from our university regarding the violence and sexual harassment against women in the campus. Similar letter has also come from the Department of Secondary and Higher Education of the Ministry of Human Resource Development of Government of India. The member-secretary of WDC has informed all of them that the university and some college level WDCs have started functioning. We have completed seven orientation programmes in which the 280 representatives of colleges of the University of Mumbai took part. Some of them have taken up cases of sexual harassment at college level. The Grievances Redressal Committee of university level WDC is currently investigating two cases of sexual harassment.

University level WDC meets every six months. For awareness generation, the colleges of our university are organizing seminars, talks, and self-defence workshops, besides poster campaigns on the issue of sexual harassment at workplace. Sociology Department of Sophia College has conducted research on this subject.

Formation of Grievances Redressal Committee of Women Development Cell

To handle the cases of sexual harassment, a seven-member Grievances Redressal Committee (GRC) has been constituted from among the WDC members as per the directive of Vice-Chancellor and the chairperson of WDC.

On March 8, 2003, the first meeting of GRC took place for hearing of a case filed by a woman employee of Marathi Department of University of Mumbai. GRC has completed a preliminary inquiry with regard to two complaints of sexual harassment.

The process of inquiry is time-consuming, tiring and emotionally exhausting. The commitment and sincerity of GRC members is gratefully acknowledged by WDC. So far, WDC has handled six major cases of sexual harassment at workplace; in three cases principals of colleges were the accused.

Poster and Slogan Competition

WDC sent circular signed by the Vice-Chancellor to the principals of affiliated colleges and heads of university departments. WDC received an enthusiastic response from both men and women students, teachers and employees from medical, engineering, fine arts, commerce, sciences and arts colleges.

Performance Appraisal

As a member-secretary of the University of Mumbai's WDC, I found the day-to-day work of WDC quite challenging. In spite of negative vibes of jeering patriarchs and cynical veterans of academia, the WDCs in the colleges are receiving popular support from students, staff and teachers. To deal with varied forms of discrimination faced by women employees, students and teachers, WDC conducts legal awareness workshops. This year we have conducted eight such workshops for teaching and non-teaching staff of the university. The colleges are organizing interactive sessions on SHW through poster exhibitions, lectures, training sessions, essay competitions and publishing articles in the college magazines.

The top-down approach (Vice Chancellor as president of University WDC and principals as ex-officio chairpersons of college level WDCs) towards WDCs has provided legitimate women's space (literally and metaphorically) for bringing out sensitive issues concerning sexuality, talked in hush-hush tone to the public realm, in the context of rigid academic hierarchies. Mandatory induction of representative of the NGO in the WDC acts as a fearless conscience keeper. WDCs have helped women's concerns to transcend the barriers of marginalization and trivialization of women's agenda. WDCs are nodal agencies, net-works and platforms for women's empowerment.

Important Initiatives at the National and Global Levels

The National Policy for Women Empowerment (2001) and the state women policies have given due weightage to the prevention of SHW and promotion of grievance redressal mechanisms in cases of SHW.

High profile institutions such as Indian Institute of Technology and reputed engineering colleges, medical colleges and public sector enterprises such as RCF, Indian Railways, nationalized banks and insurance companies have instituted grievance cells to deal with SHW.

During the last three years national and international Round Tables and conventions have taken place. National Productivity Council organized national conventions in 2002 and 2003.

Outcome of Round Table Conference (held on 8th April 2002 at USEFI) was quite encouraging. It deliberated upon the need to create awareness and break the cordon of silence that surrounds the problem. It was emphasized that sexual harassment is not about sex; it is about a phenomenon where the accused wants his victim to realize the authority that he exerts. It was also decided to study the problem of sexual harassment in a broader perspective with special emphasis on different places of work.

Likewise, outcome of Regional Conference (held on 3rd-4th September 2002 India Habitat Centre) is also inspiring. It studied and discussed the problem of sexual harassment primarily in four sectors, namely, universities, PSUs, organized and unorganized sectors. There was a unanimous agreement upon the need to create a healthy environment where men and women could work together without inhibitions. A holistic view was taken in respect of each sector/workplace, its special problems and the formulae which would cure this burning problem. Emphasis was laid on the interdisciplinary treatment of the issue.

The School of Law and Legal Studies, in association with United States Education Foundation of India, Supreme Court Bar Association and Vivekananda Institute of Professional Studies, organized a national conference on the issue of sexual harassment at place of work in 2003. The conference discussed the following issues:

(i) Sexual Harassment (Prevention and Redress) Bill, 2003

This Bill, drafted by the National Commission for Women, proposed to provide for prevention and redress of sexual harassment of women at their workplace, or arising during and out of the course of their employment or in other institutions and establishments and matters connected thereto. It arrived at the conclusion that implementation of the law is the most important factor

1. The Bill does not make it mandatory to have an Internal Complaints Committee for workplaces having 50 or less than 50 employees.
2. The Bill does not provide for *suo moto* recognition by the appropriate authority of a non-reported complaint of sexual harassment.
3. Section 7(7)(c) provides for immediate transfer of the defendant. This tool of transfer is not effective as the defendant continues with his deviant behaviour in the new place.
4. The salient details of the procedure of appeals need to be worked out.
5. The Bill does not contain any provision for the prevention of misuse by women.

(ii) Problem of Non-Reporting of Cases

- Fewer cases are being reported and a large number remain hidden. The media is playing an active role in highlighting these cases.
- Due to lack of sensitivity on the part of society women are reluctant to complain. The problems of sexual harassment belong to the silence zone.

Problems and Issues

1. There should be gender sensitization of society so that the victim is not made to feel guilty of the fact that she may have encouraged the man to sexually harass her.
2. Women should be made aware of their rights, the concept and definition of sexual harassment and the redressal mechanism available to them.
3. The victim's privacy needs to be protected.

(iii) Judicial Approach to the Problem of Sexual Harassment at the Workplace in the Last Couple of Years

- Through two landmark judgments, namely, Vishakha vs. State of Rajasthan, and Apparel Export Promotion Council vs. A.K. Chopra, the Supreme Court of India enjoined the executive, in the absence of a domestic law, to adopt certain guidelines and measures to ensure the prevention of such incidents.

- However, not many cases are being taken up by the victims to the apex court.

Problems and Issues

1. Need to gender sensitize all levels of the criminal justice system.
2. Steps to be taken to increase conviction rate in such cases.
3. Need for speedy trial procedure in relation to this issue.
4. Non-existence of any Sexual Harassment Complaints Committee, dealing with this problem, even in the apex court.
5. Need for the apex court to direct the various workplaces to form Sexual Harassment Committees within the provided time limit.

Conclusion

Sexual harassment at place of work is a universal issue. Even though occurrence of sexual harassment in workplace has been a widespread problem in India and elsewhere, it is for the first time that such a practice has been recognized as an infringement of the fundamental rights of a woman under Article 19(1)(g) of the Constitution of India: "To practice any profession ought to carry out any occupation, trade or business". Of late, the problem has assumed serious proportions and there has been a meteoric rise in the number of cases but surprisingly in most of the cases women are not reporting the matter to the concerned authorities.

In our country, Articles 14, 15 and 21 of the Indian Constitution provide safeguards against all forms of discrimination. In more recent times, the Supreme Court has given two landmark judgments – *Vishakha vs. State of Rajasthan, 1997* and *Apparel Export Promotion Council vs. A.K. Chopra, 1999* – in which it has laid down certain guidelines and measures to ensure the prevention of such incidents. Despite these developments, the problem of sexual harassment is assuming alarming proportions and there is a pressing need for domestic laws on this issue.

India is rapidly advancing with developmental goals, more and more women are joining the workforce. It is the duty of the state to provide for the well-being and respect of its human force to prevent frustration, low self-esteem, insecurity and emotional disturbance. This, in turn, affects business efficacy, leading to loss of production and loss of reputation for the organization or the employer. In fact, the recognition of the right to protection against sexual harassment is an intrinsic component of the protection of human rights of women. It is also a step towards providing them with independence, equality of opportunity and the right to work with dignity.

In the last 50 years, various international human rights organizations have been focusing on promoting and protecting women rights. It has been acknowledged by the United Nations that women's rights are human rights. The same was reiterated in the Beijing Declaration too. Most of the international human rights movements have raised their voice against abuses and violence perpetrated upon women in general. In 1979, the UN General Assembly adopted the Convention on the Elimination of all Forms of Discrimination Against Women (CEDAW). The areas where discrimination has been found to be rampant are: political rights, marriage, family and employment. The Convention emphasized that discrimination and attack on women's dignity violated the principle of equality of rights.

In 2003, the National Commission for Women (NCW) drafted the Sexual Harassment (Prevention and Redress) Bill. The Bill provides for prevention and redressal of cases of sexual harassment of women in their workplace. However, the Bill has many loopholes and they need to be plugged before it could become legislation. For any sexual harassment law to be successful in India, it is important to be aware about the difficulties confronting our society and ways to overcome them. We all are aware that India is a patriarchal society and most of the cases of sexual harassment remain unreported. Women are reluctant to complain and prefer silence due to lack of sensitivity on the part of the Indian society. There is a need for gender sensitization of our society so that the victim does not feel guilty and is encouraged to report against any kind of harassment. The victim's privacy should be protected. Both the police and the judiciary, in particular, need to be gender sensitized. There should be speedy redressal and increase in conviction rate. Women themselves should be made aware of their right to safe and harassment-free work environment. The concept and definition of sexual harassment should be clearly laid down and the redressal mechanism should be made known to women in each and every sector of the economy. Structures and mechanisms should be created for women in the unorganized/informal sector to combat SHW. Despite bold judgments by the Supreme Court, in most of the workplaces, even in the government sector, there is a non-existence of any sexual harassment complaint committee to deal with the problem. The apex court must direct the various workplaces to form such committees within a stipulated time period.

In any civilized society, it is a fundamental human right of people to be able to lead their lives with dignity, free from any mental or physical torture and to ensure this, the transgressors must pay for their unsolicited sexual advances. At the same time, we should encourage organizations such as Men Against Violence and Abuse that organizes gender sensitization programmes as well as self-defence classes to combat sexual harassment at workplace (Sadani, 2003).

To effectively prevent SHW, we need both top-down initiative by the state and employers and civil society initiatives from citizens groups, women's organizations and trade unions.

Works Cited

Chorine, Christine, Mihir Desai, Colin Gonsalves (1999), *Women and Law*, Vols. I & II, Socio-legal Information Centre, Bombay.

Combat Law (2003), The Human Rights Magazine, Special number on Violence Against Women, September-October.

Court Meeting (2003), Amendments to Ordinances and Appendices to Ordinances, No 19. XV D Sexual Harassment, University of Delhi.

Dalal, Suchata (2003), "Bias in the Boardroom", *The Sunday Express*, May 18.

FAOW (1991), "Moving.....But Not Quite There-Evaluation Report of One Decade 1980-1990", Forum Against Oppression of Women, Mumbai.

Gupte, Manisha and Renu Khanna (2002), Process Documentation of Gender Training of Dilaasa, Mumbai.

Mathew, Mini (2002), *Sexual Harassment at Workplace*, India Centre for Human Rights and Law, Mumbai.

Nair, Meera (2003), "The Seamier Side of Office Life-his Woman's Day Let's Do Away With the Groping, Lecherous Advances Made by Male Colleagues at the Workplace", *The Indian Express*, March 6-12.

Patel, Vibhuti (2002), *Women's Challenges of the New Millennium*, Gyan Publications, Delhi.

Patel, Vibhuti (2004), "Crusade of University of Mumbai Against Sexual Harassment at Place of Work", paper presented at a seminar on "An Interdisciplinary Approach to the Unexplored Areas Related to Women" sponsored by University Grants Commission and organized by Maniben Nanavati College for Women, Mumbai on 30th & 31st July 2004.

Ramanujan, Sweta (2004), "NALCO Sexual Harassment Victim takes Heart from Family and Friends – Working Woman Shows Grace Under Pressure", *The Indian Express*, February 23.

Report (1999), Workshop on Prevention of Sexual Harassment of Women at Workplaces, Department of Adult and Continuing Education and Extension, University of Mumbai.

Sadani, Harish (2003), "Man Against Violence and Abuse-MAVA", *Urdhva Mula*, Vol.2, No. 2, December.

Sadashivan (1999), Policy for Prevention of Sexual Harassment in Educational Institutions and for Dealing with Cases of Sexual Harassment", Bombay University College Teachers' Union, Mumbai.

Samhita (2001), *The Politics of Silence*, Kolkata.

Sophia Centre for Women's Studies and Development and India Centre for Human Rights and Law (2003). "Sexual Harassment of Women at the Workplace", The Department of Sociology, Sophia College, Mumbai.

The Times News Network (2003). "Disclosures: What is Sexual Harassment", *The Times of India*, June 15.

Women Development Cell (2002), Orientation Program on Women's Rights: Laws that Protect, August 6-7, 2001 organised by Department of Adult and Continuing Education and Extension in collaboration with Ghanshyamdas Saraf Girls' College, University of Mumbai.

—, Report for 1991-2001, Department of Adult and Continuing Education and Extension, University of Mumbai.

II

Re-think

Re-thinking is the second step in our frame of reference for re-defining feminisms. Re-think, at a surface level, is a kind of re-visitation. However, each of the articles in this section expands this simple act of looking back into a thorough comprehension of the **why, what** and **how** the original thinking process progressed. **Esther David** attempts an interesting second look at the famous painting of "The Original Sin". Through semantic and visual cues David's second look opens up the space for our collective re-thinking of the painting and the biblical myth. A fellow writer, **Lakshmi Kannan** projects her re-thinking process into the poetics of feminism. From the question of being a woman-of-many-roles to being a writer, Kannan's personal-artistic discourse re-thinks the politics and poetics of representation.

G.S. Jayashree combines feminist scholarship and politics of representation in her analysis of short texts by women over the last 150 years. She examines how through the submissive, progressive, regressive and assertive phases, an awareness of the gender status and a constant reiteration of a position of subalternity have framed the creative discourse. **A. Mangai** continues Jayashree's discussion by extending the arguments to explore the politics of representation, norms of theatrical conventions, aspects of space, choreography and the body politics of contemporary Tamil theatre. Mangai's arguments are harnessed from her multiple roles as academic, activist and director, feminist theatre group. **Shobhana Nair** activates her process of re-think by juxtaposing two apparently contradictory developments, namely, gender representation in Indian media and the setting up of Women's Development Cells (WDCs). Contesting our common perception that media reinforces stereotypes while WDCs collapse those stereotypes, Shobhana explores the ways in which both resist stereotypes and progress towards affirmative tendencies. **Aniruddhan Vasudevan** proceeds on his re-thinking activity by contesting essentialist categories of genders and sexualities. He situates his activist-academic deliberations in the context of alternative female sexualities within the women's and the queer movements.

5

A Second Look at Michelangelo's Painting – Original Sin

ESTHER DAVID

Novelist & Artist, Ahmedabad

Michelangelo Buonarroti (1475-1564) started painting the Sistine Chapel in Rome in 1508. The restoration of the chapel was done in 1992. Once the pollution was removed, it showed that Michelangelo had not painted in dull brown colours, but in bright colours.

We human beings often have enemies. So, it comes as a surprise while reading *The Bible* that even God almighty had an enemy in the form of Satan, often depicted as a serpent. Satan was always trying to disrupt God's handiwork or artwork, that is, the creation of earth. Satan, in the form of a serpent, arrives very early in the Bible, the Old Testament, known as the Israelite Bible or Torah to the Jews.

Most human beings fear snakes more than anything else on earth and this fear syndrome can be seen very early in the Genesis. Interestingly, the first part of the Bible has become the turning point in the story of humankind. It is written in the Bible that after God created the earth, he created

Adam from clay, fashioning him in his own image. This is a famous painting, which shows the hair-breath distance between the limp hand of Adam and God's energetic hand, as he is about to touch him with the breathe of life. This distance can be interpreted in many ways. Was it a moment of indecision on the part of God, as he may have foreseen the result and the mess human beings would create on earth?

Another way of looking at this painting is with the reference to overtones of male homosexuality in Michelangelo, as it is also about two men about to touch other. Was it his idea of divine love? In contrast, God created Eve from Adam's rib, as he saw that Adam was lonely in paradise and needed a companion of the human kind.

The Genesis also has references to the 'Tree of Life', also known as the Tree of Knowledge. After the act of creation, God tells Adam and Eve, that they had the freedom to frolic in paradise, but were not to eat the fruit from the tree of life or knowledge. As soon as this ban was put upon them, it is more or less suggested that Eve, being a woman, was very curious about this tree. It is made to appear that Adam being obedient followed God's commandment. But, Eve's could not contain her curiosity and appears to have long dialogues with the serpent or Satan, who tempts her to pluck the fruit from the tree and eat it.

An enthusiastic Eve even convinces a rather reluctant Adam to eat it. This act of disobedience eventually leads to the expulsion of Adam and Eve from Aden, paradise.

So far the serpent or Satan is always depicted or referred to as a male or neuter, as often the word 'IT' is used in the Bible. In the late eighties, when the Sistine chapel paintings were restored and the grime removed, my daughter sent me these slides. I was surprised to see that the paintings were in bright colours and I came upon a painting titled "The Original Sin", in which the artist depicts the serpent as woman. This particular painting changes the entire image of Satan from male to female. It could be analyzed, either as a homosexual artist's difficulty with women, his dislike for women or an artist's creative liberty to give the serpent a female identity?

It was interesting to study the serpent or Satan painted as a woman and tempting Eve to eat the forbidden fruit, was like an attack on women. It was a conspiracy of the artist, as he tried to show, that not one woman but two were responsible for Adam and Eve's expulsion from the Garden of Eden. With the two women in the composition, he was trying to prove a point that women were vile and scheming creatures. One male art historian even went to the extent of writing that, "it is a beautiful depiction of woman as a serpent!"

Biblically, the serpent is more or less, referred to as 'IT' or a green man with horns and a forked tail, like a serpent's tongue. But, in this slide, the possible male or neuter serpent has been transformed into a female, thus making the Satan-serpent into a female, holding women responsible for all sins on earth and also someone who spoilt the innocence of men! So, in this painting, two women become responsible for the downfall of humankind, and God becomes very angry and expels Adam and Eve from the Garden of Eden or paradise. This expulsion fills human life with sorrow, suffering, struggle and pain. In a pictorial sense, the artist seems to say that the idyllic dream or utopian existence of human kind comes to end, because of these two women – Eve and the female Satan.

Many events come to the surface with this event. The first one being that, Eve was created from Adam's rib, so automatically, she had a subservient secondary role to Adam, as God did not model her from clay like Adam. But, God created Eve with Adam's rib. The different materials used in the making of man and woman, show that God did not want Eve to have an identity of her own, so he fashioned her from a male component. The second event being that Adam was the more obedient of the two and according to the male scribes who wrote the Bible, Adam hesitated to eat the fruit and had to be seduced by Eve to eat it.

Eventually, when God expelled Adam and Eve from the Garden of Eden, a flaming sword circled it and guarded paradise, stopping them from re-entering it. God punished both Adam and Eve as he ordered them to fend for themselves, making them conscious of their nudity, so that they started covering themselves with the proverbial fig leaves.

If you read closely, the punishment is not so harsh for Adam, but is harsher on Eve, because after copulating with Adam, she is condemned to experience physical pain, akin to near-death, when she gives birth to her children. Even here, there are some positive aspects to this story. One can guess, why God decided to be harsher with Eve, because, he saw that she had the intelligence to influence her husband. May be, she was stronger as she was not made from clay, but of a stronger material like bone, Adam's rib. In a way, Adam became weaker than her, as a part from his body was taken to make Eve. He was made of clay, she-bone.

In a way, Eve also showed her strength, as she was also the source of procreation, carrying children and giving birth to them, often described in the Bible as "flesh of her flesh". And, even if the child was born from her blood and tissue, she did not in a way become weak, but remained strong and gave birth to many more children. It is interesting to note here that the forbidden Tree of Life was also known as the Tree of Knowledge. It is possible that Eve may have collected from the she-serpent, female Satan or Satan, who convinced her that it was God's conspiracy that they were not to eat from the Tree of Life, as God did not want them to enrich their lives with knowledge. Here, God becomes the jealous God, the one who may have created human beings in his own image, but did not want them to have more knowledge than him.

When Eve showed the courage of disobeying God and even eating the fruit, God must have dreaded Eve, as with this incident, he realized that she was an intelligent thinking woman and wanted to know what was so special about the Tree of Life. She did, at a heavy cost, as her life is often more difficult than that of a man.

In the Bible, the forbidden fruit of the Tree of Life or Tree of Knowledge is not described in detail. And, it is definitely not described as an apple, but known as a fruit, as Eve confides in the serpent, "it is pleasant to the eye". Her female instincts are seen at their best here as like all women, she fancies beautiful objects like the beautiful fruit. But, male scribes have come to the conclusion that the forbidden fruit was an apple, as it pleases the eye. This fruit can also be connected with the male anatomy, because Adam is often portrayed as a spineless worrying character, who is torn between the will of God and the persuasion of the seductive Eve. When he must have reluctantly accepted the forbidden fruit and eaten it with a feeling of guilt, so the apple was stuck in his throat. It is possible, the term Adam's apple, comes from here and used to describe a man's neck vis-à-vis the Adam's apple! This part of male anatomy is known to bob up and down under duress and can be easily connected with Adam's indecision, giving an impression that the apple of seduction Eve had offered Adam was stuck in his throat. In art and the advertisement world, a mere half eaten apple is often shown as a symbol of sin. It depicts how a woman tempts and seduces a man.

These are some of ways of looking at Adam and Eve and the famous painting "The Original Sin".

6

At the Crossroads

LAKSHMI KANNAN

Novelist & Poet, Delhi

Perhaps no other term than 'feminism' has had such a disquieting effect on writers and artists who happen to be women. While women who have taken up acting as a profession have successfully shaken off the gender tag by calling themselves 'actors,' writers are yet to free themselves from the oft-repeated appellation. A writer is still referred to as a 'woman writer' (while no one speaks of a 'male writer') and the matter is further confounded if she does not have a feminist agenda in some of her works. A writer's discomfort with the term 'feminist' is understandable in view of the rather facile kind of use made and the tendency to get prescriptive about issues taken. A writer justifiably fights free of this term when it stereotypes her and forcefully crams her works into a narrow mould just to fit into the blueprint that theories of feminism have for the positions they take.

At times, the term comes through as much too limiting, sectarian and therefore constricting for a writer who has her rightful place in mainstream literature. Her creativity absorbs truth in all its contradictions and may even defy the textbook 'neatness' of what is considered feminist and what is not. For instance, a writer who has the artistic integrity to portray some of her male protagonists in a positive light may not have a gender bias. Or, she may well explore general themes that have little or no feminist bearing at all. A writer at any rate is pledged to truth as she sees it, in all its bristling contrariness, its challenging complexity and multivalent points of view.

What happens when this writer writes about the flip side of feminism and exposes its ugly underbelly? She may factor in a truth that may well run counter to the standard feminist point of view that one is used to, for her truth may show some female protagonists in an unflattering light. In such cases, either such areas are overlooked and ignored, or the writer is criticized for speaking against women.

Yet in all honesty, writers who are older and who have grown up on the strength of this movement called 'feminism' over the past two or three decades, do feel ungracious about totally disowning this label because they owe much of their name and their standing to this very movement. It is not as if this writer is turning her back to it now. She is simply moving on, growing, or out-growing some of the rigid tenets that are thrown up by formal, classroom feminist studies.

What we need at this point in time is a whole new poetics of feminism that can face up to the 'post'-ness of post-feminism, a poetics that can match the complexity of creativity from writers who are women. A new poetics that can face the untamed essence of life, acknowledge versatility in *oeuvres* when it sees it, and the skills they call for to portray multiple levels of human experience. If feminism has taken us far, it has also deserted us midway with the question "After feminism, what?" We need to look afresh at works and themes but not with the same old clichéd verbiage. If feminism always wants a 'pretty picture' of women from writers, how can a writing represent the fullness of life in all its shades – grey or luminous? Art has to be viewed as art. Works cannot always conform to the blueprint of feminism scholars and I cannot think of any sensitive writer in her right mind wanting to do that.

While the movement in itself has been tremendously helpful in bringing about many healthy changes in the social fabric of India (and the rest of the world), the critical equipment is still wanting in sociological imagination and a readiness to consider a work from an artistic angle. I shall explain towards the end of this article how feministic criticism can occasionally fail to absorb the full import of a work if it sticks to its own stern agenda of "what is feminist" and "what is not", but first let me cite two main, and apparently contradictory, forces that a woman has to contend with, today.

One, like I said, is her quest for growth, her spirit of adventure with which she explores themes that may at times run counter to the formal requirements of feminism, keeping herself neutral and free of gender bias. Sadly, her quest is often stymied by the counteractive pull of the gender bias she confronts in her personal life at every step. Certain experiences play themselves out in a stubborn, world-weary, repetitive pattern. They bring a woman back to feministic experiences in the raw, so to speak, and compel her to admit that there are still many things that have not changed, that they are not likely to change for a long time to come. There is no way she can avoid these experiences, though she can of course exercise some control over them.

This is when her resistance to stereotypical patterns of feminism is chastened by the indifferent external world that keeps throwing up those very stereotypical experiences, and she finds a tedious parallel of the same in the lives of other women. She finds herself in a clichéd situation, in which the clichéd expression "personal is political" is proved on her pulse to be sadly true. It takes a lot from her to distance herself from that experience and still be herself. The experience gets to be either cloaked in silence or verbalized when she finds a suitable context for it and this context is again an invariably feminist context. She feels she has come full circle.

I can cite two (out of many other) instances from my experience that can be classified as 'typical,' if not stereotypical, for they may have happened to many other women.

The first of these experiences exposed for me the shams of the so-called educated male who is still a cave man at heart, whether he is in the garb of a colleague, a fellow participant in an overseas programme or a person with whom one has only a professional equation. I spent a term in the University of Canterbury at Kent as a Writer-in-Residence on a Charles Wallace Trust Fellowship, which is when I came across two men from India who were on the campus on a different programme. Both of them seemed to carry a large piece of the retrograde mindset from the deep, dark interiors of Tamil Nadu. When they looked a bit overly pleased to meet me, I thought it was because they wanted to hear some Tamil sounds on that proper, all-British campus. I did not know of their academic status at Kent, but I came to know that they were given single rooms in some building across where I stayed, while I, as a Resident Writer, was given a fully furnished flat, complete with a maid who would come twice a week to clean up and help around. When the men got to see my flat, they were again a bit excessively overjoyed about my well-appointed kitchen, which is when I grew suspicious of their intention. Soon my worst suspicion came true. What the two men expected from me was an invitation to Tamil meals on a regular basis at my flat as they could not/or would not do their own cooking at the modest shared arrangement in their own digs and almost always walked around with a famished look on their faces.

I decided to be cautious and emphasized the very obvious fact that I was there for a programme, that I have a pile of work with talks and readings scheduled for me in different parts of UK and will travel frequently. I told them that I definitely had no time to cook, that I generally made do with sandwiches, fruits and so on. The day they nearly begged me to call them over for a Tamil meal I was in for yet another unexpected shock. After wolfing down the dishes I had made, they clucked in sympathy and said, "Madam, we realize why you live practically on bread and fruits, for how can any woman cook only for herself when her husband is not around?" They actually believed, or wished to believe that I was living for an entire academic term on just bread and fruits because a woman can cook only when her husband is around, or when she calls some guests over, but she can never cook for herself! Need I mention that I showed them the door after that and hoped that it must have been the very last decent Tamil meal they had on that British campus?

"Woman equals food" or "woman translates into food". Period. It is an unchanging attitude that would make a feminist out of any woman, even the one who fights shy of this term. A few years later the same drama was wearily played out again, this time on the sylvan campus of Shimla's Indian Institute of Advanced Study, where I spent my term as a Fellow with a project to work on. Only this time, my husband accompanied me. Once again, we got to see a contingent of Tamil men from interior Tamil Nadu such as Salem, Tanjore, Madurai and some very small but urbanized villages. They sought my husband's company at the dining table in the general mess where all of us had our lunch. That evening, my husband said: "Do you know that all the Tamil men consider me a very lucky man. When I asked what makes me 'lucky'? They said, you've a wife and she is cooking fabulous meals for dinner every day." I hurried to correct them with a lie, so I said: "Indeed no. *It's she* who is the Fellow here on work, and I'm just living with her in her allotted flat. She is so busy at work that we mostly have bread, that's all. There's no cooking done at home. So you better watch it," he warned me, worried for my time and energy. About a week later, my husband reported, "My fortune has turned. From being considered lucky, I have suddenly become an 'unlucky' man now, and do you know why? The same Tamil men are saying, Poor man, his wife feeds him bread for dinner. How pathetic."

The second experience I shall recount is not amusing. It has to do with one's religion and culture and the moral policing that goes with it. This experience can take a woman back to her very fundamental, basic human right – her rightful place in the religion that one is born into, the right to pray as she has been conditioned to, since childhood.

Men appropriate what goes by the name of 'religion' amongst Tamil Hindus, with women of low self-esteem tacitly or openly supporting their men in perpetuating this patriarchal pattern. The recent media coverage of the controversy surrounding gender discrimination in that male bastion, the Sabarimala temple in Kerala is a case in point. Incredible as it may be when you look back at the harsh history of this temple, things led on to a landmark judgment by the court that finally decreed that women of all ages be admitted to Sabarimala and that any past notion of their alleged 'biological impurity' is defunct and simply laughable in this era of science and scientific temper. We find our sisters in Islam still struggling for their religious rights, as they are allowed to worship only within the confines of their homes. Their Tamil Hindu sisters are subjected to other sly systems of a patriarchal exclusion even within the most educated household. Only everything is done with a veneer of normalcy, refinement and utmost discretion. It would not be perceptible to people who cannot see beyond the mask of education, economic progress, refinement in behaviour and the token 'respect' given to women.

My encounter with the retrograde elements that are sanctioned as 'legitimate' in the eyes of 'religion' has to do with the issue of widowhood, with no such issue to match it when it comes to men who have lost their wives. They are allowed to get on with their religious practice like before, with no taboo anywhere to restrict their movements. For this, I need to dwell on the question of one's faith, the religion, and in the case of Indians, the question of caste that further complicates things for people. If we see a caste war tearing our young adults apart who have taken to the streets, braving baton charges and arrest in their agitation against reservation in educational institutions, there are grey areas within a single caste, and this *intra*-caste issue is no less contentious than the *inter*-caste war.

We are born into a particular faith and are conditioned to accept it as an incontestable truth, complete with the mores with which it has been fed to us from infancy, along with Cerelac or Glaxo or whatever was the prevalent brand of milk food. So, we take it as a 'plausible given' in our lives. That is how I accepted not just Hinduism, but also my caste as a Brahmin, a caste considered as 'high' but marked by its stern orthodoxy.

Later, the girl grows up, receives her education, is a professional in some area of work, and grows older on all the various changes in the decades of the multi-pronged entity called "the woman's movement". It sharpens her sensitivity to gender bias. She soon realizes that the Faith (religion) she is born into is unapologetically, unambiguously patriarchal. Even so, she learns to take it in stride with a shrug, saying it is 'no big deal' because almost every other faith that she gets to 'know' of through the people she meets is in some ways patriarchal. "It's more to do with people," she reasons with herself. "It's people who get between you and the faith." They can be maddeningly contrary, even downright retrograde, but again "it's no big deal" she thinks, because women have always got by in an unequal world. She moves on, realizing that it is easier to peel off one's skin and throw away it away, than discard one's inherited faith with a toss of the arm. Its shortcomings, its flaws may have more to do with religious history, the tortuous route that socio-political-cultural-geographic forces take, rather than with faith *per se.* She reasons with herself that to discard one's faith is as foolish as the proverbial throwing of the baby with the bath water.

All my life I learnt to bypass the patriarchal side of my cultural background in my search for the Force that sustains and holds things together, despite everything. I am aware that beyond all the bickering of these self-righteous people there is a supreme force that governs our lives and I have always wanted to stay tuned and connected to this force. As for the ways of my culture, there were other things to perk up the religious scene anyway – festivals, *utsavs* and *aartis* with all the poetry and drama that come with them. Although they are inextricably linked with the sacred, polytheistic rituals that are mostly agrarian in significance, they nevertheless gave an outlet for socializing, and generally enlivened an otherwise quotidian, routine life.

However, there was this one grainy element that prickled under the skin – the puritanical streak of orthodoxy amongst

Brahmins. It could surface startlingly in the most liberally educated, enlightened, kind-hearted individual born within this caste and raise its ugly, bigoted head. It was like a stubborn streak of paint, or stain or scar if you will, that could not be washed or wished away. There was this formalism and a frenetic attachment to rituals for instance, as if some stern dictate told them, "Do it this way, or else…" Never mind if in the process, someone is harshly excluded, or a sincere, caring friend is not allowed to touch the family silver for *puja* because he/she belongs to an allegedly 'lower' caste. Can this single, overarching system stand up to a pluralistic world-view? This question has always haunted me.

I look up at the faces of the deities in the Hindu pantheon I have grown with. They look serenely inscrutable, even benevolent. Surely, they could not have cloned these invidious stereotypes? They could not be so petty or cruel? Ironically, it was this very orthodoxy that was to effectively push me away one day into a veritable 'godless' isolation at a time when I most desperately needed my gods, my faith and people to face a crisis. And that can be explained only by recounting my personal experience – the death of my husband.

My husband was suffering for many years from a terminal illness caused by a dysfunctional liver, complicated now with a very serious condition called encephalopathy that affected his brain, his vision, his motor movements, senses, vital functions and just about everything in his system. In short, he was trapped within a body that did not work for him any more. He became an invalid, his skin ashen, his face puckered and his head tilted to a side most of the time. The hospital became his home and the ICU a kind of an extension of his bedroom. We, as well as he, knew that he did not have much time on this earth.

The standard assurances by the Brahminical people I knew ran on a set pattern: "Have faith in god, offer prayers, give expensive donations to temple trusts (never mind if your hospital bills are soaring so high that you may next have to sell your house), fast on Tuesdays, Thursdays, Saturdays (so what if you're already dropping dead with exhaustion looking after him without food or sleep?). Just pray for your husband's life (again, it doesn't matter if he finds it impossible to live within that wasted body, pierced all over with needles, tubes, the works), for what is more important is you should remain a *sumangali,* i.e., a *suhagan,* a woman who has a living husband." It implied that I should go *before* my husband. In which case, who will nurse him through this terrible sickness? Who will give him as much time, energy and patience as I do? Who will spend the huge amount of money on his treatment the way I do? "*Sshh…Just pray, fast, donate…*", I was told.

Meanwhile, my husband teetered on the very edge of consciousness that ranged between states of being in a stupor, or being semi-conscious, unconscious or plain comatose, requiring close monitoring in an ICU. He would suddenly lose his vision for a few hours, having already lost his sense of smell. If something caught fire and burnt nearby he would be unaware of it. He lived out his last days purely on dole as it were living off the plasma from the innumerable blood donations by friends and strangers arranged through the Red Cross Society.

The Brahminical ones attended his funeral ceremonies, making sure about the 'correctness' of the ceremonies in terms of formal rituals, keeping a strict count of the days after the death as the 1st day, 2nd, then on to 5th, 10th and 13th – all of which had be to properly conducted. After the 13th day, all of them vanished, without as much as leaving a trace! Who vanished? The whole lot of the obsessively conventional, puritanically orthodox Brahmins, smug in their sense of cultural superiority and homogeneity. And, they effectively took with them the entire set of gods on whose names they had asked me to plead for *sumangali*hood. Because they discreetly shunned me on festivals and special occasions as my presence was now considered 'inauspicious' for the context.

Are the gods confined only within festivals, I wondered? And how did I suddenly forfeit the right to participate in them? By living on to nurse a dying man? My family wrapped around me warmly to compensate for the 'flaws and failings' of orthodoxy. It lavished on me jewellery, cosmetics, perfumes, flowers, holidays and clothes in such vibrant hues that I have never worn even during my best years. I was very moved by their desperation to "dress me up" again and pull me out of mourning into mainstream life. Gently, the family and friends persuaded me to hold my pen again and sit in front of my computer after a very long time. But then, there is another life outside the family and one's circle of close friends.

Is this a case of faith failing a person at a time when she most needs it? Not really. It was the 'people problem' again and their gender bias. Yet I am thankful for this cathartic phase in my life when, within the silence of my home, I could for the first time look inward and take stock of what orthodox religion had to offer a bereaved woman in a moment of crisis. It was also a turning point in my life when ironically as it were, I began to have increasing faith – in myself, in the caring members of my family and in friends who came from a diverse religious background – Christianity, Islam, Hinduism, Jainism, Sikhism, Buddhism or Arya Samaj. The only religion of these people seemed to be love and I was very touched by their concern, the precious time they spent on me to nurse me back to normalcy through my darkest moments of grief, fear, loneliness and alienation. Their care and concern flowed into my being and made me whole again. The force that I was always searching for was manifest in these people. They restored my faith in people. Incredible as it may sound, different friends (who don't know each other) expressed the *same* beautiful thought: "Come evening Lakshmi, when the sun dips, my thoughts fly out to you and I wonder what you may be doing there, alone in your house", said many of them and I was speechless with surprise by the same chain of thought that linked them. What is any religion that cannot be kind and human, in the first place? Fortunately, I discovered a spiritual path that has a human face and it is Buddhism.

A feminist perspective, then, surfaces inevitably in life just as feminism is an inevitable 'ism'. It is as inevitable as Marxism was, when it exploded on the world in a big way. It gave us a certain sharp sociological perspective after which there was no looking back. Anyone who has been writing for the past four decades, and who happened to be a woman, is expected to have a feminist point of view not because it is the trend, but because too many facts are leading up to an awareness of the outrage against women and the violation of their human rights. Because, at its most basic and fundamental level feminism is all about human rights. Only, when the victim or the affected person happens to be female, the issue is taken as 'feminist'.

This awareness has since become pervasive and intensified, thanks to inputs from media, both print and visual, and the rub off on the judiciary, educational and professional institutions. With all the NGOs around us who often work in tandem with print and visual media, any woman-related issue, any happening that is perceived as an injustice to woman instantly gets voice and visibility and soon becomes a public outcry. It has permeated into the nooks and crannies of our existence with such ramifications that it is now as much 'in the air' as the general awareness in the print and visual media about health, fitness and sensible eating. They promote health awareness, teach us how to cope with diabetes, hyper tension or cardio-vascular problems, they give psychiatric counsel on stress management, time management, consumer counsel on how to move the court when cheated by an insurance policy and so on. We are living in a climate that is right for public voices to assert their right for a fair play in life. Cases such as Jessica Lal, Priyadarshini Mattoo and Nitish Katara would not have shaken the very foundations of our judiciary and the slumbering conscience of a people without the protests and a candle light vigil in India Gate.

Let me go back to the point of how feminist scholars look at texts that *do not* explicitly champion the cause of women. I have been associated with the Help Age Foundation for a long time and have participated in many of their seminars, workshops and programmes for promoting awareness of the needs of senior citizens, their health and socio-economic problems, and of how to improve the quality of their lives. We had data, statistics, case studies and research findings to go by, much like we do in women's study departments that take in women's demographic profile, their rural/urban background and other related data. The observations we culled from the

Help Age seminars were therefore not somebody's 'opinion' but an empirically proven data. One such data clearly pointed to the disturbing fact that elderly people who have become too much old to continue living on their own, and who need to be financially supplemented by their sons have a miserable time at the hands of their daughters-in-law. This is true even for the educated elderly who once occupied important professional positions and have now retired from active service. The situation at times worsens when their NRI sons take them abroad, thereby cutting off their ties with their relations and larger family in India. They do not get good food, or enough food, they are not given a comfortable space or room and are generally ignored and treated with little respect for their 'personhood'. In fact, they stand stripped of their 'personhood' and are just relegated to become a stereotype of another kind, 'the grandparent'. They are even denied an identity of their own.

In contrast, elderly people who live with their daughters are relatively better off, the data showing how it is not necessarily because a daughter is a better child, but it is because a son-in-law generally does not interfere with the parent-daughter relationship, does not plot, scheme and trap the elderly in painful situations of denial and deprivation. The men (in this case, the sons-in-law) are busy with their work. I published two stories that had elderly men as the central protagonists and both stories enjoyed a wide readership in the original Tamil as well as in English and Hindi translations. One of the stories is set in London and it went on to win an *Ilakkiya Chintanai Award,* which is primarily a critic's award in Tamil. The other is composed in a fantasy mode that includes birds, squirrels, plants, flowers and trees that can 'communicate' with each other and with the central protagonist, the elderly man of the story. This story became a favourite with Hindi readers. During a reading in Hindi, the story was enriched by the feedback about the various myths and legends curled around Indian flora and fauna coming from the erudite and culturally educated ones from the audience. In both these stories the women, i.e., the daughters-in-law of the household are shown to be predatory, harsh and selfish about their own needs. They act mean and cruel with the physically fragile, elderly men. Interestingly, the stories seemed to divide the audience into two broad groups of men and women! While some of the men swore that they have seen such a thing happening in their families, the women protested and questioned me as to why I have shown women in such poor light. "How can you, a woman writer, give such a negative portrayal of women?" I was asked. To my reply that we cannot polarize the 'negative' and 'positive' so arbitrarily, that the truth lies somewhere in between and it reflects the data from Help Age, there were women who said, "Even if it is a truth, a woman writer should not bring it out into the open, like this." At which point, it became an active duel between the women and the men, with me reduced to just a witness. The story was forgotten, the author was forgotten, what unfolded was the drama of real life, with men shouting, "This is how it is in my elder brother's house. Women can bring about a *satyanash* with their wily ways," and the women aggressively confronting the men. As I sat back to watch the big fight, I felt strangely glad (if that is an apt word for what I felt) to see my story taken as 'real' enough for them to hotly argue for – or against – it. While social scientists, researchers and media reporters cover the same data as the 'plain truth' a writer who is a woman is asked, "How can you....?"

I am aware that feminist critics and scholars watch the women protagonists in my fiction and poetry warily. It would be nice to see them round off their observations with sociological insight rather than a readymade, static blueprint that is much too artificially 'tidy' for life and its surprises, its largeness and its defiant changes. It would be a healthy growth for feminism if it were nudged closer to human rights issues.

Another peculiar backlash of textbook feminists is the way they perpetuate the 'camp' attitude, dividing critics, scholars and authors alike as 'women' and 'men'. A well-known feminist organization got us all together for a national conference with delegates from across the country and a few from abroad. Much steam was let off during the sessions and one such session attacked (women) writers who drew considerable praise and accolades from established and important male critics! "What's the reason for this?" asked an indignant delegate. "We must re-examine the works of these writers more closely and see if they are playing up to patriarchal notions of women," she remarked, like the works in themselves were suspect in some way.

Posturing and hypocrisy rules the roost in Tamil Nadu, a region I have come to know through the way authors and critics go about their work. Many of the women writers I know have a close contact with their godfathers, often an important male writer, or editor of a leading magazine. Only when the women publish their works, they scrupulously avoid having a 'foreword' written by these men, and do not even mention them in their acknowledgements. The same women swoop down on an unsuspecting (woman) writer who may have had the naivety or thoughtlessness to allow a major male voice to write a 'foreword' to her book. This writer, together with her book, will be ripped apart by the professional feminists for having allowed a 'male' name in the book. They cry themselves hoarse about 'gender sensitivity' and 'gender divide and discrimination' and go on to perpetuate the same divide-and-rule method in a way that shows their consummate cunning in assuming postures.

The thing is one cannot say anything conclusive about feminism or any other 'ism' for that matter. As an author, a woman has to keep herself open to life as it unfolds in all its untamed, wild profusion. In the process, if she records the painful fact that certain women can be caught being very chauvinistic in dealing with other women less fortunate than themselves, or weakened by old age, the poetics of feminism has to absorb that with equanimity. If in the same process, the writer records the pleasure of meeting men who are friends of women and who would genuinely go all out to help women in their capacity as a friend, a colleague, or a family member, that should also find a room in the poetics of feminism.

What is a creative writer who does not take risks with every work she writes? She cannot allow herself to be fettered by pre-conceived rigid positions. Because any risk entails a leap taken in freedom, recklessness and some innocence.

7

Courage Never to Submit or Yield: Short Stories by Women in India

G.S. JAYASHREE

Professor of English, University of Kerala, Thiruvananathapuram and Editor, *Samyukta*

To say that women have traditionally been tellers of tales would be to place them immediately in a gender-specific role. Questions like, don't men tell tales (no pun intended) nor can't one talk one's way to life as Scheherazade did by telling tales may be raised as counters. Whatever that be, all of us instinctively enjoy narrating stories and listening to them. This paper offers a brief overview of the short stories written by women in India in the last one hundred and fifty years. There are stories of love and lust, of greed and violence. Some ground us in the world of brutal reality whereas some take us to the liminal worlds of fantasy. The range that the stories cover is amazing. Though it is common knowledge that not all women are feminists, we are surprised to note that some women writers take stands against women and sympathetic to men. But we cannot generalize. In fact, the two features that figure repeatedly in the stories that women have written are an awareness of the gender status and a constant reiteration of a position of subalternity.

While sex refers to the biological differences between women and men, gender relates to what is masculine and what is feminine – it refers to the identity of women and men based on socially defined roles that are assigned to one sex or the other. As such, gender is best defined as a relationship within society rather than inherent qualities or possessions. It is these relationships, between women and men within the same household and outside, that differentiate and define the roles of gender. These differences are reflected in perceptions, roles, opportunities and the like. In a complex societal context like that of India this translates into a negotiation of power, both exercised and denied. The stratification of power, inevitable in any relationship, gradually begins to surface in seemingly innocuous ways in numerous situations. We have, in many of the stories by women, the subtle etching of relationships of power along with efforts to undermine and subvert. Gender awareness is of prime importance in such a context. It embodies an understanding of the negative impacts of gender issues and the need to address the inequalities that arise. It acknowledges the significant contribution that women make as equal participants and beneficiaries to society.

What interests us most in this theatre of power is the inevitable realization on the part of the woman of her subaltern status. We know that the history of the subaltern classes is just as complex as the history of the dominant classes. But it is the history of the latter that is usually accepted as 'official' history. This is because the history of subaltern social groups is necessarily fragmented and episodic; because their history is not recognized as 'history'. They are always subject to the activity of ruling groups, even when they rebel. In story after story that women have told we have evidence of this, the valiant but pathetic efforts made by women to overcome their limitations. We point this out not to strike a pessimistic note but to show that women have less access both to the means by which they may control their own representation and to cultural and social institutions. Many stories examine the nature of and reason for the 'spontaneous' consent given by women to the general direction imposed on social life by the dominant fundamental groups. The inevitable conclusion is that this consent is 'historically' caused by the prestige and consequent confidence that the dominant group enjoys because of its position and function in the world of money and culture. Women, whether they are from the urban or the rural milieu, find themselves excluded from any meaningful role in this regime of power. They do not have a position from which to speak. The stories that women write can be read as efforts to gain a space by wresting moral and intellectual leadership in a society where they had systematically been denied agency.

When we read the stories for a better understanding of the factors that have worked to exclude women, we find that structures of caste and class have had a negative impact on the lives of women more than anything else. The caste system in India is a rigid hierarchical order of social inequality in which one's rank is ascribed at birth. Caste and untouchability have puzzled social historians for centuries. Castes are ranked on the basis of one's 'pollution' – work-related contact with life processes such as birth and death and life substances such as faeces and blood. The greater one's purity, or lack of contact with pollution, the higher one's rank. Contact with a person of a lower caste can negatively alter one's purity and require, in some cases, a ritual procedure – such as bathing or changing clothes. A more serious defiling act can result in expulsion from one's caste. Intermarriage between castes is strongly discouraged. The stratification on account of caste is more acutely experienced in the villages. Those belonging to the 'lower' castes are often discriminated against, denied access to land, forced to work in degrading conditions, and routinely abused. They are considered 'untouchables' and may not cross the line dividing their part of the village from that occupied by higher castes. They may not use the same wells, visit the same temples, drink from the same cups in tea stalls, or lay claim to land that are legally theirs. In what has been called India's 'hidden apartheid', entire villages in many Indian states remain completely segregated by caste. Most of the people belonging to the lower castes continue to live in extreme poverty, without land or opportunities for better employment or education. It goes without saying that women suffer most in such a situation. Inequalities suffered on account of caste figure prominently in some of the stories.

Feminist scholars have elucidated the role of women and gender differences in understanding the significance of caste. Many have pointed out the mutually inclusive nature of caste and class. The perceived status of a caste certainly has a connection with real economic status. The centrality of gender inequality and male dominance in this doubly oppressive system has also been noted. Women writers are aware of the oppression that can occur if one happens to belong to the 'wrong' class, caste and gender. They offer various explanations for this system of inequality. It was generally held that the hierarchy of castes is based on distinctions of ritual purity and pollution. But such an explanation overemphasizes the role and ideas of Brahmins and neglects the resistance of lower castes and alternative indigenous ideologies. The frequent deviations of actual behaviour from these largely Brahmanical ideals are also not considered. Moreover, these theories provide little insight into the changes that are occurring in contemporary India. In principle, individuals and groups could not change their caste, but in practice there is considerable social mobility – usually involving shifts in rankings. This typically occurs when a caste or lineage acquires wealth or political power. Social privileges have followed economic well-being. Some of the stories that we have included sketch the hold caste and class have over the imagination of an entire nation. They are narratives on the contentious issue of caste as also of struggles to overcome social and economic deprivation.

Unlike western texts that proclaim that rural rather than urban areas are women spaces, the women writers of India seem to find the cities more congenial for the rigidity of conventions and traditions is less in the urban scenario. However, urban spaces too often demand a heavy price from them. Images of rural India as opposed to urban India feature in some tales in this selection. The world of rural India is rife with conventions and traditions. The caste system is rigid in villages. Intense poverty drives the poor peasant classes to the cities. Yet they are never happy there and long to go back to the cool greenery of the village. There is an interesting story by Nirupama Bargohain that traces the life of the child labourer of rural Assam, who becomes one of the working class of the new, industrial towns. The economic sub-structure becomes the 'super-structure' as Franz Fanon would have it. The condition of women in this context is even more problematic. Mobility and isolation, two crucial characteristics of modern urban life, often trigger a quest for origins. This is because the urban environment repeatedly thwarts the urge to connect. In contrast, the strength of the rural society is in its collective nature.

In order to forge a common ground, the women writers are seen to use a whole range of themes and it is possible to trace many common features in their stories. Fantasy is used to delineate perceptual experience and to trace the voyage into the mind. Most writers try to recover the self, lost in the labyrinth of tradition and social custom through the medium of writing. Fantasy is both a theme and technique that women writers employ to grapple with reality. While fantasy is frequently employed as a subversive technique, it emerges as a theme in some tales. Suma Josson has a story, *The Village,* in which the reader is lured by the visual images of the text into the miasmas of a dark and threatening world of the protagonist's mind. The reader hesitates between a realistic reading of the tale and a reading of the text as a fantasy or an illusion. Uncertainty is the very heart of fantasy and the village, in Suma Josson's tale, cannot be isolated as a dream but as a world where everything proliferates with potential meanings and becomes a source of danger. In common with all fantasy texts, ideas, objects and situations in the short story are hedged round with baffling associations as is the wall, the thermos flask and the woman in the village. All reassurance or reprieve is illusory in the face of the anxiety the reader shares with the narrator, an anxiety that arises from the knowledge that the familiar can veer on the frightening. Anxiety and hesitancy take on strange and threatening forms, sometimes too great for the mind to bear. At the end of the tale, it is not surprising, therefore, to find the narrator pausing on the threshold of madness.

Important themes chosen by the post-eighties writers include morbidity, bitterness, revenge, sensuality, death, sarcasm, irreverence, gender consciousness, de-mythologization, representation of marriage and divorce as well as love. Love has always been idealized as the finest of human sentiments and immortalized by many writers in their works. It still remains one of the most popular themes in fiction, reiterating the fact that no amount of mechanization can destroy such finer aspects of life. Love is the root of all relationships and affection and commitment to each other breeds security in any relationship. Taking into account that this is a sentiment that does not distinguish between the king and the beggar or the man and the woman, it is interesting to observe that all the various shades of love, spiritual and physical occupy prime position among the themes of fiction. It is the only panacea for the world and its occupants ripped up in the name of power, possessions, mistrust and hatred. The wonderful nature of this emotion is that it teaches one to give, not grab. The present-day women writers project the fact that men too are capable of genuine uncorrupted love as illustrated by Manak, a character in Amrita Pritam's story "Stench of Kerosene". He stands as a symbol of loyalty and love, the finest specimen of a husband. Conjugal love and understanding has become a major theme in the works of many contemporary writers. Family is here that which offers solace and comfort, relief from the turmoil of the external world.

As opposed to this sublime quality, themes of violence also preoccupy many of the women writers. Women are traditionally presented as sufferers of violence and as passive receptors. The presentation of women in the stories from all over India, carry the pain of suffering and the triumph of survival. Acts of violence perpetrated by men against women feature in a number of tales written by women. The ubiquity and the diversity of male crimes of violence underline the fact that men collectively and as individuals maintain women's oppression. Mental violence is the subversive text in many tales. While women suffer both mental and physical violence, rape is one kind of violence that affects women physically and psychologically. Rape illustrates the male urge to control and dominate women rather than the male sex drive. It subjugates women by keeping them in a state of constant fear. The representation of rape and domestic violence in fictional works is problematic for the act of violation should not be sensationalized or glamorized. The women writers, who deal with the above themes, underline the exploitation and the victimization that women are subjected to. The responses and the emotions of the victim of rape and the attitude of family and society to the victims are the concerns of the writers. Domestic violence is also a theme in the work of these writers for male violence against women is part of the manifestation of patriarchal power.

Human relationships and the human predicament become an important theme in short stories that women write. It is interesting to note the transition from the purely feminist to a more general social orientation in some of the stories. There are women writers who focus on the peculiar situation of the woman in association with man – father, husband, son or some other male member at the level of the family and her male employer at the official level. Woman is hardly ever viewed as an independent individual. This pattern is seen to have a psychological impact on the woman; she is tuned to apprise herself in terms of what others might think of her. This culminates in frustration, which is capable of destroying her relationship with others. The most telling illustration of a total disorientation of a woman, perhaps, is in a marriage where her concerns are frequently pushed to the background. Most of the writers have drawn attention to the unequal status of the woman and shown that a little sensitivity on the part of the man can work wonders to forge a weakening relationship. It has been rightly pointed out by writers like Manju Kapur that men are overly demanding in relationships and they often hurt women without knowing that they have done so. At the same time, there are men who consciously hurt women and this also has been a favourite theme with the writers.

While this is one side of the picture, it is also seen that women writers depart from this and view society objectively, thereby bringing into focus relationships where men are the sufferers and women consciously or unconsciously hurt them. These often centre on the modern working class, where man and woman are both breadwinners and the economic independence has given the woman an equal footing with her mate. Many stories by women picturize the independent woman who disregards the man, a typical reversal of roles. True representations of the parts played by women lend an aura of authenticity to the stories. They reflect the social realities of contemporary India where women are more exposed to western values and lifestyles and where both have to shoulder responsibilities.

In the larger social context, writers discuss the crisis of old age, something, which has never been a serious issue in the traditional Indian families where parents were automatically taken care of by the children. The terrible crisis of the aged is of course a consequence of the hard core commercialization which has driven people away from their native homes in search of more profitable ventures. The predicament of the diseased and the aged thus is taken up as an important theme in modern fiction. There are stories addressing the dilemma of such characters who view themselves as useless burdens in the world, as well as those who face any calamitous situation with undying hope. While pointing at this grave social issue, the writers also emphasize the need for adjustment on the part of the sick and the aged, to adapt themselves according to the pace of the modern world.

The great majority of Indians use the regional languages of the country, which can be called *bhashas*, for everyday communication. It is worth mentioning that the voice of the woman resounds more in the oral narratives of the *bhashas* and in folk songs and performances than in published or classical works. It is also possible to trace a female literary tradition as a more or less continuous trajectory from the earliest periods of recorded history to the present times in the *bhashas*. It reveals an inheritance of covert and at times overt resistance to the marginalization of the woman and to institutions of patriarchy. That this feature is visible in all Indian languages is particularly noteworthy. The ways in which the distinctive female identity is established through the oral and written traditions have many parallels in the literature(s) of the various regional languages of India.

Though feminist historiography has always maintained a stand against linear narratives based on chronology, an account of the history of women writing in the regional languages of India based on a temporal axis can prove helpful as an initial attempt. We have arrived at the following typology of women's writing in India using the literature available in Malayalam as the paradigm. An examination of women's writing in India in the regional languages from the beginning of the 19th century, when written texts began to circulate, shows a more or less four-phased development, which could be called:

1. The Submissive Phase
2. The Progressive Phase
3. The Regressive Phase
4. The Assertive Phase

This is a purely tentative classification and could be modified when more material from the early periods in the regional languages become available. The rationale for the classification is based on the attitude of the woman writer to the world around her. Caught between the need to articulate herself and the social pressure on her to remain silent, the woman writer had to formulate strategies to circumvent social norms and traditions. Initially at least, the only recourse left to her was to be within the bounds of social and literary conventions. During the first phase of women writing in India, there were hardly any innovations in themes and techniques. Most works were imitative and devout. Women wrote *sthothras* or recounted tales from the *Ramayana* or the *Mahabharata* with hardly any deviation from the norm. This phase of women's writing can only be dubbed the submissive phase. The nationalistic and reform movements that swept across the country in the first four decades of the 20th century brought with them massive ideological reconstructions of patriarchy and gender. They highlighted both freedom and bondage – a dangerous combination.

Women writers of the second phase project progressive ideas. They examine how the woman could at times exercise her agency to change or reverse her fate. The evils of *purdah* or the confinement to the inner courtyards and the hardships of widowhood are portrayed by the women writers of the progressive phase. They were aided in this by the journals that published their writings, which had gained a significant female readership. The most important of them were *Bharati* and *Bamabodhini Patrika* (Bengali), *The Indian Ladies Magazine* (English), *Savithri* (Telugu), *Sthree Darpan* (Hindi), *Sundari Subodh* (Gujarathi), *Ismat* (Urdu), and *Vidhya Vinodini, Lakshmi Bai* and *Mangalodayam* (Malayalam).

The third phase in women's writing shows a regressive rather than a progressive movement, when the woman writer, from concerning herself with the world around her, circles in on herself and her sorrows. Coming as it does in the historical period that spans the first three decades after independence, their writings reflect the struggles and counter-struggles that women writers had to face as a new world formed itself around them – a world that did not fulfil the hopes the women had during the pre-independence era. Not content by being just efficient homemakers and educated mothers, this was also the time when more women sought to work outside homes in hospitals, offices and colleges. It was an era of disillusionment for the woman in many fronts.

The fourth phase of women's writing can be termed as the assertive for it is a time where the woman had begun to write herself with more confidence than she was likely to. She had recourse to a whole range of techniques. The writers of the assertive phase wrote from the perspective of the woman and related to issues that concerned the woman most. Images of being entraped within cities and man-made orders, even that of language, are important themes in most of the fictions written in the last decade of the 20th century. Women writers to delineate perceptual experience often use psychological realism and fantasy.

The four phases of women's literature in the regional languages of India that we have identified are clearly distinct from the classification of the major phases of women's literary sub-culture in English fiction from the 1840s to the present-day that Elaine Showalter has made. The basis of this categorization is the attitude displayed by the woman writer in her works. Showalter defined women's literary output as being opposed to the authoritative mainstream literary culture defined by a patriarchal politics and aesthetics. Showalter has listed the first phase of women's writing as the imitative feminine phase, the second as the angry feminist phase and the third as the female phase that prioritizes self-discovery. The first phase of women writing in the regional languages in India shows more of the submissive attitude of the woman rather than imitative. Submission is her way of assuring for herself the space to write. The other end of the trajectory is the assertive phase where her experiences are analyzed and discussed openly, where her anger or dissatisfaction is allowed an outlet through discussions and writings. These changes – from the submissive to the progressive, the regressive and finally the assertive – are based on a change of perception of the woman writer, because attitudes largely depend on perceptions. If the woman writer of the first phase who could find recognition had a feudal background that set her apart from the common man and the central concerns of the age, the writers of the later phases were those who read and wrote against the grain and who belonged to the lower and upper-middle classes rather than to the aristocratic or the feudal classes. Social reformers and the intellectuals had advocated female education during the early decades of the 20th century and the educated middle classes formed the readership of women writers. Women writing by cutting across class differentiations had created a new world for the women to express themselves.

The Submissive Phase

The first phase of women's writing in India reveals certain common features. Women writers of the early phase, who were lucky to get their works published, were of royal or aristocratic origin and enjoyed the benefits of Sanskrit education and royal patronage. Though they had literary accomplishments, they were largely marginalized and their works were uncollected and fragmentary in character. There are a lot of works that are 'anonymous' and a great part could possibly be the works of women writers. The compositions of the women of lower classes formed part of an oral tradition and rarely if ever, found the way to print. In the choice of literary forms, most women writers preferred the conventional. Poetry written by the women of the time shows a keen sense of rhythm. The most important of the women writers of this phase include Manorama Thampuratti, Kilimanoor Uma Devi Thampuratti, Thottakkattu Ikkavamma, Kuttikunju Thankachi and Tarigonda Venkamamba.

The Progressive Phase

By the late 19th century there was a spurt of magazines for women, some of which were published by women themselves. Many articles in the journals attempted to critique the image of the woman in the *puranas* and the *ithihasas*. The image of the woman that was prevalent in the 19th century as the angel in the house or as second-class citizens and as figures of sorrow and sacrifice came under fire. For the first time in the history of women writing in India, women voiced their protest against the injustices meted out to them. They had gained a readership and won a certain degree of recognition. Women writers were strengthened by the journals that were brought out during this period; by an assurance that they would be heard and that their opinions counted. The nationalistic phase is also the era of the journals for this phase corresponded roughly to the organized attempt to regain political freedom by non-violent methods – something that appealed to the women. National movement for freedom influenced most women who wrote in the periodicals and publications of the time. Some were actively involved in the struggle for freedom. All the writers of the time were highly idealistic. Aware of themselves as the silenced and the marginalized, women writers of the time show gender-specific concerns. A conscious female selfhood is evident in their texts. In this context, we can think of the works of Sarojini Naidu, Lakshmibai Tilak, Ramabai Ranade, Mokshadayini Mukhopadyaya, Tarabai Shinde, Lalithambika Antharjanam and Swarnakumari Devi.

The Regressive Phase

A new phase of women writing emerged in the first decade of the post-independence years. The works of most women writers who lived during the age reflect disillusionment for the promise of total freedom that the freedom movement signified, did not bring about social freedom for women. On the contrary, it seemed to add to the bondage that women had to endure. Women had fought shoulder-to-shoulder with men in the struggle for freedom but the status of the woman remained the same after independence. Male chauvinism and the domination that they saw around them, incensed most and an era of subversive literature of resistance came into being. Social taboos and fears could no longer constrain them. The works of writers like Sugathakumari, Rajalakshmi, K. Saraswathy Amma, Dudala Salamma, Shivani and Achanta Sarada Devi show this element of disillusionment.

The Assertive Phase

In the post-1980s decade, women writing in India took a new turn. By this time women writing had come to its own and could use a whole range of themes and techniques to forge common ground. Most writers deal with the journey into selfhood to reclaim the self lost in the labyrinth of social customs and taboos. This *athijivan* phase is literally the phase of survival which women writers use as both theme and technique in various genres. Most writers of contemporary times have made their more significant contributions in the genre of the short story. A brief account of the writing of short stories in English would help us to know better of the literary model arrived at.

The Queen's English may have been introduced in India to create a race of clerks but the language has been cleverly appropriated by the Indians to put themselves across to the world. Ram Mohan Roy was the first Indian to write in English. His works on religion, *The Precepts of Jesus* and *The Guide to Peace and Happiness* are proof of his fluency in the language. However, his writing is more utilitarian than creative. The first Indian writer of a novel in English was Bankim Chandra Chatterjee – his first novel was *Rajmohan's Wife*. The most prominent women in the Indian English literary scene are Toru Dutt and Sarojini Naidu. Toru Dutt's novel, *Bianca or the Young Spanish Maiden* may be mentioned in this context. Her works, which appeared in the last quarter of the 19th century, blazed the trail for a phase of Indianization. She started the line of Indian women writers in English with her single volume of poetry and is reckoned among the great pioneers of Indian literature in English. She is a representative of all those women who came after her and claimed eternity, defying intense and real encumbrances such as those posed by a long and limiting tradition which benumbed their imagination and questioned their identities as women, as Indians and as writers and wrote in a language which they wielded with ease but could not really claim as theirs.

Indian writing in English, which started under the influence of the English education made available by the colonizers, soon grew to a stage when it acquired a national consciousness and served to reveal the essential India to the West. The scarcity of women's prose writing remained, nevertheless, a fact for a long time. It is in the post-independence period that the production of novels and short stories gained momentum and though it had a late start, they have advanced much more than poetry not only in quantity but also in quality. The most famous fiction writers of the early period are D.F. Karaka, Mulk Raj Anand, Raja Rao and R.K. Narayan, followed by K. Nagarajan, Bhabani Bhattacharya, Manohar Malgonkar, Khushwant Singh and others.

The list of notable women fiction writers in English now is a long one and includes Jai Nimbkar, Kamala Markandaya,

Anita Desai, Ruth Prawer Jhabwala, Nayantara Sahgal, Nina Sibal, Namita Gokhale, Chitra Bannerjee, Shashi Deshpande, Gita Mehta, Sobha De, Bharati Mukherjee, Arundhati Roy and others. Jai Nimbkar's maiden novel was originally published by Orient Longman, India in 1974, who also reprinted it in 1995. She writes in both Marathi and English. *Come Rain,* her other novel in English, was published in 1993. Nimbkar has also published two collections of short stories in English. Kamala Purnaiya Markandaya was a journalist in India before migrating to London in 1948, where she married an Englishman. Her first novel, *Nectar in a Sieve,* was published in 1954 and was critically acclaimed. Anita Desai had been shortlisted for the coveted Booker Prize thrice for *In Custody* and *Clear Light of the Day* in 1980 and 1984 respectively and for *Fasting and Feasting* in 1999. Her other notable books are *Fire on the Mountain, Games At Twilight* and *The Village By the Sea.*

Ruth Prawer Jhabvala was born in Germany of Polish parents and came to England in 1939 at the age of twelve. Later on she had settle down in India. Her published works include novels, television and film scripts, many of which are set in India. In 1975, she won the Booker Prize for *Heat and Dust,* and has two Academy Awards for her screenplays – *A Room with a View* and *Howard's End.* Nayantara Sahgal's unique upbringing in a political family is reflected in both her fiction and political writings. She has written a memoir *Prison and Chocolate Cake.* Her novels, which are often set against the background of Indian history, include *A Time to Be Happy, Storm in Chandigarh, A Situation in New Delhi, Rich Like Us* and *Mistaken Identity.* Shobha De has published seven novels, all of which have been extremely successful. The erotic content of her novels has been controversial, and there are varying opinions about her works. While some show disdain, others extol her for venturing to employ themes that were held taboo for women writers.

Bharati Mukherjee's works focus on the "phenomenon of migration, the status of new immigrants and the feeling of alienation often experienced by expatriates" as well as on Indian women and their struggle. Her works include *The Tiger's Daughter, Wife,* the short stories in *Darkness,* and *The Sorrow and the Terror*, a joint effort with her husband. *The Middle Man and Other Stories*, a collection of her short stories, secured the National Book Critics Circle Award for Best Fiction. Arundhati Roy is one of the writers credited for raising Anglo-Indian writing to new heights in the literary world. She won the prestigious Booker Prize in 1996 for her first novel *The God of Small Things*. Her novel was published in India by India Ink, a small Indian publishing house and it has gone on to sell more than 6 million copies in 13 countries. Nowadays, she works for underprivileged people. Gita Mehta has written novels like *Raj* and *A River Sutra* and non-fiction books like *Karma Cola* and *Snakes and Ladders*. Her works have been translated into thirteen languages and published in twenty-seven countries. Chitra Bannerjee Divakaruni is another significant writer who immigrated to the United States in 1976, at the age of 19. In 1995 Divakaruni published *Arranged Marriage*, a collection of short stories. In 1997, she wrote her first novel entitled, *The Mistress of Spices*. *Sister of My Heart*, published in 1998, is Divakaruni's most recent novel. The unprecedented popularity of the periodicals in the latter half of the 20th century created a record demand for short stories and in response to that many writers tried their hands in this genre of literature.

The Indian English short story writers such as Githa Hariharan, Suma Josson, Sujata Sankranti, Shashi Deshpande, Manju Kapur and Susan Viswanathan are outstanding creative geniuses whose compassion and humanism blended with a strong sense of their craft make marvellous stories, which defy and challenge societal precincts of caste, class and gender. Many among the contemporary women writers realize that myths, customs and traditions continue to be reference points for the Indian people in their daily lives. Though the women try to shirk themselves free, they have so internalized them that they are part of their psyche, their personal, religious and Indian identity.

The stories by women are unostentatious yet dramatic. Most of them have a definite local colour and undoubtedly breathe the spirit of India. These writers share a common ground in narrating the struggles of their characters against tradition. They tell the stories with sympathy and intelligence, speak of the limited options that women have in the Indian society; that for a woman to step in or out of the traditional roles, there is a very high price to pay. Shashi Deshpande, a veteran short story writer, is one who never took a conscious decision to become an author. According to her, she stumbled into writing but realized later that the vocation was ever waiting for her along the line. She, perhaps, speaks for other Indian women writers too when she says that "my stories come out of my own intense and long suppressed feelings about what it is to be a woman in our society. It comes out of the experience of the difficulty of playing the different roles enjoined upon me by society; out of the knowledge that I am more and something different from the sum total of these roles. My writing comes out of my consciousness of the conflict between the idea of myself as a human being and the idea that society has of me as a woman."

The Indians who write in English have to grapple with two real and serious problems of creation. The first one pertains to the language used. The Indians, of course, the socially and intellectually elite among them, use English for intellectual purposes. But it is rarely the language of their emotions. Secondly, in their writings, most of the creative writers deal with non-English-speaking people in non-English-speaking situations. The problems posed by these two stumbling blocks are all the more critical for women writers because they mostly tell tales about non-descript people, lonely kids, women – young and old – and even animals. They write in an alien language but the theme and the texture of their writings are unmistakably Indian. Yet, these women triumph over all their limitations and achieve a brilliance that is marvellous and praiseworthy.

While the stories by women voice the everyday experiences of the Indian woman, we can also hear loud silences in the sub-text of many a story. We learn of control embedded in the institutions of family, education and religion that women writers have to negotiate. The worst, of course, being the one imposed by gender. As a body, the stories seriously challenge the deep-rooted androcentrism of modern knowledge. They graphically depict how in spite of progress in female literacy and access to higher education, feminist consciousness is still limited, patriarchy is still intact, and is constantly reproduced in innumerable ways. They are lessons on the ties that bind gender to censorship. Censorship can come from the self, family, culture, religion and government. It is now widely recognized that censorship is when women, following a lifetime of being edited, begin censoring themselves almost spontaneously, without conscious thought or hesitation in the name of love or loyalty. They seem to have internalized the idea that they must not make their family life or the lives of people they know the subject of their writing. To do so would be to expose husband and children or even set them up for ridicule. The assumption, of course being that, when the writer is a woman, the characters she creates are necessarily those found in her private life. In story after story we read how women writers battle against customs and conventions, some pronounced, some not so pronounced. They are in fact bold accounts of self and voice successfully recovered by women writers.

8

Re-presenting and Re-visioning Engendered Bodies: Contemporary Tamil Theatre – A Feminist Perspective

A. MANGAI

(Penname of V. Padma, Tamil theatre activist and Faculty of English, Stella Maris College, Chennai)

> "To be signed with a woman's name does not necessarily make a piece of writing feminine. It could quite well be masculine writing, and conversely, the fact that a piece of writing is signed with a man's name does not in itself exclude femininity."
>
> — Helene Cixous, *Castration and Decapitation*

I begin with the basic premise that not all feminist perspectives need to begin with a gynocritical approach. That does not make it redundant or inappropriate. As I am aware of the temporal distances one has to transgress to study the discussions available in a regional Indian language like Tamil, I prefer not to adapt a survey of women's work in Tamil theatre over these years.[1]

I wish to dwell on the ramifications of feminist theoretical insights to the practice and theory of theatre as is practised in Tamil today. That would let me explore the politics of representation, revisioning the forms of theatrical conventions and their uses, aspects of space and choreography and the body politics. Representations of masculinity and femininity, performing gender, gendering stage in terms of space and choreography and the eventual omissions and constructions of gendered selves in Tamil theatre would evolve through such an exploration. In the course of discussing these aspects we would take recourse to plays, performances, themes and reception of some of the Tamil literary and performance texts.

Politics of representation leads us to the study of characterization of both male and female, and how these characters are embodied/engendered on stage. It would be interesting to study how masculinity is constructed on stage which in turn is a comment on the construction of femininity and vice versa. It ranges from actual female or male bodies occupying the universe of stage-space to the narratives of gender that evolve in the course of the performance.

Tamil play-texts do not lack female protagonists. Except some of the more popular early plays[2] of Muthusami that set him firmly on the national context as a contemporary playwright, and the new experimental plays of Muruga Bhoopathy, most of the plays worth mentioning have prominent female characters in the narrative. Almost all the early plays of Indra Parthasarathy have female protagonists. It is interesting to compare the shift from choric narrative to female voices in *Kattiyakkaran* (1981) and *Padukalam* (2002) in Muthusami and the trajectory of Indra Parthasarathy switching from female-centred plays to more historic/puranic themes of *Nandhan*, *Aurangazeb* and *Ramanujam*.

In the plays and productions of Prof. S. Ramanujam, one finds the strong female characters of Perundevi, the gypsy, Manikka Valli and Sembavala Kali.[3] Right from his earliest Tamil play *Purancheri* he has focused on the female voice. It would be interesting to add that his articles and lectures, brought out in a single collection recently, reveal that he had not dealt with these characters as female embodiments (2004). He sees Perundevi as the tragic voice of suffering due to war; Manika Valli as the symbol of chastity, though a dasi in her life. The gypsy however represents the self-sufficient, confident and nomadic voice critiquing the male order reified in the myths of Chandramathi, Draupadi and Seetha.[4] In his plays and productions, he successfully avoids treating their destinies as shaped or even influenced by their gendered bodies. The sexual identities of these women are not insisted. Therefore, the female voices become universal human voices. This omission of gendered constructions actually evades social gender as practised around us on an everyday basis. Though this treatment is the epic treatment of characterization and one, which is easily comprehensible as a universal category, it also distances female characters from realities.

This came to the forefront while we were working on *Manimekalai.*[5] It could have been easier to place her as a universal mother born to end hunger. But, the questions of her desires and the need to renounce her female bodily self to become this universal mother seemed too important to evade. The epic *Manimekalai* dismisses her sensuality in one single sentence in the original epic. "If this be the nature of desire, let it go thwarted", she says when she realizes that her heart yearns for the attention of Prince Udayakumaran. Inquilab's *Manimekalai* and the performance emphasized the difficulty of such a dismissal, the pain and agony of it all. In fact, the play presents this emotion haunting her in other scenes as well. The desiring body she loses by becoming a nun is seen as sublimated to a maternal instinct of feeding the hungry. The play-text refers to breasts and the nursing as her embodied desires. And then moves on to her decision of symbolic feeding. All women professional stage artistes, belonging to the genre of musical drama, performed the play.[6] The hesitation they had about referring to breast as 'mulai' stemmed from the perspective of treating body, sex and sexuality as taboo subjects. They actually suggested that if the word was replaced by the Sanskrit word 'sthanam', it makes it 'literary' and somehow less embarrassing.

I am a great admirer of Ramanujam's plays and productions and a student of his methodology. But, Perundevi wails with hair let loose all through the play; the female gypsy becomes the passive receiver of erotic approaches layered with mild suspicions of her whereabouts. I distinctly remember when the actor playing the gypsy in *Mauna-k-kuram* asking him as to why the gypsy just receives attention from her partner and does not participate in the erotic exchange? Why should he alone enquire about her whereabouts, while she deems it none of her concern? To that query, Ramanujam replied with a question: "Which gypsy is having this response? Is it the play's gypsy? Or is it the gypsy in you?" Of course, one had the fixed conventions of kuravanji[7] where only the male gypsy asks these questions. But, the play had reversed the narrative order of kuravanji and it was a contemporary play where breaking conventions would not have been out of place. Therefore, I think, I sense some reservations in Ramanujam's representation of gender, though he is by far the most sensitive director in Tamil in terms of not only gender but also social realities.

I must mention his recent production of Muthusami's *Narkkalikarar* in 2005. There is no specific gender attributed to the characters in this play. We have already had two other productions of the same play by Ramanujam. This production was staged during the election season. The play assumed dense political proportions. The chorus consisted of men and Chandra performed the role of the narrator. This rendered the play a gendered reading of the current political climate. The Narkkalikarar, the neutral person refusing to take decisions but is ultimately forced to take one, only to be attacked by the defeated group was performed by another woman. So, what could have evolved as a feminist concern was subtly toned down. Not halting there, he made the Narkkalikarar draw the gestus of trans-sexuals. While this can be read as a metaphoric reading of today's armchair mentality, it became a stereotyped presentation of a trans-sexual body. If gender is concerned with the way masculinity and femininity are constructed, trans-sexuals pose a challenge to every accepted classification. As one working currently with a group of trans-sexual actors, I found it offensive. It was during the same elections that they were demanding an identity card.[8]

It is pertinent here to record how having a female playing a woman's role is not enough to make it gendered. In Chennai Kalai Kuzhu's[9] *Uram,* a street play on deteriorating agriculture in the context of globalization has a farmer's wife played by a woman. As the male farmer struggles with latest fertilizers, manures and issues of producing more at a low cost, his wife comes in nagging him about mortgaged jewels. She is not shown as participating in agriculture or even knowledgeable about it. She is like any other middle class home-maker, domesticated hundred per cent. This group being the cultural wing of Progressive Writers Association belies its link to working class lifestyle. For that matter in most street plays, gender is not embodied. It is always signified as a differential marker. The male performers however are marked by social labour.

It is interesting to note the re-construction or construction of images by women writers. There seems to be certain trends established by women playwrights in Tamil even though their output is not great in terms of quantity. Personally, the gypsy, Avvai – the bard and Manimekalai – the Buddhist nun seem to depict a trajectory in my representation of gender. The self-sufficiency, mobility and participation in affairs of the world excite me to no end. Also, this string of images provides me an opportunity to dwell on realms of knowledge construction and discussion of a sexed experience of a female body.

Ambai's plays are minimal in comparison to her short stories. Prasanna Ramasami attempted to adapt her stories for stage. *Black Horse Square* gave great scope to discuss rape in multiple perspectives. *Aarrai Kadathal* (Crossing the River) represents the female images of Thadagai as the nurturer of forest and Rama as the intruder. The play was written at the peak of fundamentalist attacks on Babri Masjid in Ayodhya. The precise moment of the play expands the frontiers of gender in our responses to contemporary issues.

It would be relevant here to record Prasanna's choice of fragmented narrative in almost all her performances. She sees the connection between Gandhari, the Trojan women, Antigone, Srilankan poets' voices and a Vietnamese woman's testimony of destruction. She avoids a unilateral voice holding the whole narrative and lets it dissolve. She also returns to the same text at various times, each time changing the timbre of performance. Somehow in her treatment she prefers an abstract international humanism rather than a grounded, localized referentiality.

Pritahm Chakravarthi has given us documents of various life stories: a dhobi woman, aravani, film actress, victim of domestic violence, living with child sexual abuse and most recently Dukshala the only sister of the Kauravas. She prefers to retain her presence as a storyteller. Therefore, the texts come across as readings of these images by Pritham and her own statements. Her realistic style of performance too places these texts in a rational plane of drawing inferences from these lives/stories. These are neither documentary voice as in Anna Devere Smith[10] nor are they explorations into image-building.

One must bear in mind that as in most other regional traditions in India, female performers are not welcomed into the fold of performance genres. In Tamil the pure dance forms exclude women except in the case of Poikkal Kuthirai and Karagam; the balladic forms like Villuppattu have women taking it up; in the total theatre forms like Koothu, it is the males who impersonate female characters. Almost the whole history of theatre all over the world has encountered this tradition of male construction of female characters. I do not want to dwell here on the implications of such conventions on a female actor as I have written about them earlier.

It is relevant to recall the professional female actors in Company/special drama choosing to perform Rajaparts. Actors like Jayalatha of Pudukkottai decided to perform male roles, since their expertise in female parts far outshone the male actors and she did not get enough shows for fear of not being a 'match' to her on stage. Therefore, she performs male roles and has no problem even if she far surpasses the other actors, since she is in a male garb (Amaithi Arasu).

The younger directors and writers reveal a relative indifference to this aspect of gender. Velu Saravanan had mentioned in an interview the difficulties of having female members in the group and how as actors one of the male members can perform the female with no difficulty. And he is not wrong either. In the recent production of *Paramapadham* by Prasad, Gandhari was performed by Rajan, a male actor and of the three female characters in the play, the other two being Draupadi and Amba, Gandhari was performed with more energy and subtlety. Thanks to the traditions of female impersonation! In the productions of Muruga Bhoopathy there has been no strong presence of female body or character so far. In *Udira Mugamoodi,* though there is one female in the cast, the delivery of a baby is enacted by a male actor. It is powerfully executed and the text draws parallels between the colonized native land and a female body taken possession of. The construction of colonial identity is explored as Mother Nature violated and forgetting of the umbilical chord. It seems easier for Muruga Bhoopathy to construct the female body on the basis of polarities of nature/culture; prakriti/development. In a way, this becomes a mode of recourse to what appears to be a primeval rhetoric in the evasion of social gender.

Using the female impersonation conventions to bypass the issue of not working on a powerful female presence on stage seems to be one of the commonly practised patriarchal privileges. I do not mean to suggest that the young theatre people in Tamil Nadu are consciously adapting a patriarchal tactic. But it is a pointer towards how the system bends itself to suit the purposes of dominant ideologies. Anuradha Kapur's *Sundari: An Actor Prepares* based on the life story of Jayashankar Sundari and Amal Allana's production of *Mother Courage* with Manohar Joshi in the lead role have discussed the complexities of body politics when one operates within these conventions of performance (Subramaniam 2002).

My recent experience of directing Usha Rani in *Pani-t-thee* has made me play with these conventions. Appearing in the full regalia of Shikandi in Koothu costume and changing herself into Amba in the course of the narrative throws light on the modes of conventions prevalent in Koothu for male and female roles. And, when she performs both in the same play, it becomes a reading of these conventions. Even without making any claims, the performance subverts the norms imposed. As a note to this experience, I must add that these transgressions of conventions can remain only at the level of experimentation. They can never reach the traditional spaces of performance that easily. An example of that is the Shakthi Tappattam troupe. It consists of primarily dalit women, who are school drop-outs. It functions from Dindigul. Though it has been functioning as an all-female tappattam group for over a decade, they perform in festivals and meetings. One cannot take that group to ritual performances in temples or funeral houses. Perhaps they don't want to go to these spaces either!

Staging gender operates through space, movement and choreography. Space, which is a crucial factor in theatre both on and off stage, is wrought in gender conflicts. The fact that our choice of time and venue should change if we wanted to have more female audience, is a clear indicator as to how the notion of entertainment in the 'modern' world excludes women. Just like how the television plans to have women's programmes in the afternoon, Shakthi Cultural Group of AIDWA performed matinee shows during lunch hours in the lunch halls or in slums.

I have been preoccupied with the use of space and its implications for the construction of gender identity for long. The fact that a central character was always presented at mid-centre raised issues of prominence, power and control. In the case of female characters, while most of these were victimized roles, what are placed at the centre are those images. One cannot easily change that perception when these very characters become angry or vengeful. Added to that, would be the signs created by music, props and movement.

It is pertinent to recall how the staging of *Avvai* responded to stage (V. Padma 2000). Avvai was seated at back left on a mid-level platform. Though one might get into slight problems of visibility, we retained that. As I have already said elsewhere: "But I felt that a central character need not always occupy centre stage, and for a bard within her own community, Avvai needed to lead, not to preside....To me this space meant a redefinition of assertion" (ibid., 225). But I must admit that Avvai was brought into the stage on a vertically higher level with two men carrying her on their shoulders! That resonates with goddess images, of which we have aplenty.

Conventions of staging authority operate with distinct spatial pattern on stage.

M. Ramasami's production of *Muni* had the Arjunan Tapas maram at stage centre symbolizing Topulan Raja's power. It also represents his phallic authority. An interesting comparison could be made of M. Ramasami's Antigone performed as *Durkira Avalam* and M. Jeeva's productions of *Medea* and *Antigone*. I would call Ramasami's production as character-oriented and Jeeva's as choric. The elements of ritualistic performance Jeeva evoked in *Medea* made her agony the voice of all women who feel wronged and used in an opportunistic ways. Jeeva also tried to document and record the dalit woman's specific plight in her plays.

A very poignant portrayal of voyeuristic male gaze was brought on stage in Muthusami's *Padukalam*. The villagers peep through the gaps in the thatched screen while the performers are putting on their make-up. The scene offers a strong critique of how the gaze varies between the male and female actors. There are also snide remarks made at the looks of Bhisma – actually of the actor playing Bhisma – at the women characters – actually playing the roles of Draupadi and Ghandari. At one point the text moves on to recording how eyes gape through the branches of the trees in the grove serving as women's toilet in the Punjai village. This play had an unusually critical flavour at all the male values. It called for an uncompromising admittance of a male psyche prevalent in our everyday affairs. This aspect of laying bear the practices of masculinity became a consciously gendered activity. And I think one owes it to Muthusami to admire his courage at negotiating life in all its complexities.

In *Pani-t-thee,* Shikandi, born a female and announced a male child and growing up as one, provided excellent scope to deal with the construction of maleness. The difficulty of honing the borrowed male body into a warrior body is another story altogether. The dichotomy of polarizing male-female into polarities of sex/gender came under scrutiny in such moments of tensions. Of course, this play had Shikandi, transforming himself into Amba, while narrating the story in flashback, willingly allowed the audience to 'look at' the performer 'becoming' a woman. While *Padukalam* exposed the voyeuristic male gaze, Amba in *Pani-t-thee* challenged the same by the same means of 'putting on' make-up in front of the audience. The woman looks, instead of being looked at on stage. That dynamics changes the power structure of the act of seeing.

Choreography is another crucial aspect in theatre, which gets loaded by conventional practices and their implications. I distinctly recall how whenever there are fewer women in the group, they are 'used' as fillers positioned prominently. I myself had been subjected to stand aside and wait for the rest of the group to make the formation and fill the gap. Most often, this assigned spot is central, crucial and the most visible. But, the principle behind such choreography is to make sure that the female body is 'looked at'.

The way *Mauna-k-Kuram* was designed by Ramanujam is a text to be studied in depth for its choreographic finesse. The female chorus appears with baskets and broomsticks, while the male chorus comes in with their 'silampam' sticks. These simple props of everyday life are brought in with a deceptive innocence. But, the female chorus wields their baskets as thrones and brooms as scepters and the male chorus uses the sticks as tools and arms to fight and protect themselves. All through the performance these props are woven into intricate patterns, never once out of the hands of the chorus. They become the rocks, plants, river, swing, balcony, steps and window, and so on. I remember the uneasiness the broomsticks created in the audience, especially in Kanchipuram Koothu festival, where stalwarts of koothu form were present. Some of them even said, "May be you can bring them in and at some point put them aside in a corner." This statement clearly marked how allowances may be given but one should not break the norms.

Body politics revealed in contemporary Tamil theatre has been a relatively unspoken realm. The debate *Avvai* created about the depiction of her relationship with Adhiyaman is an example of how things are read. In fact, a controversy over the text being prescribed as a language text in Manonmaniam Sundaranar University was created by the state BJP. A popular weekly covering the news titled the piece as "*Avvai kal kudithal; kadalithal*" (Avvai drank toddy and engaged in love). Avvai's poems are the first ever documented female voice in Tamil literature. She escaped the severe parameters of codifications of cataloguing. But she could not escape the male order of imposing old age, grey hair, bent back, forehead adorned with sacred ash, didacticism, perennial piety and single hood bordering on asceticism. It is this latter image that appealed to the Tamil psyche, for reasons well known. Therefore, it is no surprise that Inquilab's *Avvai* seemed to be flouting the rules of etiquette. Bringing a young, intelligent, sensuous woman participating in the affairs of the state on stage was a unique experience. Though the style of performance is not in any way new to Tamil theatre world, this image of Avvai created a stir and shook the complacency of conventional images built around her.

It has been a revealing experience to work on *Manasin Azhaippu*, the play by Kannadi Kalai Kuzhu, a group of Aravanis. Here was the group of trans-sexuals who refuse to give up even a wee-bit of whatever femininity they were practising. They did not want to wear *salwars* during rehearsals. For them *saree* was a symbol of their assertion. Voicing their basic demands for decent jobs, dignity at work, a place to stay and minimum human concern, the group laid bear their lives to the audience. Here was a group questioning the assumptions of masculinity but choosing to lead a life within the paradigm of femininity. The play ends with one of them sharing her experience of being thrown out of a ladies coupe, as not being woman enough. The only recourse she had was to strip naked and challenge the ticket collector to verify if she had any marks of maleness in her body. That moment makes one grow chill and question what in essence constitutes maleness. The act of disrobing resonates with conventional meanings, yet signifies something utterly novel and poignant; femininity that must never show itself has to prove its existence through recourse to nudity! I am still resolving the issue of negotiating this group's notion of femininity. They choose to have a male partner, only to be faced for the most part with betrayal, being used and suffer violence. Almost every single one of them is a bread-winner and all that they long for is a patient ear and an open heart.

Srilankan Tamil theatre world is another area, which offers interesting trends emerging over the years. There is such an active theatre world among Srilankan Tamils – both diasporic and national. Kuzhandai Shanmugalingam, a Jaffna-based playwright is a powerful voice to be acknowledged all over the world. Theatre flourishes in practice and academia in Srilanka. Ranjani Obeyesekara's *Srilankan Theatre in Times of Terror* (1999) completely omits this aspect as inaccessible. This approach in the context of many published texts with reviews and photographs of performances is a disservice done to Srilankan Tamils, which is even more offensive than other exclusions imposed on that people. A very strong debate on gender in performance has evolved in Srilankan Tamil theatre over the past decade.

I can only share my own direct experience with more confidence. Evolving plays through improvisation and structuring these, as performances have been the basis of my work in theatre for long. I had the opportunity of conducting theatre workshops twice in Batticaola. My work was with Surya Cultural Group. The ritualistic kulirthi[11] was offered to all women widowed, singled and alone. While the end was consoling, the stories themselves were narrated in the form of oppari (Keaning). I did face resistances from the group. I guess I was evasive about that. I assumed that this was the first response to an emotional expression and the problem of sharing life stories of persons too close to one. As I returned to India, Vasuki, the organizer of the group and a painter, reported the deaths that occurred in many families. The members felt that these forebode evil because they tampered with the oppari form. For the first time I learnt that forms could have a life of their own.

My latest play with that group *Oru Pidi Anbu* (2002) ended with the performers moving through the audience with turmeric water, considered cooling and healing, asking each one to paste their imprint on a piece of cloth used as the curtain throughout the performance. When one of them came up after the show, she asked for the turmeric water, which did not reach till the end of the hall. It became a symbolic act of participating.

If theatre had its origin in ritual, it may never lose touch with rituals. The deal is to discover our contemporary rituals, which would have the efficacy of community living and collective signification. Perhaps, that could be the only alternative to fundamentalist agendas of dividing people on the lines of religions, castes, class, gender and sexual orientation. I can feel myself sounding like the tired voice of a possessed soul. I wish we could evoke the power of the oracle through theatre.

End Notes

This paper was first presented at the "Padma Bhushan Dr. Rajah Sir M.A. Muthiah Chettiar of Chettinad" Eighth Endowment Lecture, Department of MIL &LS, University of Delhi, March 14, 2005.

1. Entry of women in Tamil theatre and their negotiations with the conventions of female impersonation, still prevalent in traditional forms deserve a detailed study. There were all-female companies like that of Balamani Ammal (Ref: Oxford Companion to Indian Theatre, 2004) and stalwarts like K.S. Sundarambal reigned supreme on stage and screen. In modern drama, Krittika, an experimental writer of the sixties, had written and staged a few plays. Ambai has written a few plays, scant in comparison to her output in fiction. Kalai Rani, Mangai, Pritam, Prasanna Ramaswami, Gandhi Mary, Guruvammal, M. Jeeva, A.S. Padamavathi, and K.R. Usha (not an exhaustive list) have been engaged in theatre in various capacities for over two decades.

2. Muthusami's *Undhi Chuzhi* (1981) is a play dealing with the politics of reproductive mode and its implications in a patriarchal system. It was not performed as often as his other plays like *Narkalikkarar* or *Suvarottigal.*
3. Corresponding plays in which these female characters appear are *Veriattam, Mauna-k-Kuram* and *Sembavalakkali* (Ramanujam Nadagankal (Ed. Annamalai, C.), Chennai: Kavvya, 2004.
4. Chandramathi is the wife of Harischandra who suffered to keep up the promise of her husband; Draupadi is the wife of Pandavas who endured public humiliation in Duryodhana's court; Seetha is the chaste wife of Rama who had to prove her purity by entering the fire ordeal.
5. *Manimekalai* is a play written by Inquilab. It was produced by Voicing Silence with an all-female cast of professional stage artistes of Tamilnadu in 2002. The text published under the same title by Mithra (2006) is quite different from the performance text.
6. Isai Natakam or Musical drama came into vogue in the late 19th century, almost as a pan-Indian phenomenon (Ref: Oxford Companion to Indian Theatre, 2004).
7. Kuravanji is one of the Prabhanda genres in Tamil belonging to 17th and 18th centuries.
8. Kannadi Kalai Kuzhu is a performance group of transgender community and has evolved two plays so far.
9. Chennai Kalai Kuzhu was formed in 1984 as part of the Progressive Writers' Association. It operates with defined left politics. It is one of the leading political theatre groups in the state. I have been one of the founder members of the group.
10. Anna Devere Smith introduced a new style of working on documentary sources. Her Fires in The Mirror and On the Road reveal multiple perspectives of different players in the contemporary racialised context in U.S.
11. Kulirthi is a ritual performance done in Kannaki temples in the Easter parts of Srilanka. Kulirthi, literally means 'to cool down' or support.

Works Cited

Lal, Ananda (ed.), *Oxford Companion to Indian Theatre*, Delhi: OUP, 2004.

Padma, V. (A. Mangai), "Theatre of Protest and Resistance – Avvai", *Indian Journal of Gender Studies*, Vol.7, No.2, July-December, 2000, pp. 217-230.

Obeysekare, Ranjani, *Srilankan Theatre in Times of Terror*, New Delhi: Sage, 1999.

Subramanyam, Lakshmi (ed.), *Muffled Voices: Women in Modern Indian Theatre*, Delhi: Har Anand Publications, 2002.

9

Gender Representation Paradigm in Indian Media: A Post-Feminist Perspective

SHOBHANA NAIR

Faculty, S.R. Mehta Arts College, Ahmedabad.

Introduction: Feminism and Post-feminism

Feminist theory has several different theoretical approaches and positions but whether it is socio-economic, psychological or literary, its two primary concerns are power and freedom (Jain, 2001: 82). Jain further mentions that feminist struggle has been studied in three stages: the first was a concern with the right to equality and political rights and the second with emphasis on alternative perspectives and epistemological structures. The first held 'man' as central with woman being a 'no-man,' with aspirations to become one, whereas the second privileged differences, motherhood and the self. The third stage, the post-feminist one, is at one level an attempt to demolish these binary oppositions and, at another, an effort to re-define power and freedom. It is an attempt to extend the area of women's roles and of their questioning of relationships in order to drive home the point that the self does not exist in isolation. The term 'post-feminism' has thus evolved, moving from feminist to womanist to humanist. It is a move towards reciprocal change.

The present paper assays this extension of women's roles in the context of two developments:

1. The slow pace of change in gender representations in the Indian media, especially television advertising, which is the focus of this paper.
2. The setting up of Women's Development Cells (WDCs) under the aegis of universities as per the University Grants Commission (UGC) guidelines.

Gender Representation in Indian Media

Media in a Sociological Context

Media is a very integral part of our lives. This generates a lot of public interest regarding the role it plays in any society. In this respect, media plays a crucial role in almost all aspects of daily life. D. Croteau and W. Hoynes (2003) have studied the sociological significance of media that extends beyond the content of media messages into the domain of how we learn about our world and interact with one another.

Mass media messages, such as those on television, radio and print, do not allow for the intimate interaction of sender and receiver that characterizes personal communication. Croteau and Hoynes (2003) contend that audiences must rely on other resources to make sense of media messages. This point will be revisited at the conclusion of the present paper in support of the postulate regarding the potential of the television medium to influence cultural norms.

Gender Stereotyping in the Western Media

Alice Courtney and Sarah Lockeretz's content analysis of men and women in print advertising was one of the first and also one of the most widely cited research studies on the subject. These authors concluded that four general stereotypes of women existed across advertisements in eight major general interest magazines in the years 1958, 1968 and 1978:

1. A woman's place is in the home.
2. Women do not make important decisions or do important things.
3. Women are dependent and need men's protection.
4. Men regard women primarily as sex objects.

The findings from content analysis of television advertisements showed similar results:

1. Prevalent female roles were maternal, housekeeping and aesthetic.
2. Women and girls were seen less frequently than men and boys.
3. Women were shown to have different characteristics than males (such as less authoritative, decisive, powerful and rational).
4. Women were housewives or in subservient low status occupations.
5. Women were depicted as less intelligent than men.

Gender Representation in India: The Sociological Dimension

India is the original home to the Mother Goddess. Ancient India boasted of women scholars like Gargi, Anusuya and Maitreyi and the more recent past saw women rulers like Rani Laxmibai and Indira Gandhi. Even, the mythologies and folklore depicted Indian women in favourable light.

Despite the Indian Constitution being one of the most progressive in the world that guarantees equal rights to men and women, the official statistics present a dismal picture:

1. Men outnumber women in India.
2. Women have little control over her own fertility and reproductive health.
3. Only 54 per cent of Indian women are literate compared to 76 per cent men.
4. There are fewer women in the paid workforce than men.
5. Women are underrepresented in governance and decision-making positions.

Women in Indian Media

To a great extent the public portrayal of women and women's issues in Indian media is also an indication of the position women have in Indian society. Advertisement (heretofore abbreviated as 'ad') images are reflections of social reality. Over the past decade, commercials have portrayed women in diverse roles. Most of the manufacturers have created two diametrically opposed female stereotypes in their commercials. The first and the most enduring of these is that of a housewife who is often depicted as a dirt-obsessed fanatic who spends all day on her knees cleaning bathroom tiles. The other, less prevalent counterpart is an entirely different species. She is dressed for success, a single-minded careerist woman who needs a hair colour, deodorant, shampoo or beauty soap to help maintain her cool business-like image. They next targeted the women who were seeking fulfilment in both their jobs and home lives. The new woman has a much better self-image than the traditional housewife mainly because of her ability to juggle her personal and professional lives.

The progressive perceptible change in the portrayal of women in Indian commercials from weak and dependent to strong and autonomous is primarily attributed to the feminist movement. The male power structure that controls the ad agencies is not ideologically committed to or opposed to the women's movement. It is committed to the principles of profitability. Financial self-interest demanded a more enlightened approach to female consumer needs today considering the fact that their numbers have considerably increased. The portrayal of women in dignified roles is not the result of social awareness alone. The only solace is that stereotypes predating the women's movement are gradually changing, keeping up with the times to portray realistically the diversity of women's roles. Role reversal is also a new trend that further points to the breaking of stereotypes and the change in attitudes with respect to gender equality. For instance, the recent Vicks Vaporub ad shows a father nursing a sick child in the absence of the mother. With more and more nuclear families coming up, the sharing of family responsibilities is being redefined.

The Indian Advertising Industry's Response

At a social level, advertisement mirrors society and society mirrors advertisement. Several such healthy changes are encouraged/reinforced by advertisements. It also creates role models, who in turn could be the working mother or the husband who cooks food and performs maternal duty. It is only lately that the Indian advertising has incorporated the roles of a working woman and a single woman. Today, the commercials facilitate a new portrait of the Indian women who have entered different professional careers such as politics, management, technology, sales or administration, which will aid in narrowing the gender gap further. It will enable the movement for gender equality to move further from being an exclusive concern of women to being a people's issue.

Indian Feminism versus Western Feminism

Indian feminism has dissociated from western trends because of religious and cultural factors. Unlike our western counterpart, marriage and family are very central to Indian life. The political fact of India having been a colony that necessitated a common fight on part of both men and women for their rights is proof enough that women have contributed immensely during the days of freedom struggle. Even in pre-independence period, the Indian woman possessed a strong moral sense, was independent and thinking individual. Still, the ad industry took a little longer in portraying this image, where

1. women are encouraged to move into what is perceived as a male's domain,
2. women are shown as earning to supplement family income, and
3. women enjoy high status, as they are involved in decision-making affairs.

In any sphere of life change is inevitable. Indian advertising, too, cannot escape this fact. Thus, the portrayal of women in Indian advertising is no exception to this rule. But, change does not, however, come easily in the world of Indian advertising, which is emerging slowly from self-analysis and self-awareness.

A Glimpse of Indian Advertising

A brief look into the Indian advertising industry would be in order here before we talk of this change. The first advertising agency in India, B. Dattaram & Co., was established in 1905 in Girgaum in South Mumbai. After 100 years of its existence, when one looks back, the incredible change cannot go unnoticed. It has definitely traversed a long and eventful journey. When we compare it with the advertising agency in the US, which was set up in 1871, Indian advertising is hardly too far behind the most powerful nation. This era has also seen major changes in spheres such as technology, values and lifestyles, perceptions, etc. How could advertising resist change in the face of developments all around? The change is more prominent in the past 15 years than in the preceding 85 years.

Despite these changes, one aspect with regard to advertising that has shown very gradual change is the portrayal of women in stereotypical roles. This issue has been discussed and researched through the years. A careful study of ads shows a consistent picture of gender stereotyping that has varied little over time. Women were portrayed as passive, unintelligible and yielding to the wishes of others, especially the men in many commercials. In contrast, men have been portrayed as constructive, powerful, autonomous and achievers. The Indian ads continued this kind of portrayal till the late 90s without significant change.

The Study

The present paper studies television ads of two well-known Indian brands to postulate that the shift in the gender representation paradigm in the Indian advertising industry is gradual at best despite the potential of this communication tool to influence the cultural norms. The ads of Santoor (a well-known brand of soap) and Godrej Storwel (a long-established brand of furniture) that appeared over a period of almost two decades depict the shift in the role portrayal with little change in gender stereotyping.

Santoor offered two useful ingredients, sandal and turmeric, proven to be very good for skin care. Sandalwood paste and turmeric were used by Indian women for centuries as skincare ingredients. 'A mistaken identity' route was selected by the ad agency in 1989 as the most identifiable way of depicting the younger looking skin. While Indian women felt they should look young and receive compliments from others, the best representation was when a married woman with a child (the ultimate proof of womanhood) gets mistaken for a younger woman – by a group of women. The format of 'mistaken identity' was depicted in situations/places that could be easily identified by the target audience:

(1) In a book shop
(2) In a bangle shop
(3) At a wedding
(4) In an aerobics class

Fifteen years on, the ads of Santoor depict the same benefit, but with the following imagery:

(1) A mother and her girl child playing cricket in their lawns. The woman is shown breaking her neighbour's windowpane.
(2) A professional fashion designer, being awarded for her skill. The element of 'mistaken identity' as proof of the efficacy of the soap's ingredients is carried on in these series too.

The perceptible changes are:

1. Cricket, which is mainly considered a man's domain, is used as a metaphor to depict the change in a woman's role and status in one of the ads.
2. The woman is depicted as venturing out of her domestic/ conventional sphere in both the new ads.
3. The latest ad shows her as a professional designer, who is independent and accomplished in her chosen field. This woman is not depicted as dependent and needing man's protection.

In all the Santoor ads, the woman is also shown as interacting with other women and not men. In fact, of the six 'anecdotes,' only the one about the fashion designer has a man in one of the frames: a cameraman shooting the event. The irony of this situation is not to be missed here. The woman's role is certainly changing in society, but even in 2004 (when this ad was released) the ad agency did not show a woman 'manning' the camera!!

As the above demonstrates, Indian advertising certainly is coming to terms with the changing paradigms of gender representation. But, this 'coming to terms' is slow and the advertising fraternity (please note my deliberate use of this word) does not want to 'upset the applecart' by being 'too liberal' in its depiction of ordinary life situations.

I would cite another illustration to substantiate my argument. For this purpose, I shall analyze three ads in a series, of the brand Godrej Storwel that has a history of over four decades in this country.

1980s: Concept 'marriage': This commercial showed a new 'bahu' entering her husband's house for the first time in her life and being given the keys to her own Godrej Storwel.

1995: Concept 'pregnant woman': This depicted another traditional Indian custom – celebration of a 'would-be mother'. Motherhood is seen as the ultimate test of womanhood in Indian society. It can be seen on the basis of these two ads that the manner in which women were portrayed in a span of 15 years have undergone very nominal, if any, change.

2004: Concept 'young couple': This depicted a modern-day young couple at a construction site. Even the dresses worn by the male and female models in the ad depict their youth. Unlike the earlier ads that had models in traditional dresses like the sari, this new ad showed both in casuals, the girl in a bright-red frock. The images in the ad reveal that this couple is on the verge of setting up their own 'nest,' without any of their elders around. The ad begins with the line "we'll set up our heaven here" and goes on to show the man cavort around his companion and show the still-to-be-built apartment. This representation was a radical shift from the brand's earlier concepts. But, even here, the ad falls back on the stereotype of the male as the provider of the family. The female's representational paradigm seems limited to her bold, unIndian dress, as she joins in her consort's revelry.

Conclusions and Recommendations

The introduction to the paper showed the power of media in influencing cultural norms. But, the very characteristics of mass media, such as television that is the focus of this paper, require the audience to resort to other resources to make sense of the media messages. The second point covered in the paper is about the Indian feminism movement that is gaining momentum due to the concerted efforts of members from various walks of life. This impetus should be harnessed in giving the right direction to gender representations in the Indian media. As brought about in the paper, the shift has been slow at best. Though, as mentioned earlier, the change is more visible over the past 15 years than in the earlier 85 years of Indian advertising.

Women's Development Cell

I now look at the second development mentioned in the introduction to this paper: the initiative of UGC in the Indian universities in pursuance of the Supreme Court's judgment regarding women's right to gender equality, working with dignity, a work environment safe and protected from sexual harassment or abuse and appropriate work conditions in respect to health and hygiene (WDC Ready Reckoner, 2005).

The Genesis

The Supreme Court, in its judgment in the case of Vishakha and Others versus State of Rajasthan and Others, reported in 1997 (6) SCC 241, has directed all employers, the person-in-charge of working place to prevent and deter the commission of act of any kind of harassment, including sexual harassment and to provide the procedure for resolution, settlement or prosecution of acts of sexual harassment by taking all required steps. In pursuance of this ruling, the UGC has directed all universities to constitute Women's Development Cell (WDC) at both university and college levels.

The scope and purpose of the WDC, established in October 2005 at Gujarat University, are as follows:

- It will function as a nodal agency with several collegiate WDCs under its umbrella.
- It will be binding to the management/employers as well as students, teaching and non-teaching staff of the Gujarat University and the colleges affiliated to it and other recognized institutions in respect of the fundamental right of 'gender equality' and 'right to life and liberty'.

The powers and functions of the WDC (Gujarat University), as mentioned in its Ready Reckoner, are as follows:

- To ensure implementation of the policy in the university and other constituents to which it is applicable.
- To ensure and supervise the proper constitution and functioning of the WDCs set up in colleges and recognized institutions.
- To act as the appellate authority in respect of the decisions taken by the WDCs in the colleges and recognised institutions.
- To do all such acts and things as may be necessary to carry out the objects of this policy – publications, events, training and creative activities (WDC Ready Reckoner, 2005).

My suggestion for a proactive role for WDC is in keeping with the last point mentioned above, i.e., the scope of activities of such an institution. The WDC (Gujarat University) has prominent members in its Advisory Committee, including a Government Pleader and Public Prosecutor, two former Law Secretaries of the Gujarat Government, a leading academician from Mumbai University and the founder of one of Gujarat's leading NGO in the area of women empowerment – Ahmedabad Women's Action Group. With leading academicians from the university and prominent persons on board, I foresee a larger role for the top management, including the Advisory Committee, of the WDC with regard to issues of gender equality, such as gender representation in the media.

A Proactive Role for WDC

It is recommended that institutions such as the newly formed Women's Development Cells (WDCs) in universities across the country should play a more proactive role of being the catalysts of change in gender representation in the country. Mass media, such as television, will continue to hold sway as a cost-effective form of reaching the geographic, ethnic and economic diversities of the Indian landscape. Consequently, I envisage a larger, proactive role for WDC to act as a bridge between the media and the masses, in addition to the role currently defined by the UGC.

On the one hand, WDC can play the role of an advocate for better, realistic and ethical gender representation to the media industry. On the other, it can go to the masses and interpret the messages for them in a way that reduces the gender-based differentiations in society. My conviction regarding this larger role for WDC stems from its very constitution: a group of senior academicians who can command respect from various sections of society. Also, these academicians and researchers, by the very nature of their duties, are better equipped to study the latest developments in gender studies. Thus, they will be in a position to provide the necessary platform to disseminate such

Women's Development Cell's Proactive Role: The BRIDGE

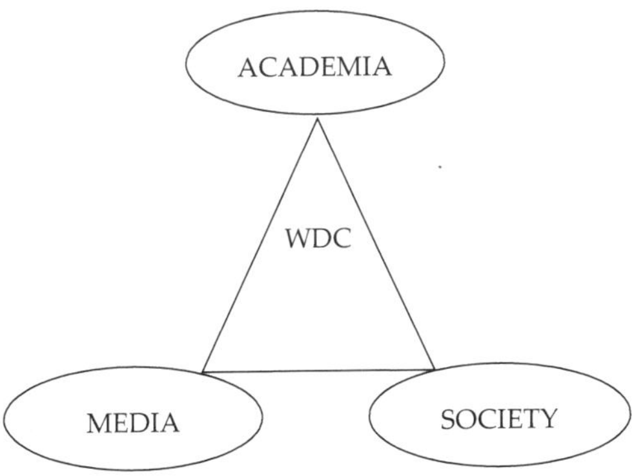

information among the target groups by way of publications, events, seminars etc. as envisaged in the role for the WDC. Such a constituent committee can have its say with both the media as well as the general public, thus acting as a bridge between the media and society.

Organizing for Success

To fulfil this larger role in society envisaged for WDCs, there can be a two-level structure. The lower level can take care of the operational aspects within the university set-up, as defined by the UGC. The upper level can comprise of senior members drawn from various departments/faculties of a university along with the advisory committee. It shall play the role of mentors to the needy and advocates of gender equality to the media. This latter level can play the important role of a bridge between the academia, media and society – a meaningful role that justifies the attempts of the post-feminist movement mentioned in the introduction to this paper.

Works Cited

Croteau, D. and W. Hoynes. 2003. *Media Society*. California: Sage.

Jain, Jasbir. 2001. *Indian Feminisms*. New Delhi: Creative Books.

Lobo, A. "One Hundred Years of Advertising". *USP Age*. December 2004.

Menon-Sen, K. and A. Shivakumar. 2001. *Women in India. How Free? How Equal?* 2nd ed., New Delhi: United Nations Resident Coordinator.

Meyers, W. 1984. *The Image Makers: Secrets of Successful Advertising*. London: Orbis.

Parameswaran, M.G. 2001. *FCB-ULKA Brand Building Advertising*. New Delhi: TMH.

Shields, V.R. 2003. "The Less Space We Take the More Powerful We'll Be". In A.N. Valdivia (ed.), *A Companion to Media Studies*. MA: Blackwell Publishing.

WDC. 2005. *WDC: A Ready Reckoner*. Ahmedabad: Gujarat University.

10

"What do we know (not)?" Alternative Patriarchies – Alternative Female Sexualities – Anti-essentialisms

ANIRUDDHAN VASUDEVAN

(Performer, Researcher, Activist based in Chennai)

Alternative female sexualities – lesbianism, bisexuality and several unnamed desires – force both theory and practice of feminism and the queer into self-reflexivity and realignments. This essay explores the why, how and what of this, with specific reference to anti-essentialist approaches and patriarchies within alternative thinking.

Hey! Why are you ogling at him?

Chee! I am not a lesbian.

This exchange between two 'kothis' (the pan-Indian term) – for effeminate gay men who prefer macho, usually penetrating, partners – is symptomatic of uninformed, ill-informed and, sometimes, misogynic attitudes that very often surface in the queer male mind. The above response does not only innocuously point to the speaker's sexual preferences but to the fact that he thinks love between two 'kothis' not a valid one and also equivalent to a lesbian relationship at the same time. This does justice neither to gayness nor lesbianism! It betrays an assumption that a valid gay relationship is only between a 'kothi' and a 'panthi' (macho, active, usually the penetrating partner in sex) and an idea that there are no such differences in women-women relationships. One can say without sounding farfetched that this postulates a single undifferentiated femininity, a monolithic category 'woman'. It has also, by difference, constituted a restrictive identity of what 'man' is. In the given instance what has effected this is a certain knowledge (or its lack thereof). And here, by knowledge, I mean the unconscious, internalized, unreflective ideas. These cannot be ignored, just as any powerful, possibly violent, notions about any other cannot be ignored.

As a foil to this knowledge, is another kind of knowledge. Anti-essentialist feminist scholarship has radicalized thinking about sex, gender and sexuality by liberating categories like 'man', 'woman', 'male' and 'female' from the socio-cultural and political essentialisms that they are usually tied down to. That is, anti-essentialist approach has given feminism the necessary impetus to wrench such loaded terms away from the way they had been hitherto unproblematically deployed. It disabled talking about 'man', 'woman', 'masculinity', 'femininity' etc. in terms that would posit unquestionable essences to these identities, and signaled the birth of the social consructionist approach and theories of gender, and sexuality subsequently. Eve Kosofsky Sedgwick sums it up:

> The charting of a space between something called 'sex' and something called 'gender' has been one of the most influential and successful undertakings of feminist thought. For the purposes of that undertaking, 'sex' has had the meaning of a certain group of irreducible, biological differentiations between members of the species Homo sapiens who have XX and those who have XY chromosomes... 'Sex' in this sense – what'll demarcate

> as 'chromosomal sex' – is seen as the relatively minimal raw material on which is then based the social construction of gender. Gender, then, is the far more elaborated, more fully and rigidly dichotomized social production and reproduction of male and female identities and behaviors – of male and female persons ...(Sedgwick, 27)

In short, the most radical contribution of anti-essentialist feminism has been in rupturing our assumptions of linear, consequential relationships between sex, gender and sexuality taken in that order – therefore, you are a woman or a man not because there is a hidden essence in you that makes you so, not because you have the reproductive organs corresponding to the male or the female, but because there are socially constructed, discursively produced codes, narratives and acts that make you so.

This approach has certainly been a whiff of fresh air. Lesbian and Gay Theories take off exactly at this point of de-essentializing sexuality, gender, and even sex. Sexual attraction to the opposite gender/sex is not a preordained, 'natural' reality anymore when the very foundations of defining that gender have been shaken. When one's sex is not one's essence of identity, when gender is not a 'natural' category, sexuality cannot be 'naturally' mapped anymore as sexual attraction between members of opposite gender/sexes. For the 'naturalness' of that gender and the determinative power of that category sex in defining the identity of an individual have been called into question. So, maleness, femaleness and sexuality need not relate one-to-one with man, woman and gender/sex respectively. Are there problems with this liberating epistemology? Does it, in anyway, address the day-to-day lived oppressions that continue to treat these same categories as rigid, immutable, non-transcendable essences of identity? Pulling the meaning out of the category 'woman' poses a problem for all women. But heightened so for women who are forced, more than others, to reclaim that identity. For example, coloured women, butch women, lesbian and bisexual women in general etc. They were not safely ensconced in that identity before it was de-essentialized. Their (authenticity of) womanhood was (and still is) already in question from many heterosexual quarters.

Ignorances and Knowledges – unManichean

Ignorance is the most violent element in society reads a bumper sticker. The truth of it rings aloud. Sometimes insensitivities and injustices do not spring out of some vicious deliberateness, but out of *not knowing*. The word *ignorance* resonates with a certain degree of pity and the possibility of condoning. *Not knowing* not only seems to catch the problem by its throat without mincing words, but also gives a space to do something about it. When I do not know something, I can start getting to know it. On the other hand, *knowing* something radical does not always lead to things radical. There might be a good deal of gap between that knowledge (system) and 'reality,' which sometimes might turn into a breeding ground of violence.

In this essay, I bring two processes under observation, in the context of the positioning of alternative female sexualities within the women's and the queer movements: (1) queer communities' and theory's grappling with questions of identity, identification, and difference; and (2) the problems posed by anti-essentialist feminist theory to identity and identity politics. Both are, primarily, questions of knowledge – of epistemology, of both systematically and consciously produced and possessed knowledges as well as internalized knowledge matrices and scripts. In the case of anti-essentialist feminism, the problem comes out of a theoretical knowledge system that is unable to engage with certain 'realities', while in that of queer collectives, the issue is that of ignorance. But, of course, "these ignorances, far from being pieces of the originary dark, are produced by and correspond to particular knowledges and circulate as part of regimes of truth" (Sedgwick, 8)

What are "We"?

By choosing men as their sexual and romantic partners, gay men stay outside traditional definitions of 'family', that epitome of heteropatriarchy and heterosexuality. By opting out of this structure, how do they alter their relationships with women? Do the other familial, social and professional relationships that gay men have with women get fundamentally altered because of this absence of sexual violence between them? Does the same-sex choice of these men breed coterie-formation and misogyny? Are these men, minus the male-gaze, the stereotypical best pals of women as some movies have represented? How understanding are they towards the same-sex choices of women? Do the larger gender intolerances of heteropatriarchy get replicated within the alternative, queer communities? These are questions being self-reflexively raised within queer collectives – not only by lesbian feminists and pro-queer feminists, but by all who resist all forms of oppression. Instances like the one that I started this piece with are many. They will fall anywhere on a continuum between lack of understanding and misogyny.

In some instances, this lack of sexual interest towards women spills over and manifests as a total lack of interest with anything that concerns women. The following cyber conversation is an example:

A: was reading an article on Mumbai by a Tamil writer

B: I hope he had something good to write about

A: boy! how can u assume it is a "he"???

B: anything related to a she doesn't really interest me

Of course, lesbianism and bisexuality are yet to find adequate positioning and support even within the women's movements. That, however, need not stop queer communities from engaging with such issues as queer men's unhealthy attitudes about women; not only their sexuality but their very being.

It is not unusual to hear men, even queer men, joke about how there is no penetration in lesbian sex and how that somehow makes it incomplete. As mentioned earlier, these attitudes and comments are double-barreled. They not only betray their insensitivity towards women's same-sex choices but also their basic internalization of ideas of what is complete (later *legitimate*) sex and what is not. This sets about a dangerous hierarchy. It creates what I am tempted to call an *alternative patriarchy*; a *homopatriarchy* may be, as opposed to *heteropatriarchy*.

The point I am trying to make is that there is something equally, if not more, threatening as sexual violence. It is a sort of epistemic violence – not just a thrusting of an episteme over a reality but the violence of ill-formed epistemes over a reality. It is a question of knowledge: What do people know? If the question is asked internally in groups like the lgbt communities, about their own members, what it highlights is alarming. If queer communities believe in the need for sustaining the collective politics launched, such questions have to be repeatedly and endlessly asked and addressed. It is imperative to do that if alternative communities envision for themselves structures different from the usual centre/periphery or hierarchical models. To break away from a structure only to end up replicating it is a meaningless act. Queer communities are progenies of radical rethinking of categories like sex, gender and sexuality that are otherwise naturalized, internalized and normativized. To act out similar or the same internalized scripts within these alternative communities is self-defeating.

The question is whether queer theory concerns itself with these issues of identity politics at all. Being fundamentally on anti-essentialist modes, queer theory sometimes tends to discredit identity politics itself, as we will see later in this essay. So, the paradox is that, while deconstructive approach helps liberate the category sexuality from its normativized and naturalized state, it also proceeds to collapse the foundations of identity politics itself. If our identities are free-floating signifiers and if all we have are multiple affiliations that get differently foregrounded at different times, in different contexts, why do we feel the need to assert of our right to one particular identity – say, as a queer individual or as a woman over that of being a teacher or a writer? Amartya Sen touches this nerve when he remarks, "Sometimes a classification that is hard to justify intellectually may nevertheless be made important through social arrangements....the social world constitutes differences by the mere fact of designing them" (Sen, 27). Queer theory's approaches to issues of identity, if they have to be of continuous relevance to queer politics, must "go beyond the purely intellectual into contingent social significance;" they need to "take note of the social context and contingent relevance of being in one category or another" (Sen, 27-28)

I think; therefore you are

I was not a man until she insisted on pointing out I was.

A 'male' friend who was upset that a 'female' friend refused to take him for anything else but for his being 'male' uttered this remarkable statement. She chose to see him as 'irredeemably male', as he dejectedly put it. He was, for her, what she thought he was. Of course, it could have been the other way round as well. His obvious androgyny and his feminism were not of much help in the face of how someone chose to see him. In the crucial gap between how we choose to see ourselves and how most others continue to see us, violence might happen. Amartya Sen touches upon this aspect of identity in his recent book, *Identity and Violence: The Illusion of Destiny*:

> The constraints may be especially strict in defining the extent to which we can persuade *others*, in particular, to take us to be different from (or more than) what they insist on taking us to be .... The freedom in choosing our identity in the eyes of others can sometimes be extraordinarily limited" (Sen, 31).

Thus, when Judith Butler says "If one 'is' a woman, that is surely not all one is; the term fails to be exhaustive" (Butler 3), it is as important for the subject to *know* it as for the others. That is, when someone sees you only as a woman, only as your gender and sex, even your own ability to see yourself as more than that may not be of much help. In the case of lesbian and bisexual women, their womanhood becomes a bone of contention both from the patriarchal angle as well as from the anti-essentialist perspective.

Where do we place these on-the-face realities with respect to anti-essentialist understandings of sex, gender and sexuality that destabilize these identity markers?

Identities and Differences

Questions of identity and difference have variously concerned feminist and queer scholarship. Let me give a bird's eye view of some of the major conceptual understandings that have a direct bearing upon our subject(s) of discussion. These are from both feminism and queer studies, and many of them have significantly taken place in the intersections of the two. However, not all the theorists and critics whose work I quote/discuss here are, what is often called, 'representative'.

I am (not what you are not)

Luce Irigaray's influential article "This Sex Which is Not One" represented a break from Freudian understanding of female sexuality as always dependent upon male sexuality for its existence. Her positing female pleasure as independent of male sexuality, as auto-erotic, has marked a radical shift in understandings of female sexuality as not just a relational category always referring to the male, but also a function of individual desires: "A women 'touches herself' constantly without anyone being able to forbid her do so, for her sex is composed of two lips which embrace continually. Thus, with herself she is already two – but not divisible into ones – which stimulate each other" (Irigaray, 28). This theorizing of the autonomy of female pleasure has effected a major realignment in thinking about gender and sexuality.

You do, so you are

Judith Butler's poststructuralist incursions in *Gender Trouble: Feminism and the Subversion of Identity* discuss the centrality of the performative aspect of gender. The accepted ontological, essential identity of a gender is, she analyzes, a result of stylized bodily acts that constitute an identity when repeatedly performed over time. Importantly, she sees the act of performing gender not as a conscious or a voluntary one but as something determined by what Foucault has called *regulative discourses*, discourses that *discipline and punish*. Together, these acts create the illusion of a stable gender identity. So, the signified 'gender' slips over the signifier 'sex'.

Homo/Hetero

The first breakthrough in queer understanding was the dissolution of the difference (or differance) represented by the hetero/homo binary. Eve Kosofsky Sedgwick takes issues with it in her *Epistemology of the Closet* at the very outset:

> ...homo/heterosexual definition has been a presiding master term of the past century, one that has the same, primary importance for all modern Western identity and social organization (and not merely for homosexual identity and culture) as do the more traditionally visible cruxes of gender, class and race (Sedgwick, 11).

Sedgwick's argument here is that all our understandings and reworking of several such sets of binaries like 'natural/artificial', 'wholeness/decadence', 'same/different', 'domestic/foreign' etc. are incomplete without the consideration of the homo/heterosexual definition as well. She argues that these other categories have been 'ineffaceably marked' by the homo/heterosexual definition. In placing this alongside gender, class and race, Sedgwick has at once demonstrated the 'irresolvable instability' of the homo/hetero binary construction. This has been the necessary first step.

Come in ....Stay out

Diana Fuss provides a spatial understanding of this binary opposition in her introduction to *Inside/Out – Lesbian Theories, Gay Theories* (edited by her). She explains how the "structural symmetries of these seemingly fundamental distinctions," like the hetero/homo one, are based "on a logic of limits, margins, borders and boundaries" (Fuss, 1). She argues that such polarities may actually be indispensable models in understanding how cultural meanings are constructed: "...the denotation of any term (is) always dependent on what is exterior to it (heterosexuality, for example, typically defines itself in critical opposition to that which it is not: homosexuality." Hence, "Inside/outside functions as the very figure for signification and the mechanisms of meaning production" (Fuss, 1).

Conceptualizations like that of Diana Fuss' point to how complete dissolution of such binary oppositions might prevent us from seeing how inclusive and, hence always, exclusive territories are charted; how and why something falls 'inside' and the rest fall 'outside'. Such a framework enables engaging with issues of identity politics. This facilitates discussions like that of Steven Epstein's, which ring the warning bell: "... it seems clear enough that the gay movement will never be able to forge effective alliances with other social movements unless it can address the inequalities that plague its internal organization." Ed Cohen expands upon this and points to a general unfortunate reality concerning identity politics: "...no matter how sensitively we go about it, 'identity politics' has great difficulty in affirming difference(s)" (Cohen, 76). He, in fact, calls for a redefinition of identity politics itself and emphasizes the importance of remembering that any collective identity is "constantly and self-consciously in the process of inventing, multiplying, and modifying" (Cohen, 88) itself.

Whose Theory?

Suparna Baskaran, probably informed by her ethnic 'difference,' looks at how anti-essentialist thinking discredits all forms of identity politics, and even identity itself, and how this problematizes addressing issues of identity-based violence:

> The logic of gender-skepticism seems to imply that day-to-day lived oppression is perhaps a problem for some women – poor women, fat women, women of color, lesbians, women who are not able-bodied – but the immediate problem for poststructural feminists is the fine tuning of their theory of deconstruction and linguistic arbitrariness (Baskaran, 192).

Her argument very crucially points not only to a knowledge-reality gap, but to the unevenness of theoretical practice itself. It raises the question of who produces it and who cannot afford to consume it. When these questions are raised, there is a space available to discuss, account for, and register differences. In the particular context of this essay, that of the positioning of alternative female sexualities, Cheshire Calhoun's following analysis catches our specific concern:

> ... in focusing on lesbians' and gays' shared status as sexual deviants, the gay rights movement was unable to address the connection between lesbian oppression and women's oppression...it tended to equate gay with gay male and failed to address the patriarchal attitudes embedded in the gay movement itself (Calhoun, 201).

Mary E. John and Janaki Nair echo the same:

> Sharp lines have come to be drawn between positions that view heterosexuality as the very core of women's oppression, on the one hand, and more liberal lesbian criticisms that see a focus on sexual violence alone as being unduly alarmist, an obstacle to speaking about women's pleasure (John and Nair, 5).

What does this lead to? In a sense, it leads to a politics of non-identity where lesbian and bisexual women find neither the women's movements nor the queer movements offering sufficient non-marginal space.

Many of the above-said developments in thinking have happened at the intersections of feminist and queer approaches. Issues of gender and sexuality, fortunately, have not been neatly parcelled out to feminism and queer theory respectively. In spite of the acknowledging the fact that sex and gender is not the same thing, the contingent inseparability of the two has been recognized in these approaches.

Queer and Feminist Studies' Engagements

"To be lesbian today means to face violence as a queer and violence as a woman."

"To be lesbian today means to be invisible...hidden from a world whose sight is monochromatic and patriarchal; hidden even when we are out and powerful, by a world that is obsessed with the relationships between men" (Vaid, 799).

Urvashi Vaid in her speech entitled "Let's Put Our Own House in Order" delivered at the National Lesbian Conference, Atlanta, Georgia (1991).

That sums up the concerns.

In what kind of spaces have these issues been addressed?

- Largely in the intersections of feminist and queer concerns.
- In intersections of gender-centric and sexuality-centric conceptualisations

This is not to say that we need a 'premature' and 'foreclosing reintegration' (Sedgwick, 16) between feminist and queer analysis. We are now aware of the fact that "although sex and gender are related, they are not the same thing" (Rubin, 308). However, this essay puts forward the view that another healthy intersection of modern feminist and queer theories would offer a space where issues facing alternative female sexualities can be addressed and provide a framework to understand the complex co-workings of heteropatriarchy, heteronormativity, homopatriarchy etc.

To meet or not to meet

On the one hand, we have the endless project of queering that continuously expands the horizons of the term 'queer' and bring within it any position or gesture that challenges the heterosexual norm. The need for a larger vocabulary, conception and theorizing of sexuality and sexual practices has been stressed. That the destabilization of the hegemonic sexual order is not sufficient in itself has been recognized. On the other, the homogenizing tendencies of the term, its glossing over internal differences and inequalities are being resisted from within.

On the other side is modern feminism's anti-essentialist radicalism, which disables any conceptual reworking wherein a category can be used in different matrices of meaning and politics. Theoretical deflating of concepts does not result in simultaneous dissolution of oppressions that have the same concepts for their loci. For instance, as long as lesbian and bisexual women are seen as less of 'women' by heterosexual women and men, and as 'women' – and hence almost already inferior – by men, the category 'woman,' I guess, has to hang around for them to rework it and reclaim it if they want to. Women of alternative sexualities at once benefit and suffer from anti-essentialist approaches. The very tool that seeks to legitimize their sexuality also destabilizes their gender identity. The tension is in affirming the legitimacy of their sexuality in the face of fundamentalist essentialisms while also continuously reclaiming their right to womanhood.

This is not an exclusive concern of the lesbian feminists. Both feminist and queer theories and scholarship find themselves situated outside the issue of alternative female sexualities. Is it a question of feminist theory and movements engaging with the dominance of heterosexuality (even within their structures) along with its war on patriarchy in general? And, a question of queer theory and movements dealing with patriarchy (even within their structures) alongside their fight against the heterosexual norm.

The reality that connects these two seemingly diverse processes – the modalities of anti-essentialist feminism and alternative patriarchies, with the issues concerning alternative female sexualities situated between the two – that I have brought under observation, is the fact that queer theory and politics are largely on anti-essentialist modes; are, in fact, offspring of deconstructive analysis. But there are perils of premature thrusting of theoretical perspectives on gruesome 'realities,' which refuse to go away however much we quote-unquote them. But, as demonstrated, both feminist and queer theory, scholarship and politics are oriented towards an engagement of rethinking their strategic positioning vis-à-vis patriarchy and heterosexuality, not only respectively. Another intersection between these two knowledge systems will help throw light on these issues, particularly in the context of alternative female sexualities. Dangers that lurk in the way of these projects are primarily questions of knowledge – to know, to unknow, to understand the gap that sometimes crops up between specialized knowledge and experience.

Works Cited

Baskaran, Suparna. "Physical Subjectivity and the Risk of Essentialism". *Our Feet Walk the Sky: Women of South Asian Diaspora*. Ed. Women of South Asian Descent Collective. San Francisco: aunt lute books, 1993.

Butler, Judith. *Gender Trouble: Feminism and the Subversion of Identity*. New York and London: Routledge, 1990.

Calhoun, Cheshire. "Separating Lesbian Theory and Feminist Theory". *Feminist Social Thought: A Reader*. Ed. Diana Tietjens. New York: Routledge, 1997, pp. 200-218.

Cohen, Ed. "Who are 'We'? Gay 'Identity' as Political (E)motion – A Theoretical Rumination. *Inside/out – Lesbian Theories, Gay Theories*. Ed. Diana Fuss. New York and London: Routledge, 1991, pp. 71-92.

Epstein, Steven. "Gay Politics, Ethnic Identity: The Limits of Social Constructionism". *Socialist Review 17*. 3. May/August 1987, p. 19 (as quoted in Cohen)

Fuss, Diana. "Inside/Out." *Inside/Out – Lesbian Theories/Gay Theories*. Ed. Diana Fuss. New York and London: Routledge, 1991, pp. 1-10.

Irigaray, Luce. "This Sex Which is Not One". *This Sex Which is Not One*. Trans. Catherine Porter. New York: Cornell University Press. 1985, pp. 23-33.

John, Mary E. and Janaki Nair. "A Question of Silence?" Introduction. *A Question of Silence?: the Sexual Economies of Modern India*. Ed. Mary E. John and Janaki Nair. New Delhi: Kali for Women, 1998, pp. 1-51.

Sedgwick, Eve Kosofsky. *Epistemology of the Closet*. Berkeley: University of California Press, 1990.

Sen, Amartya. *Identity and Violence: The Illusion of Destiny*. London: Allen Lane, 2006.

Vaid, Urvashi. "Let's put our house in order." *We are Everywhere: A Historical Source Book of Gay and Lesbian Politics*. Ed. Mark Blasius and Shane Phelan. New York and London: Routledge, 1997, pp. 798-807.

III

Re-view

Re-view, like re-think, involves the act of looking back. In our frame of reference, re-think interrogates the canons and representations, while re-view attempts an assessment by combining different spheres of experience. In our scheme of things, re-view is an effective doubling of re-think, thus providing an across-the-discipline trajectory on literature and society. **Jean D' Souza** mirrors Esther David's analysis in the re-think section in her study of the feminine facets of Christ, which she argues is a *construction of convenience* to suit the patriarchal structures of the Church. Jean's questioning of the religious construction is continued by **Balaji Ranganathan** in his analysis of the historical reform movements in India during the 19th century. Moving ahead from the arguments of Dipesh Chakrabarty and Partha Chatterjee, Balaji situates his arguments within the double bind of colonialism and modernity. **Vaijayanti Shete** applies Esther's interrogation in the earlier section to the Indian context. Traversing a very broad spectrum, she covers medieval sites like Khajuraho, Modhera and Konark and arrives at an interesting conclusion that the female figures in these sites are representatives of multiple disciplines. **Indira Nityanandam** brings forth the surreptitious re-entry of cultural stereotypes in the media. This article complements some of Shobhana's arguments in the previous section. Both the contributors emphasize the need to look beyond the binaries. Our next contributor, **Vidya Rao,** also analyzes the stereotypes that define the personalities and positions of women athletes. The focus here, as in Indira's paper, is on the notion of gaze: "The attentive eye has nowadays shifted its focus from the court's baseline to the skirt's hemline." Our re-view process has not only identified and interrogated stereotypes but also positioned them differentially in the in-between spaces between disciplines and spheres of life.

11

The Feminine Facets of a Masculine Christ

JEAN D' SOUZA

Faculty, H.A. College of Commerce, Ahmedabad

I've been told that being a man entails more than having a penis. It involves – and this word is spoken, when I hear it, with a lot of stress, force and a glint in the eye – 'masculinity,' virility, machismo. Agreed, that this may be a pulp-fiction, popularist description of manhood, but when looking at Jesus Christ as a man, we definitely are categorizing him as one not simply because of his anatomy. Christ's maleness expressed itself through traits in his character to such an extent that it would be downright foolish to think of him as anything less than masculine.

Yet there is so much more to Christ's masculinity than his sex. In this paper, I wish to discuss these masculine/male traits in Christ, and show how, instead of these, it is the stereotypical feminine qualities that are given to the faithful believer as emulative ideals. Christ portrays a distinct manhood as well as a strong feminism, but the power structure of the institution offers only those ideals of Christ to follow, that suit itself.

The Christ in the Gospels is strong, powerful, attractive, dependable, public and authoritative – most of these being stereotypical masculine qualities. His power and strength are seen in the incident in Mathew (8:22-27) where he is in a small, rickety boat in the middle of a stormy sea, and he stands up, "rebuked the winds and the sea," which result in an amazing calm. A similar fearlessness and authority are seen in the various incidents where he drives out demons and evil spirits, leaving the impression that they are all supposed to listen to him and obey his command.

Power is a key element in Michel Foucault's discussions of discourse. Rather than assume that power is control, restriction, possession, violation and/or prevention, Foucault analyzes power as being capable of producing restrictive as well as other possible forms of behaviour. In the introduction written before he discusses the 'repressive hypothesis' he writes: "...... my main concern will be to locate the forms of power, the channels it takes and the discourses it permeates in order to reach the most tenuous and individual modes of behaviour...... all this entailing effects that may be those of refusal, blockage and invalidation, but also incitement and intensification" (Foucault, 11).

Having stated this in the first section of *The History of Sexuality* (Vol. 1), Foucault goes on to show how power may **not** only be about preventing someone from doing what they wish, but also about changing possible modes of behaviour. It is perhaps power in this sense that is expressed through some of Christ's actions. This productive model of power can be seen as resembling the creative spirit of the cosmos in genesis. In his essay titled "Jesus in Christian Doctrine," Alan Torrance writes:

> Just as in the event of creation God imposed forms on the forces of chaos (symbolised, for example, by wind and water), so Jesus exercised parallel power over those same symbols of chaos-calming the storm, driving out evil spirits and delivering people from physical and spiritual dysfunction (Torrance, 204).

Power, strength and authority, then, highlight Christ's maleness but not as patriarchal traits that restrict and violate. Christ's power and masculinity seem, in Foucault's words, to incite and intensity forms of behaviour and thought.

The twelve apostles who followed Christ, leaving all they had behind, could possibly touch a homosexual nerve of post-modern times when the celibacy of Christ is proving to be more unacceptable. It could even be seen as a patriarchal cult, which ignores women. But Christ's female following shows us a different view of this story. When women find him attractive, his masculine appeal is emphasized. For examples of women who were fascinated by him, we have the Samaritan woman at the well, who with her coy and coquettish dialogue with him, thought she would enchant him, but instead found herself captivated by his personality; we have Mary Magdalen, who could not contain her emotions and publicly displays them with her tears, hair and perfume; we have Martha, who cannot tolerate her sister Mary being so close to Christ while she was busy preparing a meal, probably because she too wanted the same; and we have the various named and unnamed women who followed Christ around, to the extent that when he died, there were only women at the cross, with the exception of one male, the disciple John. There is also the repeated reference to Christ as the bridegroom, which Margaret Starbird discusses at length in *The Woman with the Alabaster Jar.* Though theology might consider the bridegroom image as symbolic and not real, it still creates an aura of masculine appeal and charisma in the figure of Christ, which will be discussed in detail later.

His charisma brings us to the public nature of the figure of Christ. If he fascinated women, the masses were drawn to him. Christ's public addresses and sermons, his miracles, his outrageous rebuke to the villains of society and his interaction with crowds were all assertions of his masculinity. In a sense, it manifests his fearlessness and boldness – both of which are stereotypical masculine qualities, and not only in his times. Perhaps, one of the qualities that endeared him to the masses was that he could stand up against the ones who tried to subjugate him and from this viewpoint, he was a rebel leader.

One only needs to look at the way he attacks the temple with a whip made out of cord and drives out all the moneychangers from it, shouting "stop using my father's house as a market," to realize his fearless rebellion. He breaks the Holy Sabbath in front of the authorities, he calls the leaders of society names – hypocrites, vipers, fox, etc., he bends every law that is laid down and raises humanity above legality. Kahlil Gibran (1974) writes in "The Crucified":

> The Nazarene was not weak! He was strong and is strong! ... Jesus never lived a life of fear, nor did he die suffering or complaining... He lived as a leader; He was crucified as a crusader; He died with a heroism that frightened His killers and tormentors.

The Gospels emphasize all the evidence that establishes Christ as the son of God, but he always refers to himself as the son of man, in other words, a human son. The idea that Christ was man enough to stand up and contest an established power structure because he wanted to show that there were other possible models and discourses of strength, power and masculinity, seems more plausible to me than his miraculous, divine, metahuman image that the church tries to convey.

Christ truly was a man. If the Gospels' primary focus is on his divinity, then the secondary focus is essentially on his manhood. But what is a glaring omission in the Gospels is regarding his sexuality. If Christ's gender can be established so firmly, then why is his sex and sexuality hushed up, concealed even omitted in his life stories? The Church has been categorically insistent about his celibacy, but with more and more evidence coming to light today in the form of the *Dead Sea Scrolls* and the *Nag Hammadi Gnostic Gospels,* that claim to Christ's celibacy seems suspect. Starbird, quite convincingly elucidates the possible probability of Christ having had an active sexual life, and even being married to Mary Magdalene. Though this cannot really be proved, like so many other events/things in the life of Christ, yet the fact that this 'heresy' survived two thousand years in spite of relentless persecution means that it must have something more to it than mere imagination. We have very hazy details in the four Gospels about Jesus' life before he became a public figure, but there is information, nonetheless, about the various stages of his human life – the pre-natal stage of his mother's pregnancy, his birth and infancy, his childhood/boyhood, his youth, his public ministry, and his suffering and death. Two stages, however, are pointedly missing – his marriage/sexual initiation, and old age. The absence of old age can obviously be explained in the fact that he was killed young, and also perhaps in the belief that the "Son of God" could not be shown to be growing old and dying. Alan Torrance understands this belief as a "fear of confusing Jesus' divinity with a humanity conceived as transitory, changeable, corruptible, mortal" (Torrance, 210). Starbird writes about a Sumerian ritual where a king was tortured, 'killed' and buried because he was a reflection of his people, his kingdom, and could not, therefore be allowed to become old and weak. "If his power and strength were to ebb, so would theirs" (Starbird, 42). Such an idea could explain the absence of old age in the life of Christ. But what could possibly explain the unnatural utter silence about the sexual life of an otherwise perfectly 'normal' young Jewish man? We see Jesus satisfy all his other physiological drives of eating, drinking, resting, being afraid, feeling calm etc. except for his sexual drive. If God could descend into humanity at some points, then why not at all points, one might ask. Jack Miles in his book *Christ: A Crisis in the Life of God* puts it very aptly: "Would the experience of sex be any less proper to the condition of being 'in every way like a man' than the experience of birth?" (Miles, 60).

The major reason for the elimination of sexuality in and by the Church is that the Church identifies it as evil. But there are other possibilities of why it is not mentioned in the *story* of Christ's life. Perhaps Christ's 'celibacy' was supposed to underline the dichotomy between the divine and the human, where divine indicates asexuality and human, sexuality. Perhaps celibacy was accepted as the natural state for holy men and sages in those times. Perhaps it was believed that God's 'bachelor' state must be represented in his son. The Christian God is the single 'Father', who has no consort, but a symbolic bride in his chosen race – Israel. Even though Mary is the mother of Christ, and God is his father, yet Mary is not God's wife or consort. But the greater probability than all this is that Jesus' sexuality was perhaps edited out of the Gospel stories. Why would this happen? When something very important is not to be conveyed, then every attempt is made to see that all trace of it is deleted, erased. The canonical Gospels show not a single explicit sign of Jesus' sexual life, but when one looks into the non-canonical Gospels, we could see what the canon was trying to suppress.

Marina Warner, in her book titled *Alone of All Her Sex: The Myth and the Cult of the Virgin Mary*, and Margaret Starbird both write about the Gospel of Philip, which says, "there were three who walked with the Lord at all times. Mary – his mother, her sister, and Magdalen, the one who is called his companion. Mary Magdalen is described in this ... ... (as) the close companion or 'consort' of the Lord, who often kissed her on the mouth" (Starbird, 53). Warner also mentions the gospel of Mary, where she is portrayed as "a supreme initiate into Christ's mysteries and the teacher of the other apostles" (Warner, 229). But none of this is even hinted at obliquely in the canonical gospels. However, the fact remains that in establishing Christ's divinity, his humanity is censored, halved.

Notwithstanding the thick screen covering Christ's sexuality, there exudes a certain distinctive maleness from his personality that simply cannot be missed. Having said that, it needs to be said too that there is also a definite feminine sense to his mentality. Miles writes: "... and though he remains male, and celibate in his uniqueness, he has, particularly in discharging certain functions, a distinctly female aspect" (Miles, 214).

We see these feminine facets of Christ in those qualities that are given as ideals to his followers. The Church advocates certain attributes of Christ, which a faithful follower should emulate. This is taught through prayers, sermons, catechism, but more effectively through hymns sung in the Church and most of the marks of an ideal Christian happen to be the traits stereotypically associated with women. Note how the lyrics of these hymns foster some feminine qualities in the followers of Christ:

> Oh the love of my Lord is the essence.
> Of all that I love here on earth.
> All the beauty, I see he has given to me.
> And his giving is gentle as silence.
> Every day, every hour, every moment
> Have been blessed by the strength of his love,
> At the turn of each tide, he is there at my side
> And his touch is gentle as silence.

In other words, silence is a way of life one should adopt. Silence and gentleness would be Christ-like.

> Take and receive, O Lord, my liberty,
> Take all my will, my mind, my memory,
> Do thou direct and govern all and sway,
> Do what thou wilt; command and I obey.

Obedience, without a supposed a will of one's own, is again a stereotypical female quality to be learnt from Christ because as St. Paul says, Christ became obedient unto death.

> Make me a servant, humble and meek
> Lord, let me lift up those who are weak
> And may the prayer of my heart always be
> Make me a servant, make me a servant
> Make me a servant today!

Meekness and humility are two more qualities that Christ's followers must learn from him. In other words, one should always remain docile and retiring/mild.

> Just like a child who trusts his father dear
> And who delights to feel his presence near
> Just like a child whose mind has not a doubt
> And whose heart is never proud
> Here I come, O Lord
> Here I come just like a child
> Here I come, O Lord
> Here I come just like a child.

Faith is something one must learn from a child, because Christ loved children. But when have we seen a child that asks no questions, a child whose mind has no doubt? Then, is child-like faith actually a childish belief?

Jesus always loved his own
And he showed it to the full
He has set us an example
That we do as he has done.
Can a servant greater be
Than his master Christ, the Lord?
If we know and do this, happy we shall be.
Know, my people, what I've done to you:
Lord you call me. It is what I am.
If then I, your Lord, deigned to wash your feet,
You should do the same and wash each other's feet.

Humility and service seem to go hand in hand, where the implications of service turn into becoming a servant, and not just any servant but one who is humble and meek. In other words, one who will not retaliate.

Lay your hands gently upon us
Let their touch render your peace
Let them bring your forgiveness and healing
Lay your hands, gently lay your hands.

Touching again a very distinct feminine quality is one that is worshipped in Christ. Asking for his touch-gentle touch-appeals to his feminine side, perhaps.

Greater love and friendship has no man than this
That he die for others, give his life for all
No more are you servants, I have called you friends
All my Father told me, I made known to you
Without you I am nothing
My weakness needs your strength
So speak, Lord, to your servant
I'm waiting for your word!

The primary lesson taught through the life of Christ is love. But as the lyrics rightly point out, it is not like a 'man' would love. Is this probably because only a woman would lay down herself for another as in childbirth?

> Unless a grain of wheat falls into the ground,
> It still remains but a grain of wheat.
> But if it falls and dies, then it bears much fruit,
> So it is with those who lose themselves in me.

Anyone who suffers becomes Christ. That makes suffering valuable, worthwhile. But, in Christogising suffering, what is actually learnt by the believer is a passive and fatalistic attitude towards it.

The qualities of silence, meekness, love, suffering, child-likeness, touch and service are taught by the Church to the Churchgoer. All these are qualities, which are stereotypically feminine in nature. For my purposes, two points are made here. One, that Christ was a man with feminine traits as well, and so he could not ever be a 'patriarch' who ignored women. And second, against the backdrop of his rebellion, fearlessness, power and strength, these feminine qualities taught to the mass of believers, even though they are the qualities of Christ, reveals the discourse of power implemented by the institution. In other words, against the lead-up to authority, individuality and conviction that we see in the life of Jesus of Nazareth, the Church chooses to portray a Christ of faith with the ideals of submission and obedience, and thus creates a power structure in favour of itself because it enjoins upon the believer an imitation of Christ. At the same time, as a corollary, it is those stereotypically 'feminine' qualities that embody ultimate ethical value, it enjoins the invitation of Christ on all humans, the more so on its own officials too, but theology and practice are quite far apart here.

The Christ of faith is somewhat different from Jesus of Nazareth. Of course, neither will be a truth in itself, as Francis Watson says in his essay titled "The Quest for the Real Jesus" that "images of Jesus are always contested" (Watson, 156). To say that Christ was God's son, who died and rose again from death, requires a different mindset from stating that Jesus lived in Jerusalem around 30 A.D. and was killed by the Roman authorities. However, neither the Christ of faith nor the picture we have of Jesus of Nazareth can be accepted as complete truth about the figure of Jesus today. This is perhaps the mistaken concept that the Church created. Stephen C. Barton says in his essay "Many Gospels, One Jesus?"

> That there are four gospels standing side by side in the canon, none of which has been subordinated to another, is an invitation to recognise that the truth about Jesus to which the Gospels bear witness is **irreducibly plural** without being either incoherent or completely elastic (Watson, 170).

As an institution, the Church has deliberately picked and projected certain aspects of the figure of Jesus Christ for its members to follow in order to suit its own purposes, which seem to be those of maintaining a male-favoured hierarchy and an absolutism of itself. Christ was a man with definite feminine traits. His androgynous nature is highlighted in his masculine traits of strength, courage, authority and power, and in his feminine values of love, forgiveness, service and humility. But instead of his androgynous completeness, only a part of his personality are deified and idealised. This incompleteness falsifies the Jesus of the Gospels. Perhaps it is the androgynous wholeness that Christ personified, which the faithful believer needs to emulate, and which the world at large needs to recognize.

The title of Jack Miles' book *Christ: A Crisis in the Life of God* (2001) suggests that the figure of God was perhaps making a statement through the incarnation of Christ. The word that became flesh is more than just any word – it is a testament. "… … God's action in Jesus is to be seen as communicative action, an action in which a communicative intention is constitutive and primary, not secondary and incidental" (Watson, 161).

Depending on which side of faith one is, that testament could be read as a testament of God's love for humanity, or a crisis in the relation of God and humankind, a rectification of what has been going wrong, or just a plain cosmic coincidence of a stray birth in a random period.

Through his life, works, teaching and death, Jesus too makes a certain statement. His identity as the Christ as well as his other possible identities – a prophet, a leader, a rebel, a messiah – as someone who is 'not-Christ' are both related to this testament of his life. Again, the reading of the statement of Christ's life depends on whether the historian or the believer is active in the reader.

The Church reads both these statements made by God and by Christ in its own way and interprets them, resulting in the rules and laws it lays down for its followers. Thus, the Church makes its statement or proclamation, formulated on what it chooses to adopt. Among other things its statement may be read as an absolutist confession of the Church being the only means of salvation, of Christ being understood only through the Church, and of its own 'God' being the only true God.

This causes us to think that the Church seems to have created a figure of Christ that is drawn from the gospels, but is not entirely the same. The statement made by God in the incarnation of Christ, and the statement made by Christ in his life, do not necessarily result in the statement made by the Church in its laws and rules. There are other possible conclusions that can occur from the testaments of God and Christ. Even the Jesus of the Gospels is one who opens up possible means/forms of behaviour and though, and this kind of 'Jesus' seems almost a stranger to the 'Christ' shown to us by Church. Simone Weil, in her book *Letter to a Priest*, writes about the possible misunderstanding of the Church which is what caused the construction of a single, authoritarian structure, whereas the Jesus in the gospels would never have promoted power-centric or autocratic values.

> When Christ said: 'Go Ye therefore, and teach all nations, and bring them the glad tidings', he commanded his apostles to bring glad tidings, not a theology. He himself, having come, as he said, 'only for the sheep of the hose of Israel', added these good tidings on to the religion of Israel ... But the command was misunderstood ... (Weil, 16).

The Jesus depicted in the Gospels had an openness, a 'limitlessness' and a perfect balance of the divine and the human. So perfect was his balance here that it is impossible to presume that the divinity is greater/more than the humanity.

This balance could also be translated as one between the feminine rationale of acceptance and empathy, and the masculine one of power and strength. With this balance, it is as if Christ is rectifying the masculine patriarchal image of the monotheistic God.

The 'divine feminine' was a prominent concept among the people of the Mediterranean region before Christ. But, eventually, the male 'God' took over, and after Christianity took hold as an institutionalized religion, Goddess worship was eliminated completely. Simultaneously, the Goddess' human expression in the form of flesh and sexuality also started being regarded as sinful and immoral as against the mind and reason, which were noble and lofty aptitudes. The qualities associated with the Goddess were degraded, and those qualities not associated with her were praised because they came to be known as the qualities of the male God. The basis for sex as sin was laid right in the *Old Testament* where the "Book of Leviticus" states that a lamb must be sacrificed by anyone suffering a disease in which there were involuntary eruptions or discharge from any part of the body. In other words, the focus was on skin eruptions or sexual discharges like menstruation, transmission of semen etc. This indicated that there was something morally offensive about such natural conditions of the flesh.

The sacrifice of the lamb, thus, is a ritual that seems to "take away the sin" of any passive or uncontrollable condition of humanity. In the *New Testament*, Christ is called the "lamb of God" who has been sent into the world to take away its sin. This sin that applies to all humanity is the 'original sin' that Adam and Eve committed and passed on to the human race; the sin that "Genesis" tells us is the sin of sexual knowledge. God 'curses' Eve with childbirth and punishes her with sexual desire because of the sin of disobedience incurred when they both ate from the tree of knowledge to know more about sexuality. In order to take away this sin of humanity, the word needed to become flesh, God's son needed to become a human being. Only by entering humanity, could he save it from its inherent sinfulness. If only Christ entering humanity could cleanse the human sin, would it not also imply that Christ entering sexuality could only cleanse the 'sexual sin'? Humanity and sexuality are passive and involuntary causes of the same root – sexual regeneration in mortal humans; both have their roots in the Genesis Garden of Eden; and God cursed both of them, when he was disobeyed. God could not redeem the human race of its mortality by remaining God. Likewise, Christ would not be able to redeem humanity from sexuality be remaining asexual. If Christ's birth as a human could lift the curse on humanity, then Christ's sexuality too would lift the curse of sexuality.

The Church deems marriage a sacrament, and Christian brides and grooms are taught to draw their parallels from Christ and his bride, the human race in general, the Church in particular.

> Wives should be subject to their husbands as to the Lord, since as Christ is head of the Church and saves the whole body, so is a husband the head of his wife; and as the Church is subject to Christ, so should wives be to their husbands, in everything. Husbands should love their wives, just as Christ loved the Church and sacrificed himself for her... This is why a man leaves his father and mother and becomes attached to his wife, and the two become one flesh. This mystery has great significance, but I am applying it to Christ and the Church (Ephesians 5:22-25, 31-32).

Perhaps, the Church as the bride of Christ implies a lesson of submission and obedience. Perhaps it teaches that just as the Church obeys Christ, the believer must obey the Church. But again there is a power structure evident here.

When it is a relationship with a higher/greater authority than itself, the Church seems to adopt the bridal, submissive stance. But when relating with the masses, who are not as powerful as the institution, it adopts, the hierarchical, authoritarian and absolutist stance. In treating the members of the Church as a flock of sheep that need to be kept submitting and faithful, that need to be taught only a singular doctrine of faith through the one institution of the Church, the Church adopts thus an authoritarian, absolutist stance.

However, the point is that the figure of Christ as a bridegroom is repeated more than just a few times throughout the *New Testament.* In fact, Starbird looks at this bridegroom figure in the *Old Testament* too. Whatever the level of symbolism of the bridegroom-Christ, the implicit sexual implication of the metaphor of marriage and union – "... ... and become one flesh" – remains. Thus opening up a possibility yet again, of a sexualised Christ. This likelihood is expressed more poignantly in the "Book of Revelation", the last book of *The Bible.*

> Let us be glad and joyful and give glory to God, because this is the time for the marriage of the lamb. His bride is ready, and she has been able to dress herself in dazzling white linen, because her linen is made of the good deeds of the saints" (Rev. 19:7-9).

The bride in this case is implied to be human race. Jack Miles writes:

> And so it happens that the comic epic of Christianity ends, as so many comedies do, with a gala wedding. The lamb Triumphant arrives at long last at his wedding day, taking to himself his eternal intended, the human race itself (Miles, 260).

In other words, it would seem that the sacrifice of the lamb of God, who took human form to save humanity, can only be complete and accomplished if the original sin of 'cursed' sexuality is wiped away, cleansed. And that original sin of sexual knowledge can perhaps only be absolved through the marriage of Christ with humanity. Even if one may still believe in an asexual Christ, his marriage with a sexualized humanity wherein "the two become one flesh" would necessarily either asexualize one, or sexualize the other. And, since the former has not taken place in the narrative of the Bible nor in reality, it is only logical to assume the later.

To conclude, the Christ of faith is a 'man' in actuality, with qualities that are masculine. True, but he is also the 'Jesus of Nazareth' we read about in the canonical gospel stories, who did not fit into the stereotypical masculine model of his times because of his rebelliousness, and more importantly because of his feminine aspects. This suits the ones in power just fine: the patriarchal power structure with the male human being at the top as superior over the female can be maintained with the argument that Christ was a man; at the same time, the mass of followers can be taught his feminine qualities of obedience and subjugation so that the power structure of male superiority may be reinforced. The patriarchal Bible does teach feminine qualities, if one would only look deep enough. But are these only instruments of male domination? Is the androgynous Christ not revealed to the masses only because of the fear of toppling the masculine power structure?

Works Cited

Barton, Stephen C., 2001. "Many Gospels, One Jesus?" *The Cambridge Companion to Jesus.* Ed. Marcus Bockmuehl. Cambridge: Cambridge University Press.

Foucault, Michael, 1980. *The History of Sexuality, Vol. 1: An Introduction*. Trans. Robert Hurley. New York: Vintage Books.

Gibran, Kahlil, 1974. *A Treasury of Kahlil Gibran*. Trans. Anthony Rizcallah Ferris. Ed. Martin L. Wolf. Great Britain: Mandarin.

Miles, Jack, 2001. *Christ: A Crisis in the Life of Christ*. London: Arrow.

Starbird, Margaret, 1993. *The Woman with the Alabaster Jar: Mary Magdalen and the Holy Grail*. Vermont: Bear and Co.

The New Jerusalem Bible. Standard Ed. St. Paul's Publication.

Torrance, Alan, 2001. "Jesus in Christian Doctrine". *The Cambridge Companion to Jesus.* Ed. Marcus Bockmuehl. Cambridge: Cambridge University Press, 2001.

Warner, Marina, 1976. *Alone of All her Sex: The Myth and the Cult of the Virgin Mary*. New York: Alfred A. Knopf.

Watson, Francis, 2001. "The Quest for the Real Jesus". *The Cambridge Companion to Jesus.* Ed. Marcus Bockmuehl. Cambridge: Cambridge University Press.

Weil, Simone, 1951. *Letter to a Priest*. Trans. A.F. Wills. London, New York: Routledge.

— 1989. *With Joyful Lips*. 12th Ed., Bombay: St. Paul's Publications.

12

Nineteenth Century Social Reform and the 'Women's Question'

BALAJI RANGANATHAN

Faculty, N.C. Bodiwala College, Ahmedabad

This paper looks at the reasons for the social reform within the 'Women's Question' which had occurred in the 19th century. It will also assess its impact on the society at the time.

The 19th century India had seen the global effects of colonialism. It was global in the sense that much of the ideological social changes, which had occurred within India, were actively implemented in Europe. The changes included the fields of education, family life, religion and the role of polity. The 19th century became a contesting ground for the dispensation of ideology – be it imperial or nationalistic. The psychology of colonialism was geared on the notions of gender. The victor is always designated within culture within the paradigms of manliness, alpha roles and role models. This is true of all cultures where the role of male gender and charges of effeminate behaviour excite the same response. Colonialism engendered the myth of a super race and in tandem super males and the notion of masculinity. The myth was engendered through the means of conquests and the construction and the suppression of historiography. This involved the process of hegemonic practices, which was indoctrinated through the means of force and an elaborate use of imperial ideology. The idea of superiority engendered via the Enlightenment, utilitarianism and the notions of progress, which comprised the ideology, was reinforced through the process of education and the vastly influential works like the James Mill's history and the translation projects undertaken by the Asiatic Society of Bengal and the Serampore Press by William Carey. The entire response of the 19th century praxis has been to either approximate or capitulate towards this construct.

Modernity, which was experienced within the 19th century, had far-reaching effects in terms of social change. India then as now had to be seen within the structures of the caste system and the traditional positions taken around it. The nature of caste and the problems of losing it were permanent. The caste system along with its hierarchies was pitted against the flow of modernity which had permeated Bengal. I mention Bengal as the starting point of the British imperial rule in India. Modernity with its notions of progress and the process of education with the establishment of the Fort William College and the Sanskrit and Hindu colleges in Calcutta and the Sanskrit college at Benaras had led to the Young Bengal Movement which had with Henry Vivian Derozio created uproar within society. This was a young group, which had brought about the worst fears within society. Casteless, beef eating young men had brought out the worst effects of colonialism in popular opinion then. Society turned its back on this through its women. By protecting women from the onset of modernity, an attempt was made to prevent the cultural onslaught. The entire notion of 'Grihya Laxmi' takes root here. Women are made to approximate the Goddess of plenty in the sense of *Jouissance* at home. The home becomes the battleground to face the changing world outside. The notion of the sanctity of women was observed within 'sati' practices, child marriages and the banning of education for women. The 'sati' practice now has been deciphered to have taken place over the problems of property and not to the ideas of tradition but in the 19th century it was also a means of upward social mobility. This was largely practised by the upper class Bhadraloks and communities, which wanted to inch upwards on the social scale. So much so, the practice of 'sati' had achieved a stage where it decided the status of the family. The family then had to be understood as a joint family structure and patriarchal in nature. The role of modernity was two-fold. It undermined all traditional means of knowledge and positions and at the same time brought about a broadening of the vision. The notions of progress and education had brought out the problems and the evils within society – the most visible being the role of women and their status within society.

Women in the 19th century generally married before they were ten. They had no access to education; there was a belief that the husband was likely to pass away if the women were educated. There was a debate between two views that commentators have commented on. One was the traditional view, which had the laws of Manu which formulated the role and the status of women within society. The other was what is now commented on as the New Feminism, which had more progressive views towards the system of the women's education and their emancipation. Most of the social reforms, which took place centred on this. The most visible of the social reformers were Raja Ram Mohan Ray and the Adi Brahmo Samaj, Keshab Chandra Sen and the Brahmo Samaj of India and Ishwar Chandra Vidhyasagar.

The British had a policy of non-interference with socio-religious issues within India. William Bentick had banned 'sati' only after numerous petitions were made against the practice. The foremost of this was the petition by Ram Mohan Ray against the appeal for 'sati' in the House of Commons. He mentions:

> That your petitioners have, however, learned that a number of natives professing to be attached to the ancient practice, have prepared a petition to your honourable House, soliciting the re-establishment of the rite of burning their widows; and therefore to prevent your

> Honourable House from supposing that their sentiments are those of the whole native population, your petitioners respectfully present themselves to the notice of your Honourable House and pray that the Regulation of the local government may be confirmed and enforced (Ray).

This marks the action out as being within the New Feminism construct. The agitation by Ray was informed by his education and his interaction with the East India Company as a businessman. The very idea of the Brahmo Samaj is informed out of the idea of the Enlightenment. The idea of monotheism, the absence of idol worship and the Christian ideals, which governed it, were largely informed by the modernity of the Enlightenment. Role models of the Memsahibs, who were a part of the ruling class, inform the battle of Keshab Chandra Sen for the marriage ages of the women with the society. There had been a constant comparison with the colonizer in the reconstruction of the colonized subjects by the colonized. Keshab Chandra Sen could not keep up with the change when he allowed his daughter aged 14 to get married with the Maharaja of Coochbehar. This led to a further split with the Brahmo Samaj of India with the formation of the Sadaran Brahmo Samaj, which was against the dilution of the reform practices. Ishwar Chandra Vidhyasagar had campaigned for the role of women's education. This as I had mentioned earlier went contrary to the popular belief of death for the husband with the education of the wife. I would read more into this as involving the role of property and inheritance rights. Women were not allowed to inherit ancestral property. By keeping women sequestered like this without education the financial control stayed with the men and with the practice of 'sati' the property remained undivided. This has to do with the high mortality rate in Calcutta and Bengal in particular and in India in general due to pestilence in the 18th and 19th centuries.

There was also a trend of publications or prescriptive journals, which delineated the manner by which the women should live. These are largely referred to as the domestic manuals. These manuals become the contesting ground for the New Feminism. They are elaborate in their themes but unified in a single point of constructing womanhood and their status. The topics moved from the art of taking care of husbands, child rearing, homes, cooking and the role of education. Surprisingly, the wave of New Feminism where the husbands take the role of educators petered out by the late 19th century. Most commentators feel that the movement had largely succeeded and women had begun moving out of the previously sequestered lives and this had led to greater exposure to education and travel. This also saw the beginning of the nationalistic movement where women had played such a sterling role.

Coming now to the central thesis of my paper: how does one analyze the formation of this discourse? Most commentators – from Partha Chatterjee to Dipesh Chakrabarthy – have examined this as the demarcation of the public and the private spheres. The home becomes the private sanctum where the masculinity is preserved. There is an underlying problem that has not been explored systematically. There was an effeminate imprint outside the home at the hands of the colonizer, which led to the masculinity imprint within the homes. All the constructors of New Feminism absorbed the qualities of the colonizer and in a way approximated them within their homes and in social reform. Social reform here blurs the notions of traditions, the past and cultural and social contracts, which was in a way an implicit part of the aim of imperial discourse.

Does one take social reform in the 19th century as a logical continuation of the colonial process that sought intellectual occupation and the reformers the players who were unwittingly led by the currents of modernity into reform? Or could we say that it was the seed of the nationalistic movement? 'The Women's Question' which dominated the early and the mid-19th century was hardly seen or noticed in tracts, pamphlets or public forums by the end of the 19th century. The 'Women's Question', as I mentioned before, had been resolved into the nationalistic one.

As I mentioned earlier, the Indian male was facing an identity crisis. He was labouring under an effeminate label. This was apart from the colonial ideological transformation of the colonized subject. The 'Women's Question' in the 19th century takes its roots within this conflict with modernity. Colonialism had brought out the problems of an indigenous knowledge system that had taken the colonial modernity head on. The indigenous system was a social contract that was sanctified by age-old customs and social codes. The codes themselves were religious in origin. The codes of Manu decided the social space of the men and the women. This was further compounded by caste biases. The Enlightenment modernity was scientific in nature. There was a total reliance on reason as a governing principle, which 'gazed' and recorded the perception of reality within a mathematical paradigm. This saw the beginning of a statistical reorganization of the empire in the form of surveys, gazetteers, educational enterprises, the growth of museums and reforms in educational and social terms. This clash between two knowledge systems of indigenous knowledge versus an imported European concept of reason as a sole guiding force brought out the response both in confirmation of the new mode of thinking and a conservative counter-response to it. The conservative counter-response was based on a fear of the destruction of an old social order, which was being displaced by the rationality induced by western education and a broadening of the worldview, which characterized the Enlightenment. On one hand, there were the liberating effects of education and material benefits within modernity and on the other hand there was the problem of this compromise and the notions of the destruction of the caste within their homes. The problems of perceived masculinity and the charges of effeminacy had further eroded the Indian male psyche. The problems of losing culture at the workplace and the contact with the foreigners led to the sequestering of the women. The home became the sanctuary where colonialism could be battled and the women and their bodies became the battleground against colonialism.

Social reform in the 19th century is a part of the wave of modernity that struck with the Enlightenment project. It had a positive effect in terms of women's liberation from the kind of life that had been endured. It saw a limited number of women like Krupabai Sattaianandan, Pandita Ramabai and Anandi bai

Joshi come out from their limited spheres into a very different world where men inhabited. Modernity, which had a positive effect on the women's movement, should also be read to be a part of the imperialistic exercise which began with the process of education and the occupation of mental space. The social reformers in India had received their training to articulate within this modernity paradigm. In a way it had been a logical culmination of the British imperial process that began with the Charter Act of 1813 and the subsequent 1835 Minute on Education by Macaulay and Charles Grant.

The point that is often missed out when reading into the positive effects of social reform on the Indian women in the 19th century is the role of the women in Europe during the same period. The basic problems, which afflicted the women within the patriarchal structures, were the same. Journals and letters addressed by the early settlers in India always stress the role of chastity, virginity, obedience and an angelic innocence within the role of marriage. The freedom, as experienced by the British women in India, was a notional one. The only difference that existed between the women of the two nations was the role of education. Still intelligence in women was not a prized virtue in the role of British marriages in India. The idea of keeping a good home and maintaining the domestic set-up and upholding the British aura was more important. The British white women became the site of resistance to counter the Oriental gaze. This can be noted in E.M. Foster's writings and the British narratives of the 1857 Mutiny.

Indian women were pushed into the public sphere through the modernity paradigm. Women like Mrs. Ranade, Anandbai Joshi, Cornialia Sorebji, Pandita Ramabai, Madam Bhikaji Cama and others were encouraged to enter the public spheres by their families who had experienced the liberating effects of education. The women who came out into the public sphere belonged to a particular group of the Indian elite. They do not represent the vast percentage of women who managed to come out into the public life during the Swadeshi and the Quit India Movement. The nationalistic movement actually becomes the stage where public life for women in India actually cut across castes, religion and work biases. The notion of public life was also coupled with the gender biases and patriarchal structures within the home. The women in public life were expected to have a multiple role as a homemaker also. Kasturba Gandhi and Kamala Nehru bring out this curious double bind where they are a part of the public sphere and are in many ways unacknowledged in relation to their husbands and are also associated within their domesticity.

The very modernity that had sought to strike at the heart of Indian traditions saw its articulation in a counter-discourse of nationalism. Imperial modernity in a way was transformed into the nationalistic one with the articulation and the strategies of writers and social reformers like Bankim Chandra, Sri Aurobindo, Vivekananda, Bhartendu Harishchandra, Joythiba Phule, Gandhi, Subramaniam Bharti and poets from Gujarat like Narmad, Dalpatram and novelists like Goverdhanram Tripathi. This leads to a further problem, which I am not expanding here, of the feminist discourse with the freedom struggle which was fought over the body politics of a woman with the construction of the nation as a mother.

Works Cited

Chakravarthi, Dipesh, 2001 *Provincializing Europe: Post-Colonial Thought and Historical Difference*. New Delhi: OUP.

Chaterjee, Partha, 1989. "The Nationalistic Resolution of the Women's Question". *Recasting Women*. Ed. Kumkum Sangari and Suresh Vaid. New Brunswick, N.J.: Rutgers U.P.

Ghose, Jogendra, 1906; Rpt. 1982. *The English Works of Raja Rammohun Ray*. 4 vols. New Delhi: Cosmo Publications.

13

Identical Expressions in Visual and Literary Experience with Reference to Female Space

VAIJAYANTI D. SHETE

Faculty of Fine Arts, M.S. University, Baroda.

Walking through medieval sites like Khajuraho, Modhera, Konark etc. the connoisseur moves on towards finer modelling, fuller figures and increasing loveliness in the array of alluring female representations in the temple premises. The exterior walls display highly sensory experience that allows visitors to enjoy flowing vitality in the architectural domain. This is the space that goes beyond just utility. Herein aesthetics is understood by the female presence engrossed in distinguished activity, the same space that is interactive. In fact, all these sensuous, voluptuous figures are always attention grabbing. Of course, herein matters the monumental art decorative monument and a magnificent testimony to the heartfelt carvings prevalent in the group of temples those built up centuries ago. Artist creates a living form that is with well-defined lines.

When to talk about these erotic-challenging figures, the concern is rather on different groups of representations, though always interpreted in male perspectives. Within a definite existing form and structure artists have adapted novel ideas, and thus thereby introduced in the whole programme. Woman looking in a mirror, playing with parrot, or playing with a ball, putting collyrium in one eye, participating in a duel fight and teaching to the student and taking part in cutting the wood, are exceptionally denoting a different world wherein her efficiency or her caliber is highlighted. Such standardized female representations are known by the term 'Nari-yantra' or 'Alasa Kanyas'[1] in the ongoing temple activity. A very large and a very fine part of the sculptures on the temples consist of exceptionally attractive and elegant feminine figures where beauty has personified itself in the feminine form. Khajuraho women are tantalizing[2] and provocative. The Bhubaneshwara female is classical in her stance and proportions.[3] In some temples she is a stronger and of a more virile build, radiating more energy as she should be! Who are these innumerable females? Some of them posing as goddesses? Others, as apsaras, entertaining the gods! What are they doing there? Are they Devadasis? Ministering the needs of the deity? Or are they just women?

Resources from 'Shilpa' texts help to us to categorize them in different expressions. Shilpa Prakash, though very late text, defines and instructs on each one, viz., Anjandharini, Salbhanjika/Dalamalika, Darpana, Nupura, Shukasarika, Akhetika, Mugdha, etc. Probably, in course of centuries, the concept of woman went undercurrent in a manifold and multiform change and development. It is all this which got represented one way or other in abundance adding thought to their presence.

Let us now have a closer look at these unforgettable female representations:

1. In Solanki period, apart from the religious and iconographic depictions, Chaulukyan artist has masterly carved the secular themes to some extent. For our purpose female duel fighter (wrestler) is significant.[4] A woman taking leading part in duel fight exemplifies female power

working in a totally new field altogether. She is known as 'Akhetika'. Hoysala art is also rich in depicting secular practices. An art-lover is amazed to see a tribal woman examining an arrow, decked up in a tribal costume. This illustration also leads to a woman participation in actual fights.

2. Orissan art is unique in representation of a lady in teaching activity.[5] She may be called 'Acharya'. It is an interesting example, which suggests women followed teaching profession in the medieval period.
3. Konark temple incorporates an uncommon structural figure, which displays a woman cutting the stones.[6] Her name is mentioned among the shilpis around 13th century AD. Baya Chakada, a valuable record, which highlights on the number of shilpins appointed for the construction of the temple.[7] This record also refers to the economic policy or monitory distribution for the creative surplus. More than three hundred women worked hard for this religious programme, among them the name Radhi stands out! This is how Radhi seems to be a master sculptor. In Hoysala art, the name Mahshamardini is recorded, who was a famous and successful sculptress. Her family background (guild) is described in the Hoysala inscriptions. Similarly, the ancient inscriptions of Kshatrapa period inform us that the image of female sculptor, namely, Naganika, is housed in a museum.

   Moreover, in 11th century, King Vishnu Vardhana's queen – Shantaladevi – herself is personified on Hoysala Temple, who was expert in dance and music, still Chalukyan artists carved proto types of queens who motivated construction of the temples.
4. Again, an extraordinary representation of a young female has a new address. To visualizing a fully decked up woman eagerly waiting for her lover asking the maidservant about him is really fascinating. This dramatic experience on a Lingaraj Mandir seems modernistic and elegant. This representation complements to the nayikas' moods and behaviour, which finds parallel adaptation in

the nayaka-nayika theme, which handled by the Rajasthani painters at large.[8]

5. One more overall effective illustration is traced in Paramara's time in the iconographical narrative. It is the depiction of an innocent woman, usually known as Mugdha nayika. Paramara artist picks up Kalahantarita nayika[9] from kavya, which is none but a commentary on dramatic display in a different medium. The colours succeeded in creating an interesting background but stone chisellers adopt the same theme.
6. Further, the other renowned group of nayikas is located in conventional parameters. These so-called nayikas are always interpreted and explained as decorative motifs on the exterior of the walls. They are represented in various postures. Eye-catching female figures like holding a mirror (darpana), dancing or playing with a bird (suka), hanging to a branch of a tree (sala bhanjika), inserting a collyrium or anjana in a eye, playing a ball (kanduka krida), collecting flowers and so on, have reading influence on visitor's mind.[10]
7. This group, though stimulating but highly effective, makes us to think over a lot. However, the general rule of their evolution is related to carnal love and entertainment. Still, if they are analyzed in a different paradigm, it finds an outlet to these remarkable female figures. Herein some debatable issues are explored with the help of Rasa Chikitsa School. Architectural motifs or temple activity is an amalgam of so many existing trends, practices, religion, philosophy, technology etc. Secular themes of war, processions of infantry and cavalry, dance and music performances, groups of disciples and teachers as well as ceremonial work, trees and herbs, focus on various exceptional social features amidst the religious carvings.
8. Thus, to clarify anjandharini symbolizes alchemical ideas and practices which mark the transitional phase from the tantrik practices based on mercury sculpture esoterism. The use of herbs and their extracts in the Ayurvedic treatment with the help of minerals and metals was

common in the medieval period. Have a close look at this figure where she is applying collyrium in one eye. Rasarnavakalpa[11], especially a rasa text based on Rudra-yamala tantra, mentions some processes for preparing collyrium. In this method, collyrium is prepared from the root of Trna-jyoti plant; the root of this plant is rubbed with milk, mixed with the juices of bhrnga and matulinga. The whole mixture is made into a paste. Therefore, the very text instructs that if such a collyrium is used in an eye, it gives miraculous power of invisibility. Similarly, products of yellow Devadali and Chayateru trees result into the same effect. Another surprising situation is brought to the notice that the use of the sweet juice of Ucchata plant enables one to see the treasures deposited in different places. This is how Rasavadins prescribes unique application of a collyrium prepared out of herbs and plants. The same phenomenon may have been entered into creative field and got personification artistically.

9. Here is a representation where a lady is putting tilaka[12] on her forehead, holding a mirror in her hand. Again, the text discussed above makes us aware about the mysterious effects of tilaka prepared from the Devadali plant and other substances. Especially making a tilaka on forehead hints to the social belief that tilaka hypnotizes a man.
10. Next figure is playing with a parrot – it is informed that the suka cancu and the juice of Hemsanghri plant is used for rubbing mercury. Such mercury is kept in the hole of the feet of curlew and then it is roasted thrice in puta. One more method is mentioned for killing mercury. The killed mercury is to be roasted in puta on being kept in the hole of the beak of parrot. Such mercury helps us in the transmutation of base metals into noble metals. It is to be noted here that the technique of changing one metal to other metal was already known in the medieval period. Thus, this particular representation inculcates the technical information.[13]

11. One more illustration, which seems most erotic on the face, involves the process of the fixation of mercury in it. Here stands a female figure from whose breast showers of milk are visible. In the iatrochemical preparations human milk is an important ingredient since the hard mineral like mercury is killed for the use. Hence, mercury is rubbed with the bulbous root of Rakta-knachuki, and pressed with human milk. Then, this substance is roasted in a closed crucible finally attains fixation. Another reference to the human milk is traced when the roasted mercury is pressed in human milk with the seed and leaf of Vrscika plant is prescribed for internal use. It is to borne in mind that mercury was used for curing a disease in Rasacikitsa School. Hence, this uncommon representation suggests technical orientation.
12. This nayika is playing with a kanduka. It is a famous poetic convention.[14] Nayika is playing with a ball in Sanskrit dramas! The word 'kanduka' may hint at some mechanical apparatus used for liquefaction of minerals in medicinal practices.[15]
13. Salabhanjika – a woman beside the Sala tree – became architectural motif. A female figure holding the branch of a tree is known as Dalamalika. This motif may suggest application of plant products in Ayurveda; the above said tree cannotes to yellow flowering Devadali. It is recommended for easy childbirth in Rasacikitsa. Dalamalika is commonly visualized in early Buddhist sculptures also.

The Rasavandis regard certain plants and their extracts as the most effective ingredients. No doubt, the whole discussion juxtaposed with Rasa School is thought provoking, however the context needs to think deeply. The mystery is hidden in prevalent terminologies, which have lost their basic intention.

Therefore, it may be observed that these nayikas have much wider connotation within the broad framework. It is difficult to say since when metallic preparations, inorganic alloys, particularly the preparation of mercury, began to find use in the medical treatment. It is well known that alchemy, the

Darpana Nayika

Darpana Nayika

Shalabhanjika

Shalabhanjika

Anjandharini

Anjandharini

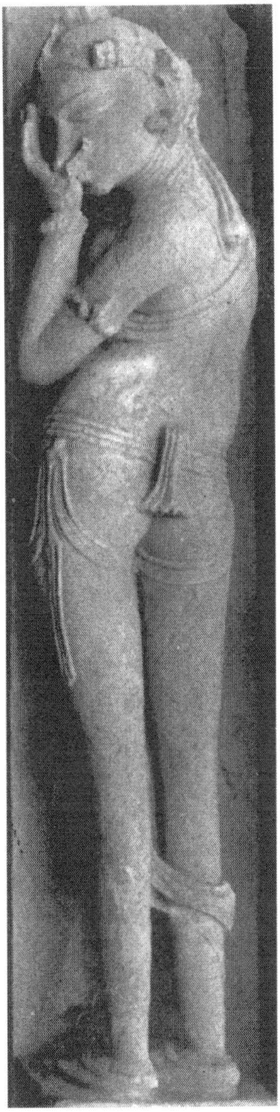

Mugdha Nayika

Payodhara

Sukasarika

forerunner of chemistry and aerator-chemistry,[16] was inexorably mixed up with the religio-philosophical thought of the culture area concerned. In India, alchemy seems to have developed, receiving sustenance from the tantric practices. Hence, the above discussed female figures may be said the representatives of multidiscipline. Thus, it is to be borne in mind that while redefining feminism, other branches of knowledge need to be explored.

Notes

1. Alice Boner and Sadashivaratha Sharma (ed.), Shilpa Prakash.
2. Marutinandana Tiwari, *Khajuraho ki Madhyakalin Murtikala* (in Hindi), Vishwavidyalaya Prakashan, Varanasi, 1991.
3. Lal Kanwar, *Temples and Sculptures from Bhuwaneshwar*, Delhi, 1976.
4. Stella Kramrisch, *Indian Sculptures*, Calcutta, 1933.
5. Marutinandana Tiwari, op. cit.
6. N.K. Bose, *Temples from Konark*, Cuttak, 1976.
7. Baya Chakada.
8. Marutinandana Tiwari, op. cit.
9. Ibid
10. C. Sivaramamurti, *Mirrors of Indian Culture*, Archaeological Survey of India, No. 73, Delhi, 1970.
11. A. Roay, Rasarnava Kalpa.
12. Ibid.
13. C. Sivaramamurti, *Medieval Sculptures*, Madras, 1971.
14. D.M. Bose, *A Concise History of Science in India*, Indian National Science Academy, New Delhi, 1971.
15. Ibid.
16. S.K. Maity, *Masterpieces of Hoysala Art*, Taraporwala, Bombay, 1978.

14

Women in Soap Operas: Devi, Demon, or?

INDIRA NITYANANDAM

Faculty, S.R. Mehta Arts College, Ahmedabad

They are rich, they are beautiful. They wear gorgeous clothes – sometimes designer wear, Western or ethnic. Their jewellery is heavy and chunky – would drive our medieval princesses to envious rage. Their houses are palaces. They live in the lap of luxury. They have everything or so it would seem to most of us (and to women viewers, in particular, those who sit glued to their television sets watching these soaps everyday they are aired). But, if we pause for just a moment, we may well be tempted to, forced to, ask: How real are they? Do they show any interest in anything beyond their own immediate limited interests? Their dress? Their home? Their kids? Do they have any idea of the outside world? Are they aware of happenings in their immediate neighbourhood? Their city? And, the world? An occasional serial may have a successful doctor or executive, but for the most part they are all merely dolled up puppets going through the motions of living in a society that is as unrealistic and unbelievable as they themselves are! Most of them have never heard of words like equality, gender bias, feminism, the marginalized or empowerment. Do they have a say in the way they live their lives? In matters that affect them directly? In the way in which they live or want to live? In the future of their children? With no knowledge of all this, almost all of them for the most part know nothing of and have no power. What is the message that these serials wish to or succeed in getting across to their viewers? Are they interested in the women they hope to address? Are they in the process of a social duty, which can be referred to as the empowerment of women? I would like to define empowerment at its very simplest in the words of Jill M. Bystydzienski: "Empowerment is taken to mean a process by which... persons gain some control over their lives by taking part with others in development of activities and structures that allow people increased involvement in matters that affect them directly" (42). And, to what extent are these women characters representative of this?

Let us begin by looking at the aims, which guide these makers of soap operas. Many of my arguments may sound simplistic but I hope to get across my fears of the harm that is being caused. The only aim, to my mind, is that of attracting attention. Media culture seems to believe in maximizing audience attention, which includes catching attention, deepening attention and then holding attention. The quality of attention has never been an important criterion because what counts is the time spent by the audience in viewing a particular programme, in this case, a serial. Having succeeded in holding the attention – in trapping the audience which now becomes a captive, with the serial being the captor – the serial maker seems to have attained his/her objective. We need to ask: What is being transmitted? What is the culture that is being projected and hence absorbed? Though we may agree with the dictum, "some culture is better than no culture", we need to see that in these operas culture is more an absence, and sensationalism is interpreted as a synonym for entertainment. I constantly refer to those serials where women are presented in significant numbers, but not realistically or positively. Women are everywhere and there is such a proliferation of women in our serials today. However, numbers do not mean anything because though they are seen they are not heard – visibility does not automatically lead to a voice. They have to be allowed to move to centre stage in more ways than one. Though they are exalted purely and merely by gender identity, they do not have a say in any important matters and they are far away from their second freedom, which is economic empowerment. The stories, if they do exist, are always the same – power struggle with villainy of the worst kind. Homicide or man slaughter is no crime if it helps these TV characters achieve their goal – in most cases, 51 per cent share in a company, break-up of a rival family, ensuring that one's rival can never reach his/her goals etc. All these are sought to be achieved only through deceit and slander or any other unlawful, immoral means that a human being (the serial maker, in particular) can think of, dream of. If ends justify the means, here neither seems justifiable.

Interestingly, in the early years of TV entertainment in our country, we did have very meaningful programmes, about women for women. In the early 1980s, for example, Doordarshan did have serials that would nudge the collective social consciousness of Indian TV viewers and help them see women more realistically and not merely as faceless mothers or mere playthings. There were serials such as *Adhikar* (about legal rights for women), *Aur Bhi Hain Rahein* (about career opportunities for women), *Udaan* (about a woman cop), and *Kashmakash* (about women's struggle). However, such serials have been totally eased out of the popular time slots for reasons best left un-discussed.

Let me now look at some of the women characters in our serials. She can be a glamorous goddess or a devil-incarnate. The family is certainly a primary source of gender inequality and as many of the soap operas are family stories, we see a constant reinforcement of the same. I do not intend to name the serials or the characters but they can all be easily identified – so loud and pronounced is their portrayal. I am convinced, as most of you too must be, that these characters can be easily seen as typical one-sided representations, which I would like to now compare with some well-known Western as well as Indian mythological characters.

Hence, there is the modern Savitri – who can single-handedly enter into any combat. If the mythological one could face Yama once and leave him with no option but to bring her husband back to life, the modern one faces a hundred Yamas, while the men-folk in the family just watch on speechlessly; and she brings her husband back to life after a few hundred episodes (not because she wants him back, but probably because the viewers refuse to accept his death), meet the villains in their own territory, shout down any opposition that she may have to encounter and all the while the *sindoor* is exactly half-a-centimeter without being smudged and the *mangal sutra* dangling prominently as proof of her *suhaagan* status.

Naturally, we have Sita – the silent sufferer, symbolizing sacrifice as the greatest virtue for a woman. Her infinite forbearance is appreciated as it fits in with patriarchal traditions, her suffering is an everyday reality, equality is almost an absurdity. She, in the modern context, accepts her husband whenever he decides to come back, whatever his transgressions are and however many they may be. She allows herself to be trampled upon and never questions everyone's questioning of her. Whether she is financially independent or totally dependent does not in any way affect her personality. She remains the sweet, malleable, ideal *pativrata.*

Our present-day Hindi serials lend themselves equally well to Western, basically Greek and Roman, mythological parallels too. Take the case of Leda, who was transformed into a swan to avoid detection. Innumerable are the women who undergo plastic surgery to avoid detection. Leda had a double set of twins since she had spent the same night with both Zeus and her mortal husband. Many of our women characters have children foisted on them whenever the producer decides to do so. Paternity is questioned often and in some of our serials, even maternity begins to seem suspect.

If Atlanta would marry only the man who could defeat her in a race, our women characters too set up many such tests to choose Mr. Right. In spite of their intelligence, they are unable to see through the deceit of their suitors, just as Atlanta had failed to do when she stopped to pick up the apples that were tossed so as to distract her. In addition to that, these women themselves indulge in deceit which the suitor alone cannot see through. In more than one serial, the woman is a total fraud – detestable too – but she goes on sailing through the serial with no one any the wiser.

We have our own version of the legendary Pandora who opened the box/jar that was forbidden and allowed evil to spread all over the world. The modern Pandora lets out evil with everything that she opens – she seems to have such an infinite variety of them. She exudes a spirit of evil herself and yet hardly ever does she have to pay for her sins or crimes, her machinations and schemes. She is able to cause harm to the best of people and still get away with it. There is no hope for the viewers that this will ever change. I could go on and on with these examples but just this handful is enough for the argument that I wish to emphasize.

What is it that characterizes the audience that remains glued even to serials that have such a portrayal of women? Do all of them share certain characteristics of place or social class or political views or are they similar in their interests? The answer is obviously in the negative. And yet, they are all hardened-compulsive viewers. Of course, media theorists point out varying degrees or levels of participation or involvement. In the present scenario, there are three levels:

(1) All those who have a TV set (not all of them may view that particular serial).
(2) Those who actually watch that particular serial.
(3) Those who actually internalize what they have watched. Obviously, it is the third group that should cause the maximum worry to society.

Among the many reasons for this increasing popularity of the soaps for women is that the inscribed viewer has a gender identity. Modleski (1982) argues that watching soap operas habituates women to distraction and fragmentation. Redundancy and repetition make interrupted viewing possible.

Hobson (1982) is of the opinion that many women watch these because it is a necessary part of lunchtime or kitty party discussions. Oscillating between distance and involvement, these serials give women an opportunity to indirectly talk about themselves. It is possible to play god because the omniscient position of the viewer in informed speculation. It has been suggested that the enjoyment of soap operas may arise from a position of superior knowledge – as audience we are more fully informed (than the characters) about who is doing what to whom and why, we can evaluate the decisions that individual characters make, and guess ahead what the consequences will be. Another important reason that has been suggested for the popularity of soap operas among women viewers is that the 'fragmented structure' of these serials echoes the pattern of a woman's life. Ambivalence and contradiction in plot leave soaps open to multiple interpretation. As there is no single narrative line and as the narrative is not linear, as each serial is merely several stories woven together, women can join in at any time. It is interesting to note that in spite of many other genres being closely related to the soap operas as a genre today, the soap is seen as basically a feminine genre because: (1) soaps delay resolution and do not have a sense of closure; (2) not much happens; (3) no single hero; and (4) dialogue blurs and delays. It in the context of this argument that any criticism of this form is seen as 'culturally elitist'.

Most serials work as a filter allowing the audience to see only what the producer-director wants them to see and hence fail in projecting a realistic picture of women or society today. These serials prove time and again that the media is fond of over-simplifications. Freedom and independence do not seem to figure in the dictionary reserved for women. The melodrama that is an integral part of many of these serials is unashamedly subversive and does great harm to the women's movements that are gradually taking roots at different levels in different parts of our country. In exaggerated black and white terms, they indicate a sneaking enjoyment of what is openly condemned. What men want, women have been conditioned to wanting too but is this what the men today want? This leads one to wonder, who wants such a portrayal, which is not actual reality but a manufactured version. The minimum requirement that one would expect of any serial is that it should have a quality of accuracy and authenticity, that it should reflect social conditions realistically, that there should be some depth and originality and that audiences should not be manipulated. And yet, what we see in serial after serial, day in and day out, is a complete distortion; for the sake of sensationalism, women are represented in a non-factual, fallacious manner, in a biased, regressive manner, in total contradiction to what is and what should be. None of them provide a platform for women to be defined by them and to present their attitudes and perspectives in a progressive way.

What is the effect of such a portrayal on the social health of our country? Are women viewers questioning such kinds of portrayal? Are they raising their voices to protest against such a portrayal? Considering the viewer ratings that these serials claim to have, the answer would be a loud and emphatic NO.

In the present scenario, the question that needs to be immediately addressed is, "How can we (as women) change this depiction that is detrimental to the cause of women?" The need to re-define ourselves is as important as the need to change the 'gaze' of society. Women's education may go some way in bringing about a change. Education as a means of empowering women to take decisions, make choices, give a direction to their lives may go a long way in women being able to stop seeing themselves as the 'other'. From the position of being an 'object,' she has to become the 'subject'. Pre-conceived notions about gender-based biases need to be seen as major hurdles in the process of women's activities as individuals. Insecurity and fear of disapproval by patriarchal norms have to be replaced by the strength to speak and act as women. Hence, these very same serials need to critique age-old ideas to provide the appropriate milieu for change. Feminist concerns must provide the basis for at least some of the serials made by women for women. Women need to redefine themselves on their own terms, if they want to make their lives meaningful.

Works Cited

Hobson, Dorothy, 1982. *Crossroads: The Drama of a Soap*. London: Metheun.

Leslie, Julia and Mary McGee (Eds.), 2000. *Invented Identities*. New Delhi: OUP.

Macdonald, Myra, 2001. *Representing Women*. London: Hodder Headline.

Mcquail, Denis, 1987. *Mass Communication Theory*. London: Sage.

Modleski, Tania, 1982. *Loving with a Vengeance: Mass Produced Fantasies for Women*. Hamden: Archon.

Oakley, Ann and Juliet Mitchell (Eds.), 1997. *Who's Afraid of Feminism*. London: Hamish Hamilton.

15

Mis(re)-presentation of Women Tennis Players on and off the Court

VIDYA G. RAO

Faculty, R.A. Bhavan's College, Ahmedabad

This paper attempts to represent the ways in which the female body is (re)presented as both objects and subjects primarily for male consumption in sport, especially tennis. Feminine attributes, such as attractive figure, flawless skin, slender and sexy legs and long hair, are generally the focus of the visual and print media, which sexualize women athletes by focussing on their physical appearance.

The attentive eye has nowadays shifted its focus from the court's baseline to the skirt's hemline. And that gaze seems to be a powerful one. And it's got stuck there. With the growing popularity of tennis, especially women's tennis, with the spectators, the media and the marketers of various fashion statements, the female tennis stars are making their presence felt with their 'off-court strokes'.

How do we, as tennis lovers, look at the female players on and off the court? Appreciate her sports (wo)man's spirit on her defeat or success, praise her sporting prowess or clap for her superb shot? Not quite. The hawk-like eye gazes on her body language, her feminine presence and her sexuality. These female tennis players have willy-nilly come to symbolize all those repressed, unfulfilled desires of the collective unconsciousness.

They are the new fashion divas on the block. They have finally arrived and plan to stay on that way. They are no longer the uniformly dressed, in the conventionally prescribed white outfit, assumed to be comfortable and necessary for any sport. Players nowadays propagate a whole range of fashion, style, grace and attitude, which is not only popular but also acceptable by the masses.

In an interview[1] that was appeared on the Internet, an interviewee asked Sharapova after her second-round win at the 2005 US Open: "I met a lot of people who came here not to see really the game, but to see you. How do you feel about it? How do you feel about being like a superstar more than a tennis player?"

Sharapova replied: "It's very flattering. ... I hope that people come out and watch me for my tennis. But, you know, I can't control the reason why they come out. Not too much I can do about that. I'm a tennis player. With being a popular tennis player comes a lot of other things. That's part of it."

Sharapova is well aware that looks are as important as winning. In another article[2], she says, "Beauty sells. I have to realize that's also part of why people want me. I understand it. It's fine. I'm not going to make myself ugly."

The historic assigning of value to women's bodies, according to culturally imposed physical standards, is an expression of power relations, with many of the traits seen across centuries as 'beautiful' largely symbolizing certain female behaviour that males deem desirable. "Beauty lies in the eye of the beholder," as John Keats said. The point is that there is no 'right' or 'wrong', 'acceptable' or 'unacceptable', physical beauty is a matter of cultural preferences and popularity. The sexualization of women tennis players in written texts, visual images, or spoken words portrays them as objects and subjects available for male consumption.

Forbes' list[3] of Celebrity 100 describes Sharapova as "a dazzling 6-foot-tall blonde in a sleeveless T-shirt and shorts who grunts each time her racquet smacks the ball to deliver a blinding, blurry serve". Or check the visual images such as the change in the colour of Kournikova's knickers or Serena Williams's body-hugging outfit showing her curves being given substantial coverage in sports pages of all newspapers. Also adjectives such as Sexy Sharapova or Buxom Serena or Leggy Blonde for Kournikova connote them as an object of male desire.

When this happens, the recurrent images of these women flashed across the social arena often sexualize and trivialize their efforts. Surely, the years spent at practising the game and accomplishing the goals, their dreams are marginalized and sometimes even undermined. For instance, according to her own admission, Sharapova's 12 years of six-hour practice days, constant travel and the exclusion of anything close to a normal childhood.

The female tennis players are materialized conveniently as marketing tools. The kind of all elusive, distant, incredible, out of the world images encouraged by reports in newspapers do not see these accomplished sportswomen as independent, professional women carving out their careers, but are rather suggestive of images controlled by and for others, especially men. Surveys, spectators and TV audiences prove that the number of males watching a women's tennis match is much, much more than females watching men's tennis.

Maria Sharapova's win in the women's final at the Wimbledon in 2004 covered her success but with a focus excessively on her appearance. Newspapers like *The Observer*[4] wanted "Offers please ... for the girl who is the world's hottest sports prodigy." Or her looks enraptured and made *The Independent*[5] "swoon".

Sharapova's combination of dazzling looks, steely determination has metamorphosed the Russian beauty into a sports icon, a marketing phenomenon, which transcends her game. Her ability to scoop 20 million-dollar endorsements, to sell everything from signature perfumes, clothing lines and mobile phone has the strategists calculating her earning potential. Or even consider India's Sania Mirza who catapulted to dizzying heights of fame and glory with the world waiting with baited breath for some more from the 'glam slam' girl. Adman Alyque Padamsee claims that Sania has everything that comes as a good package. She has become a brand name not just because of her talent but also because she is attractive.

Beauty, as represented by Sharapova, Sania Mirza or Anna Kournikova, signifies corporeal beauties who are idolised, and yet (male) authority is the social force used to tame, control and channel this pure female power. Though Sania is loved by the masses, there are the 'moral police' who consider her clothing as 'blasphemous' and going against her religion. Kournikova's off-court activities attract more attention than her on court struggles. Her relationship with ..... and her endorsement of .... have more news value.

Although what is considered beautiful has been proven to vary across cultures and changed over time, yet there always exists a dichotomy for women's bodies, along with beauty standards conditioned by varying assumptions of 'natural' womanhood and 'moral' parameters as prescribed by patriarchal fancies. For instance, most parents would give a doll – symbol of motherhood – to a young girl and probably a ball or a bat to a young boy. At a tender age, children are given gender stereotypes and roles. We give fake make-up kits to young girls making it obvious how "beautiful and fair" is important for her when she grows up. Young boys get action figures for they need to become "strong and powerful" as adults. Thus, our children are conditioned to be like everyone else, intentionally or not.

Yet, there are females who have overcome this "culturally imposed" conditional barriers and entered male-dominated territory, wherein just as in society, both domination and power are contested terrains. 'Tall and dainty' Sharapova and 'attractive'" Sania are just some of metaphors used to gauge a woman's beauty. It is important to highlight the inherent discrepancies evident in such stereotyped constructs of beauty. The feminine images, archetypal[6] models of behaviour have, in fact, been formed by men and therefore do not represent a woman's idea of femininity. This idealization, as exemplified by Sharapova or Sania Mirza as iconic figures of beauty, talent, and thereby acceding to the patriarchal power structures, has in itself ambiguous power relationships.

On the one hand, there is a metamorphosis of 'beauty' and on the other there is a transformation of the 'not so beautiful'. Sharapova is the perfect lady-like athlete who outscores Serena Williams. Perhaps, Serena is not feminine enough.

There are also reports on how Williams has failed to impress off the court, in that most important and womanly of tasks choosing what to wear. According to the *Sunday Times,*[7] Sharapova "beat Williams in grunts, dress sense and tennis". Serena is never the 'golden', 'shimmering', 'dazzling' girl of tennis.

Such metaphorical praises are not for her. And yet the Williams sisters are equally overwhelmingly popular, have fashion endorsements and fan followings. This representation serves to deconstruct the marginalization inherent in the traditional concepts of beauty. Female tennis players like Serena and Venus Williams succeed in effacing the duality between the chaste, radiant and dainty images of archetypal[8] beauties with the dark, compelling and robust images, thereby reconstructing the cultural inscription of feminine beauty.

In the *Sunday Times,* in a supposedly humorous article, Jasper Gerard writes that "the ladies" who have "even grown quite good at tennis" should be paid more because "the entire male world is in love. Or lust".

In fact, sports can be a liberating experience for women, a chance for women to be in control of their own bodies. By refusing the stereotype, of any kind – physical, mental, or even sexual – women tennis players can have access to a greater diversity of experiences that shape body image and self-concept. And hopefully this will lead to a more equitable sporting environment, one in which she will be applauded for her sporting skills rather than any other superfluous reasons.

Women need not be male-fied (if I may coin a new term like classified) – to be cut, and trimmed according to specific requirements.

End Notes

1. www.mariaworld.net
2. Forbes.com
3. Peter Kafka in a story titled "The Hot Shot" published in Forbes.com
4. *The Observer*, 4 July 2004, p.3.
5. *The Independent*, 4 July 2004, p.1.
6. Chapter I of *Archetypal Patterns in Women's Fiction* by Annis Pratt:

   The term archetype derives from the Greek archi, a beginning or first instance, and typos, a stamp, and denotes the primordial form, the original, of a series of variations. This etymology contributes to a confusion between archetype and stereotype, a printing term designating the original plate from which subsequent imprints are made and connoting an excessively rigid set of generalisations. Carl Gustaf Jung defines archetypes as primordial forms in that they spring from the preverbal realm of the unconscious, where they exist inchoate and indescribable until given form in consciousness. ... Archetypes thus constitute images, symbols, and narrative patterns that differ from stereotypes in being complex variables, subject to variations in perception.
7. *Sunday Times*, 14 July 2004.
8. In *Humanities Through The Arts*, Carl Jung describes archetypal patterns as "the psychic residua of numberless experiences of the same type."

   Homer's *Odyssey* has an abundance of archetypal women patterns. Penelope, the good woman; Athena, the soul mate; and Kalypso, the bad woman.

IV

Re-mark

The final frame in our process of re-definition is re-mark. We believe that the constant negotiations in the re-design, re-think and re-view stages enable a re-marking of disciplines. In this collection, the chosen discipline is literature. Grasping the ideas discussed in the earlier sections, our contributors journey back to their palimpsest texts to mark and highlight hidden spaces. **Sachidananda Mohanty** effectively combines the discussions of Lakshmi Kannan and Jayashree to analyze the notion of female agency in the Oriya literary context. His conclusions of this exploration are interesting because he invests the space between the private and the public not only with power but the burden of the power as well. **Rupalee Burke** continues the observations of Shilpa Das, Mangai and Aniruddhan in her study of the representation of Dalit women in Dalit texts. She uses the issue of caste and gender marginalizations to study the politics of representation. **Smitha Sivadasan** works along similar lines of arguments in her examination of the patriarchal incursions into the matrilineal space of the Nair community in

Malayalam literature. **Kavita Patel** builds on Mangai's repertoire in her study of Indian women's theatre. Providing the matrix of Kavita's arguments on transformation are playwrights such as Usha Ganguli, Mamta Sagar, Varsha Adalja, C.S. Lakshmi and Rasheed Jahan. **Darshana Trivedi** displays a practical application of the concepts discussed by Vidya Bal, Lakshmi Kannan and Balaji Ranganathan earlier in her analysis of Gangasati. Moving beyond an insight into the familial and social restrictions of the times, Darshana offers a psychodynamic perspective. In a similar vein, **Javed Khan** marks new boundaries in his analysis of Kamala Das' poetry. His insights use the metaphoric and metonymic expansions of the looking glass image in her poetry.

A collection of this type benefits by the eclectic contributions. What amazes us as editors is the running thread of continuity in the arguments, even when it is an interrogation of essentialisms and monolithic constructions. Whether it is a boon or bane is unclear but there is enough material for a sequel.

16

The Burden of Shakti: Female Agency and Literary Creativity in Orissa*

SACHIDANANDA MOHANTY

Professor of English, University of Hyderabad, Hyderabad

The issue of women and cultural icons is a complex and contentious one as yet insufficiently explored. It has far-reaching cultural and political ramifications. The view that the male and the female of the human species represent distinct categories and that certain gender roles could be valorized has been held with deep suspicion for long by many feminists. To equate man and woman with attributes like the intellect and intuition (in popular culture "men are from Mars and women from Venus"

---

* An earlier version of this paper was first presented at the National Seminar on "Women and Cultural Icons", held at Women's Studies and Development Centre, University of Delhi, on 24-25 February 2004.

I gratefully acknowledge support received from Professor Malashri Lal and her team at the Centre.

for instance) is seen in many quarters as part of patriarchal thinking.

And yet, the claim that women are possessor and upholder of particular kind of power, and that indeed women can incarnate such power as the great creatrix seems to be common to many traditions of the world. This despite the claim of arguments of authors like Dan Brown who in his *The Da Vinci Principle* contends that "organized religion has systematically suppressed the centrality of the female principle in the order of creation" (ToI, 22 February 2004).

Differently conceived and realized, however, categories like Purusha-Prakriti, Shiva-Parvati and Ishwara-Shakti of the Indian tradition seem to parallel the mythic, philosophical and cultural constructs elsewhere such as Apollo-Dionysus or Zees-Athena of the Greek pantheon.

Celebration of motherhood as emblematic of life and fecundity are viewed in many pagan and tribal traditions in the form of the fertility sites. Nature, the empyrean and the vast cosmos are seen in deeply feminine terms. But, what does female power mean in the context of today's 'metrosexual', the term first used by the British writer Mark Simpson in 1994 to suggest "the urban man who is eager to embrace the feminine side". What can it signify in the context of the emerging possibility of female cloning and redundancy of males in the biological process.

According to one report, "Charting the chromosomes, researchers say men have reached an evolutionary *cul de sac* and will eventually eliminate themselves from the planet. Indeed scientists have already discovered a type of tiny water animal, the rotifers, who through genetic selection have not only completely eliminated males but have succeeded in diversifying into more than 300 all female species, saying A – men to men" (ToI, 22 February 2004).

Despite this, however, there is a persistence of the view that as a special manifestation of female power, Shakti is integral to much of the Hindu belief and practice. We see this in our beliefs and rituals, in our folk and popular culture, and in our dance, legends and temple iconography. The celebration of the cult of Radha or Rukmini as a necessary concomitant or correlative to the metaphysique and worship of Krishna, for instance, shares affinities in the Shiva-Parvati or Ram-Sita of the Hindu pantheon.

In the 19th century, we witness a similar trend in the case of Sri Ramakrishna and Divine Mother Sharada Devi (Kishwar, 25). Here, the Master deifies his companion as Shakti. Worship of the Master is incomplete without the simultaneous acceptance and surrender to the Divine Mother. And again, in the 20th century, Sri Aurobindo, the philosopher-visionary, deifies the French born mystic Myrra Alfassa as the Mother. He writes a booklet explaining the significance of her advent upon earth. As the creatrix, the Mother takes physical charge of the Ashram named after Sri Aurobindo. This is what Sri Aurobindo says in the book *The Mother*:

> The Mother is one but she comes before us with differing aspects, many are her powers and personalities, many are her emanations and vibhutis that do her work in the universe. The one whom we adore as the Mother is the divine conscious force that dominates the existence.
>
> The one original transcendent Shakti, the Mother stands above all the world and bears in her eternal consciousness the Supreme Divine (*Sri Aurobindo*, 27-29).

The metaphysical or spiritual truths behind much of what we know today as Shakti remain unclear and indeterminate, although its use in the popular domain continues. After all, Indira Gandhi, seen as Goddess Durga, goes back to East Bengal's war of liberation of 1971.

However, many feminists like Simone de Beavoir remain skeptical of gender constructs like the male and the female. Others disagree and maintain that female identity and iconography cannot be reduced to simplistic categories like 'progressive' or 'regressive'. In this paper, I shall look at instances of some of the outstanding literary women of India. Caught at the intersection between gender, the nation and the empire, they embraced icons as superior role models and articulated their concept of the self, and the nation in a diverse manner. I shall suggest that although my analysis focuses on a specific historical context of India, the late 19th and early 20th century, some of the implications of my enquiry can be applied with modification in the case of other cultures as well.

Arguably, historical and ideological specificities seem to militate against the drawing of easy parallels between cultures. And yet there exists an astonishing set of commonalities that bind women's experience together and make the study of women as cultural icons so exciting. The unique mode and manner in which female education came to India by colonial rulers and native male reformers is one aspect that is common to woman's history in many post-colonial societies. Similarly, the juxtaposition of the cultivation of the mind with the making of the home and the hearth, is a phenomenon common to colonial India and America. "The season of instruction", Mary Kelly aptly observes, "gave mixed signals to female students *vis-à-vis* their male counterparts":

> From the beginning the signals the literary domestics received from their society were not designed to encourage young women in formulating uniformly self-respecting and clear conceptions of them selves as intelligent.
>
> Those signals that invited comparisons between female and male educational training or that heightened the contrast between the lines envisioned for the literary domestics and those of their male counterparts were neither consistent nor reassuring. Women's educational experience went no further than home and the seminary, and no future was promised beyond the walls of domesticity. Given the inflexible promises about adult male and female activities and roles, to be performed within clearly defined public and private spheres respectively, intellectual aspirations and ambitions on the part of females generally were regarded as gratuitous, perhaps abnormal (Kelly, 55-57).

Indeed, mixed signals are what constantly governed the fate of great many of early literary women in Orissa. Their desire to strive against adverse circumstances for literary creativity and participation in public space was often achieved by consciously emulating superior role models and embracing icons such as Shakti for empowerment. In some, the gap between the words of public professions and the reality of their private self, led to anguish and agony. Others learned to overcome the contradictions, and scored triumphs in personal and public life. But there was none that did not have to struggle to harmonize contradictory pulls and allegiances: personal love versus public service, the drudgery of domestic life versus the desire for literary creativity, the loyalty to a married partner *vis-à-vis* the attraction to a true companion of the soul, intimate sexual longing and the demands for public chastity. Women as cultural and spiritual icons, embodied in various ways the principle of Shakti, and quite inevitably they learnt to carry its burden as well.

For most literary women, the world of creative writing and publication was a deeply political act. They knew the complexities and the magnitude of the difficulty involved, and consequently negotiated the terrain with care and caution. They took the help of sympathetic men, fathers, brothers and spouses even as they wrote in spirited and fiery language and took up public positions that were bold and contentious. In approaching members of the British establishment and princely class known for their patronage of art and letters, they did not compromise with their artistic or moral integrity, but attempted to enlist support from enlightened quarters for publication and dissemination of their work. Thus, the 'dedication' pages of many books by women bring in the question of literary and financial support. For instance, in a letter dated 30 July 1906, addressed to the king of *Badakhamundi* in the Ganjam district, poet Annapurna Devi regrets that she has been falsely accused by newspapers and magazines of seeking assistance from the king. Her declaration is a subtle appeal for help as well:

> My husband works for Your Highness. From time to time he may be getting some help by appealing to your royal self. But I do not understand why my name was

> unnecessarily dragged into the papers. I would not have been in this plight if the Maharaja had thrown a cursory look at my poetry. I sincerely hope your good self would not be angered by seeing my poetry in the papers. It is important to follow duty in life and I must follow my own rightful path by always reposing faith in Your Highness! (Annapurna, 20, my translation).

Similarly, Bidyutprabha (1926-1977) affirmed a bold female voice in her romantic poetry and held up a superior role model for literary women of Orissa. In the poem "Pratighat" the poet is able to overcome the constraints of domestic life for the sake of creativity:

> Writing is the balm
> for all my pain.
> It's the glory of my sorrow.
> Writing is rain-soaked woods.
> It's the music of cloud bursts
> during the month of *Shravana!*
> I wish I could speak of
> the joy that gathers in my heart!
> Like a flame
> in the mouth of storm
> my poetry
> a luminous lamp!
>
> (Bidyutprabha, 390-91, my translation)

It is interesting to see in this context that in an early publication before her marriage, in the dedication page of *Kanakanjali*, 1948, this is what Bidyutprabha had to say:

> To His Highness Kishore Chandra Singh Deo:
>
> Respected Sir,
>
> Thanks to your kindness, the work of many poor and talented poets of Utkal could come to light. The attention that you have paid to an unknown writer like me is an index of your generous self. I enter the world of Oriya literature, with *Kanakanjali* in my hand, with a mixture of fear and trepidation. I shall forever cherish your

sympathy for me. Before I place my modest effort at the fact of Utkal's Saraswati, I can do no better than the offer it to your noble self. I sincerely hope and pray that as a connoisseur of talent you will accept this small offering as a sign of your greatness!

Yours
("Gunamugdha" Bidyutprabha)

(Bidyutprabha, 92, my translation)

Seeking patronage while affirming the icon of Shakti, female power was common to women's experience in India. A letter dated January 23, 1909 published in an early Malayalam journal by women offers an interesting example (the note is addressed to Mrs. Catherine Booth, the wife of General Booth, the founder of Salvation Army):

To

Mrs Catherine Booth Tucker,

Esteemed Madam and Beloved Sister,

We the members of the Ladies' Association, Trivandrum, offer you a warm welcome and thank you very much for allowing us this opportunity of meeting you here this afternoon. Our association began its existence ten months ago as the result of an informal private consultation held by some of us. Its aims are modest, its beginning humble and its achievements lie hidden in the womb of futurity. Being still in the stage of infancy, the Association is a mere dreamer and prattler, but it hopes in course of time to outline the blunders, weaknesses and indiscretions of childhood and youth…

… Your presence in our midst is particularly encouraging to us. It is a tangible proof, if proof were needed of your sympathy with and interest in all movements calculated to advance womankind, to whatever country and community they belong.

While embodying Shakti many public women alternated between self-affirmation and self-doubt. In some, the contrast was sharp and dramatic. They upheld Shakti as a conscious ideal in life and action. In others, the difference in mood swing between exuberance and diffidence was more subtle and unobtrusive. In Oriya feminist Kuntala's case, this seems to be a recurrent motif. As a Christian girl who sought to become a Brahmo for the sake of her mentor Kailash Chandra Rao, she faced persecution and ostracism in the hands of her co-religionists and approached the district magistrate Mr. Shaser and his wife with an exemplary sense of courage:

> I am a Christian girl, being oppressed by men of my own nationality. I have come to you. You are an honest Christian. Is it anywhere written in the Bible or religious codes that Christians cannot change her religion? In the last part of the 19th century, Swami Vivekananda spoke in the All World Religious Conference and it was at his forceful words that numberless Christians turned to Hinduism. Can the ruler of the civilized English people tolerate this sort of behaviour of a cruel group of Christians on a lonely girl!
>
> (Mohapatra, 140)

Kuntala's life alternated between private grief and public activism. The letters she wrote from Delhi, published serially in the Oriya journal *Sahakara*, constantly exhort the Oriyas to more on a vigorous path of economic, cultural and political rejuvenation. She reminds them of their glorious tradition and legacy of Koshala and Kalinga, their maritime ties with Ceylon, Bali and Sumatra as well as the reign of Kharavela and Ashoka. It is by consciously invoking and embodying Shakti, she argues, that we can overcome the present Tamas, the defeatism and despair that have gripped contemporary Orissa. As she declares in passionate terms:

> Only one appeal! Wipe out this name "Oriya"! Banish it for ever! We are the people of the great Kalinga! Why should we be known as ignoble Oriyas! Drown the name Oriya in the Mahanadi! Revive Kalinga and its greatness! Why should Kalinga not be a source of our riches! Agitate

> in public and change the name Orissa! Delete it from government records and stationery! Write Kalinga instead! "Kalinga-Keshari, Taruna-Utkal! Why should you be the Oriya Coolie! You are the youth of Kalinga, glorious and radiant! You are the lion's cubs in the forest of Kalinga! (Kuntala Kumari, 1969: 459).

She continues with equal ardour:

> The Rajput is dead but his history is not dead! He is only aged and feeble! Nurse him so that he can rise again! Dream for a larger Kalinga – Ganjan, Singhbhum, Medinipur, Kanthi, Phulghar,
>
> Jaipur, Bastar – all are Kalinga after all!
>
> Borneo, Bali, Java, Lanka carried the drums of war. Kalinga, its leonine army, ship loads from Tamrahpti marched ahead, the hero-warriors! (ibid).

Kuntala's exhortations are not for the sake of Mohapatra's linguistic fanaticism or jingoism. Her interventions are best seen in the historical context, to preserve, protect and promote Oriya consciousness that was under threat from a combination of British and Bengali colonialism. Although Orissa was granted statehood in 1936, parts of Oriya-speaking tracts such as Saraikala, Kharasuan, Singhbhum, Mandinipur were about to be merged with Bengal and Bihar. They eventually did. From the vantage point of Delhi, Kuntala could survey the national scene. She participated actively in the women's movement and the freedom struggle that was not oblivious to the cultural and political plight of the Oriyas back home:

> Arise O Bhagiratha! Bring the sacred waters of Ganga! Come, O' the monarchs of Kalinga! Purushottam, Kapilendra Mukunda, Kharavela, banish the dust, weakness and squalour! We have been buried under the *Bilati* weeds and malaria. Angel, only you can clear up this dirt! You! The valiant women of Kalinga! Alone, you can throw out and trample upon the weeds from Bilati! (ibid).

In the letters from Delhi published in *Sahakara*, Kuntala assumes the title of "Birashree" and "Birashrimati" and concludes:

> O You the people of Utkal! The time for your rise has come! No longer will you be half dead in famine, flood and pestilence!
>
> You are a heroic race! Be therefore known as heroes! Men should be "Birashree" and women "Birashrimati".
>
> – Your sister from Utkal
>
> – Birashrimati Kuntala Kumari Devi
> (Kuntala Kumari, 1969: 496)

The idea that it is Shakti or power that can save the land of Utkal, that women are best placed to effect the change by embodying this Shakti and that by so doing there could be gender equality, social reforms, and Utkal play its rightful role in the political emancipation of the country – is a recurrent theme in the writings of many outstanding women in Orissa – from Sarala Devi, Rama Devi to Malati Choudhury – despite the differences in ideology and rhetorical style.

In Sarala Devi there is a pronounced note of this kind. She wrote two biographies entitled *Biraramani* and *Bishwabiplabini* whose purpose clearly was to provide heroic role models for Oriya women. Other works of her's such as *The Rights of Women* and *The Economic Independence of Women*, argue for political and economic independence without which female heroism would merely remain a slogan.

The letter that Sarala wrote from prison in 1931 not only talks of her political life but also of her son and family members back at Jagatsinghpur in Orissa. It shows that for literary women like her who took part in women's issues, politics and the freedom struggle, Shakti involved fortitude and forbearance.

In this regard, the life history and work of Oriya women seem to parallel their counterparts elsewhere, like Pandita Ramabai (1856-1922), Binodini Dasi (1863-1941) and Lalithambika Antherjanam (1909-1987). Thus, for public women, upholding Shakti or female power was for the most part joy, for many women it was inevitably a burden as well. The burden of Shakti!

Works Cited

Nityananda Satpathy (ed.), *Bidyutprabha Grantabali,* 1983, Part I, Cuttack: Friends' Publishers.

Kelley, Mary, 1984. *Private Woman, Public Stage, Literary Domesticity in 19th Century America,* New York: OUP.

Kishwar, Madhu, 1997. "Women, Sex and Marriage: Restraint as a Feminist Strategy", *Manushi,* No. 99.

Mohapatra, Chakradhar, 1972. *Kuntala Kumari, Jiban Charita,* Cuttack: *Grantha Mandir.*

Panda, Radhacharan, 1938. *Narikabi Annapurna Devi.*

Sabat, Kuntala Kumari, 1969. *Kuntala Kumari Granthamala,* Vol.I and II: Cuttack Students' Store.

Sri Aurobindo, 1928. *The Mother,* Pondicherry: Sri Aurobindo Ashram, rpt. 2001.

Tharu Susie, Lalita K., 1991. *Women Writing in India: 600 BC to the Present,* New Delhi: OUP.

17

Literary Cross-dressing: Portrayal of Women in Gujarati Dalit Short Stories by Male Writers

RUPALEE BURKE

Faculty, Shree Sahajanand Vanijya Mahavidyalaya, Ahmedabad

> A woman is defined and differentiated with reference to man and not he with reference to her; she is the incidental and the inessential as opposed to the essential. He is the Subject, he is the Absolute – she is the 'Other'.
>
> – Simone de Beauvoir

Dalit literature deals with dalit realities and has sociological implications. Not so when the dalit woman's question is concerned. The double marginalization of dalit women on account of caste and gender discrimination has not yet found adequate representation in regional dalit literatures. G. Arunima notes:

> To say that both women and lower castes are oppressed would be a mere commonplace in the context of India. Nevertheless, there is little evidence from either history or

> contemporary Indian politics to show that there have been attempts to find a common ground between patriarchy and caste oppression. In contemporary India, neither feminist politics nor the Dalit movements have been able to address adequately the issue of Dalit women's oppression (Basu, 219).

Dalit women are victimized by 'male power politics' in the status denied to them in society and literature. Thus discrimination of dalit women and their marginalization in political, social, educational, religious and economic spheres is an issue that is common to the caste and gender discourse. They have been marginalized even in the dalit discourse. Dalit ideologues are yet to deal with the dalit woman's reality seriously. As for male dalit writers, not all, have only cursorily dealt with it; mainly because they are preoccupied with other themes and pursuits for obvious reasons. And now sadly enough one finds that the very caste based discrimination the dalits revolted against has crept into their own rank and file. Gender discrimination, however, always existed both outside and within the dalit fold. Liberation or emancipation is a distant dream for dalit women. It is really with women writers that the theme of the doubly oppressed dalit woman finds expression. In Tamil dalit literature Bama has written blatantly on the subject as also Sivakami. The dalit woman's two-fold misery has found more authentic expression in autobiographies in Marathi dalit literature by Shantabai Kamble and Kumud Pawde. Since there is yet a Bama or Sivakami or Shantabai or Kumud Pawde to rise on the Gujarati dalit literary horizon the dalit woman is represented by male dalit writers.

This is precisely why this paper attempts a reading of male-authored Gujarati dalit short stories with specific reference to the portrayal of women characters in them. The paper is divided into two sections. The first section deals with the woman-centred short stories while the second section comprises a discussion of not specifically woman-centred short stories.

Gujarati dalit literature is of recent origin compared to Gujarati mainstream literature. Dalit writers in Gujarat are still first generation writers, majority of whom are male, belonging to the Vankar caste and the urban middle class. Women writers are conspicuous by their absence with just a couple of them writing intermittently. Justifying the dearth of women writers in Gujarati dalit literature in *The Silver Lining*, Mohan Parmar, a leading Gujarati dalit writer, says:

> The question of Dalit women writers is a far-fetched one. The dalit community is an exploited one. In addition to this, the minimum level of education in the female population is reason enough for the apathy of women towards literature. Gujarati dalit literature can boast of five women writers which is a consolation in itself (Burke, 85).

Suggesting remedial measures he continues:

> The organization of literary camps could be instrumental in helping the *dalit women to get rid of their narrow mindedness and inferiority complex and empower them to be able to stand shoulder to shoulder with the dalit men* (emphasis mine) (Burke, 85).

One cannot help noticing the arrogantly patronizing and protectionist tone of the male dalit writer, which extends to the androcentric bias in the short stories that they write and this is substantiated in the discussion that follows.

Dalit literature is not pure literature but one that has sociological implications. Thus, Gujarati dalit short stories become social texts. Harish Mangalam, a foremost Gujarati dalit writer, observes in *Tongues of Fire*:

> The sentiments of the dalit community, the feelings, the social, economic, political and cultural problems of the dalits occupy centre stage in Gujarati dalit short stories. The mission of Gujarati dalit short stories is *to sweep society clean of cobwebs, mobilize social change and adopt new values* (emphasis mine) (Trivedi, 167).

The fact is that very few writers have given due consideration to the aspects mentioned in the quote above. The portrayal of dalit women characters without any attempts to empower them belies the claim made above as the triple oppression that dalit women have to suffer is reflected in the short stories discussed in this paper and is problematized further when there is clearly a deliberate attempt on the part of the male writers to write from a 'feminist' position. This is evident of their 'literary cross-dressing', to borrow Showalter's term with a change. The gender power politics inherent in the portrayal of women characters is borne out in the discussion of the three short stories in this section. Three other short stories by the same three male dalit writers will be discussed in the next section.

In Dalpat Chauhan's *Ba Valu Aljo* (Some Leftovers Please), the female protagonist Shantu has a drunkard husband Jivo whose inability to fulfil his role as breadwinner forces Shantu to provide for the family by begging for leftovers. Both husband and wife work as municipal sanitation workers. While Shantu comes directly home after work, Jivo returns fully drunk only late in the evening. Shantu's ambition is to educate her son Samudo and make him a teacher. The death of Samudo without getting to eat the rice he was craving for makes up the tragic end of the story.

> Although Shantu is shown fulfilling the twin roles of co-breadwinner and housekeeper i.e. efficient both in the 'public' sphere of work and 'private' sphere of home, the writer does more disservice than service to her. Shantu's experience is specific to most dalit women's lives today.
>
> As P.C. Jain points out in *Scheduled Caste Women*:
>
> Although women from the lower strata enjoy greater freedom as compared to women from the upper strata, yet the lower caste women have to live a life subject to the authority of the males of the family (Jain, 16).

The implication here is of the interplay of power and love in male-female relation in marriage as also of the caste-gender nexus affecting dalit women. The 'third dimension of power' identified by Stephen Lukes is explained in *The Gender of Power*:

"Absence of grievances does not mean that power is not involved, the power relation could be latent" (Davies, 35).

The fact that Shantu endures mutely, has no grievances and can do nothing to change her lot relegates her "squarely to the position of 'cultural dope,' that passive and unenlightened victim of circumstances beyond her control" (Davies, 81). Shantu's economic independence does not do anything to redeem her from her husband, the oppressive 'Other' within, nor grants her equal status. The fact reiterated by this story is that dalit women are more clearly victims of gender than of caste.

B. Kesharshivam's short story *Rati Rayan Ni Ratash* (The Red Berry) deals with the female dalit protagonist Keshli putting up resistance against sexual harassment by an upper caste male, the oppressive 'Other' without. Scores of Guajrati dalit short stories take up this archetypal theme. Unlike the 'dasi' image of Shantu in the previously discussed story, Keshli's image is that of 'devi'. She is shown turning the gender power equation upside down by making most of the situation unlike Shantu. Keshli exerts control over her oppressor Dipa who has been hounding her and desires to have an illicit relationship with her. She assumes the castrating form of Jogmaya [God's *Shakti* (power) that creates the world; Goddess Durga] in the market square and threatens him: "You bastard! If you are bred on lioness's milk, come, take my hand in marriage. But if you are the son of a eunuch, come, suckle me, touch my feet, call me Mother and be gone" (translation mine).

A little later in the story we read:

> Dipa had no qualms about calling her Mother or even touching her feet for that matter but it was the suckling part which gave him the shivers. Had it been an isolated spot he would have gladly suckled her but to do it in public was just impossible (translation mine).

The underlying horror of the above lines cannot simply be ignored. The Jogmaya image of Keshli instantly melts away to make way for the notion of the dalit female body as a contested site for upper caste men, dalit women as the 'Object,' the oppressed 'Other'. Before hastening to glorify Keshli's female chastity in her seemingly obvious victory over Dipo who epitomizes male brutality and force, a cautious re-evaluation of events in the narrative is necessary. The very fact that Keshli is a victim of sexual advances reveals her vulnerability and inferior status. The point to be taken is not the humiliation of Dipo at the hands of Keshli (i.e., what she does/achieves) but the violation of Keshli's dignity by Dipo that is prevented (i.e., what he does not do/achieve). Keshli like Revi in Mohan Parmar's *Thali* (*Beyond the Threshold*) and Shavli in Harish Mangalam's *Talap* (The Craving) becomes the sexual object, the object of male desire and male gaze, i.e., the upper caste males, males of their own caste as well as the dalit writers themselves. The dalit woman's chastity or purity is ironically defined only in the face of sexual exploitation, never in its absence. No attempt is made towards the social emancipation of dalit women characters.

In Pravin Gadhvi's *Matsyagandha,* the female protagonist by the same maiden name is of Shudra origin. Shantanu, the king of Indraprastha, is bewitched by her beauty and undertakes a fast unto death to bring his mother to agree to allow him to make Matsyagandha his chief queen. Indeed, a victory for the Shudra girl in terms of elevation of social and political status. However, Matsyagandha (rechristened Satyavati) regrets all the while her ineffectiveness in using her power for the welfare of the community. At the end of this lengthy story we read:

> Imprisoned for years – centuries Matsyagandha's wings were severed, blunted. An aged Satyavati – Matsyagandha walked out of Hastinapur Fort – a virtual prison. Supported by Krishna Dvaypayan she walked with tottering steps to the boat. Her son rowed the boat away from the injustices, oppressions and sexual exploitations of Indraprastha. She was on her way to merge with the Shudras without caring a damn about the wrath of Bharatvansha (translation mine).

The female protagonist is doomed to become an object of possession, a sexual object; her only virtue being her beauty, her body becomes her identity. She may be liberated from the throes of poverty and untouchability by gaining access to the palace but it becomes a virtual cage. She fears after Shantanu's death that she will be turned away from the palace by his brother Devratta but is amazed when she is allowed to retain her rightful place. Such incidents gloss over the reality. Much in keeping with the Manuvian diktats, Satyavati-Matsyagandha's life rolls on under the tutelage of her husband, brother-in-law and sons. The moral of the story is that political empowerment of a dalit woman, even when she rises to the stature of a queen, is a far cry.

It is therefore logical to conclude from the foregoing discussion that no attempts are made by male dalit writers with regards to the socio-economic-political empowerment of dalit women through dalit literature, given its specific aims and ramifications. What obtains are stereotypical images of women as either 'angel' or 'monster'. In either case women characters are constructed to suit the whims of males, including the writer himself. The notions of the 'chaste' dalit women in resistance and the 'dutiful' dalit women, in other words, the foregrounding of their respectability are concepts borrowed from Brahmin patriarchy as part of the Sanskritization process. B. Kesharshivam states in *Nari Chetna Ni Navlikao*: "The Shakti image of the women characters in my stories stems from their dutifulness, devotion towards the family, ethics and morality" (translation mine).

The middle-classness of the dalit writers intersecting with their dalitness is at the root of their perspective that women are only meant to be providers of sexual, emotional and material needs of men. As a corollary, the sexual, emotional and material needs of dalit women are yet to find articulation. Toril Moi's observation in her essay "Men against Patriarchy" in *Gender and Theory* becomes extremely relevant at this juncture: "Clearly, males and females do not – and cannot – take up the same position in relation to female experience. In this sense, they cannot be feminists in the same way" (Moi, 83). She goes on to elaborate:

> Feminism, then, is something *more* than the effort to express women's experience: it is at once, a relatively comprehensive analysis of power relations between the sexes, and *the effort to change or undo any power system that authorizes and condones male power over women* ... Men can therefore be feminist. But – and this is crucial – they cannot be women (emphasis mine) (Moi, 183).

Is it fear of disintegration of patriarchal authority that compels the male dalit writer to write the way he does? Is he allowing himself to be read through the women he writes, their experiences and reactions? Has collective consciousness any part to play in the entire process? Is the portrayal of women realistic or fabricated? Is he being pseudo-sympathetic towards women's plight? These are questions that arise in a context where caste and gender intersect in the dalit context.

II

In the short stories, which are not specifically woman-centred, the male dalit writers are caught off-guard and their explicitly patriarchal stance is revealed in the way in which they portray women characters. Women are shown to be victims of neglect in crucial areas of physical and mental well-being, girl child education and reproductive health.

In Dalpat Chauhan's *Ba Nu Mrutyu* (The Death of Mother) Suresh does nothing to free his wife Shobha and his mother from the constricting situation they are in, till the ailing mother passes away. Whereas Shobha is driven to desperation with a mentally unfit mother-in-law to look after, it is as if Suresh has no duty to discharge. He muses indifferently: "As mother's health ... Oh! Her madness is getting worse so is Shobha's irritability and hostility. It is very difficult to say who is mad at which moment" (translation mine).

B. Kesharshivam's *Gomti* is about the horrific end, which the young and tender girl Gomti faces. Andal N. notes:

> Education has been identified as the panacea which will enable girls and women with the means to initiate a

> process of social change ... Socially empowering them through education is equally important. The girl child not only has the right to survive, but also the right to be free of malnutrition, ignorance, disease and poverty ... A comprehensive movement has to be activated to transform the cultural values and institutions that negatively affect girl children. We can no longer silently consent to a generation of our daughters growing into physically, intellectually and socially disinherited adults (Andal, 76).

The above quotation serves very well to be juxtaposed with Gomti's plight under Ganesh, her uncaring and selfish father. He gets her engaged at the age of six. His employer's advice on the ill-effects of child marriage on the reproductive health of the girl child does not have any effect at all on Ganesh. Ganesh sits puffing beedis while his daughter waters the freshly cemented walls and runs all errands for him. He also sends her as a domestic help to four houses in the neighbourhood. Ganesh's employer Ramesh is shocked to find that Ganesh idles away with the excuse of having T.B. while both he and his son Bijal are given to heavy drinking. Under these circumstances, the family often goes to bed hungry. Gomti's misfortune culminates in her rape by her brother's friend. When her prospective in-laws call off the engagement her father sells her off.

Ganesh's act of selling his daughter is an extreme case of misuse of patriarchal power. The reader sympathizes with Gomti for being victimized by her own father more than for becoming a victim of rape. Once the initial shock is overcome, one wonders, which target readership is aimed at by the writer of the story. With the given portrayal of the girl child the story has nothing to imply to upper caste readers. In the case of dalit readers, there is hardly any moral or positive message to offer. Is it then a case of exoticizing dalit way of life?

A reading of Pravin Gadhvi's *Marad Kasumbal Rang Chadhe* (Machismo) is attempted in the light of the power principle inherent in Jeff Hearn's remark below:

> Structured relations of oppression exist in the domination of labour powers and appropriation of their products. The

> characteristic form is men's oppression of women's various reproductive labour powers.
>
> In addition, men do have agency. This is so in two senses. Firstly, men are *agents* of oppression ... Secondly, men *can act differently, independently; even contrary to the demands of structured relations* (Hearn, 96).

The story graphically captures the elements of domination and subordination in terms of the upper caste male's 'hegemonic masculinity' vis-à-vis the dalit male's 'complicit masculinity' and the dalit woman's 'complicit feminity'. The dalit woman is explicitly compliant both to the upper caste male as well as the dalit male.

> The male protagonist Dudo is a drum player. His wife and daughter went to Babooji's field for weeding while Dudo sat at home tightening the strings of his drum. He had never held a sickle in his life. It was for his wife and daughter to bring home firewood and cook. As for Dudo, he was the king of the drum, a devotee of the tamboora (translation mine).

Once when Dudo's wife is down with fever she sends their daughter to the field alone. The girl is raped by Babooji. When Dudo's wife confides in him about the untoward incident, he goes beserk and begins to abuse his wife calling her a 'bitch' and their daughter a 'whore'. He is mad with rage and breaks his poor wife's back for no fault of her's. He grabs his daughter by her hair and smashes her bones. Thereafter, he confronts Babooji in his wrath. Ironically enough, the writer describes it by saying, "Kalka (Goddess Kali) was invoked in him". Dudo is charred to death by Babooji. However, it is the dalit women who are the worst hit both at the macro-social level and the micro-interpersonal level.

Clearly, dalit male writers do not practice what they preach. Their short stories contribute to reinforcement of stereotypes. Most of these writers are educated and bourgeois, therefore distanced/different from their poverty/exploitation experiencing caste fellows. This is reflected in their extradiegetic-heterodiegetic mode of narration (i.e., narrators who are in no sense participants in the stories they narrate). Thus, it can be said by way of conclusion that in the six, dalit male-authored short stories discussed in the course of this paper:

(1) Women characters are defined in relation to the men they interact with and never on their own accord.
(2) They are hardly considered to be real human beings with real needs, feelings and desires entirely their own. They are not allowed an existence (portrayed) outside the 'culturally given/adopted/valued'.
(3) The portrayal of women characters reflects their position in society. A great injustice is integral to the representation/articulation of dalit women's experiences and reality since the male dalit writers are not native speakers of the situation. What happens to the women's perspective?
(4) Dalit men themselves are agents of dalit women's oppression and not their emancipation. Dalit short stories in which dalit men are supportive and encouraging in arenas where power lies with them are hard to come by.

Dalit women suffer double oppression, i.e., patriarchal and caste oppression. This is explicit in G. Arunima's observation below:

> While within the home or 'private' sphere Dalit women may suffer from verbal and physical abuse at the hands of their fathers and husbands, outside in the 'public' realm, forced, unpaid and often indentured labour conditions are compounded by sexual harassment, and a real risk to physical life (Basu, 218-19).

Thus, it can be concluded that dalit women are the dalit of dalits, i.e., oppressed by the upper castes and dalit men as well. In their struggles in the public sphere as well as the private sphere, it is as *women* that they are the worst hit by gender bias. Their being *women* makes them the more downtrodden within the dalit community. The foregoing discussion of the portrayal of women by male writers in Gujarati dalit short stories clearly indicates that the dalit woman's oppression is in Gail Omvedt's words 'specific' and 'simultaneous'. The specificity and simultaneity of the double oppression of dalit women is that they are *marginalized victims of the caste-gender nexus* in which their lives are caught. Since the two forces are inextricably mixed, they have to be combated together. The social implications of this two-fold struggle of dalit women's emancipation are very and many and could form the subject of a separate paper. However, it may suffice to say at this juncture that no one movement, i.e., either anti-caste or anti-patriarchy, would alone work for the dalit woman's cause or question. Both factors have to be combined in order to grant them an existence of dignity. It was Gandhiji's dream to see a Harijan girl as the President of India. Given the foregoing it remains to be seen whether and when his dream will come true.

Works Cited

Basu, Tapan (ed.) 2002. *Translating Caste*, New Delhi: Katha.

Burke, Rupalee (ed.) 2003. *B. Kesharshivam Ni Nari Chetna Ni Navlikao*, Gandhinagar: Bhargav Omguru.

Burke, Rupalee and Darshana Trivedi (tr. & ed.) 2000. *The Silver Lining*, Ahmedabad: Gujarat Dalit Sahitya Akademi.

Chauhan, Dalpat, 2002. *Munjharo: Short Stories*, Ahmedabad: Harsh Prakashan.

Davies, Kathy et al. (eds.) 1991. *The Gender of Power*, London: Sage Publications.

Gadhvi, Pravin, 1996. *Antarvyatha: A Collection of Short Stories*, Ahmedabad: Gurjar Granth Ratna Karyalaya.

Hearn, Jeff, 1987. *The Gender of Oppression: Men, Masculinity and the Critique of Marxism*, Great Britain: Wheatsheaf Books.

Kauffman, Linda (ed.) 1990. *Gender and Theory: Dialogues on Feminist Criticism*, Oxford: Basil Blackwell.

N. Andal, 2002. *Women and Indian Society: Options and Constraints*, Jaipur and New Delhi: Rawat Publications.

Trivedi, Darshana and Rupalee Burke (tr. & eds.) 2000. *Tongues of Fire*, Ahmedabad: Gujarat Dalit Sahitya Akademi.

18

Powerless Matriarchs: A Hidden Truth

SMITHA SIVADASAN

Researcher, Kerala

The hunger for power is inherent in all and therefore power politics has become a part of our life. Man's desire for power and thereby a comfortable life in the society gave rise to patriarchal culture. It is his selfish motive that resulted in the oppression of women. Though gender-specific roles make her different, she is not weak. The greater physical strength and money helped man to gain dominance and superiority over woman. He had created the 'ideal woman' image so that she remains submissive and silent. Moreover, the customs and rituals are made in such a manner that the men can retain their authority in all walks of life. Therefore, it has become necessary that the women should break their silence and raise their voice against oppression. Feminism, as a social movement, tries to eradicate gender inequality by promoting women's rights, interests and issues in the society.

John Stuart Mill, an English philosopher, believed that the liberty of women is necessary to the development of society.

Like most Victorians, he too believed that the family was the model and the source of all social behaviour, and he maintained that the masculine domination of the family was a corrupting influence, making boys selfish and girls abject. In his most controversial work, *The Subjection of Women* (1869), he wrote:

> ". . . that the principle which regulates the existing social relations between the two sexes – the legal subordination of one sex to the other – is wrong in itself, and now one of the chief hindrances to human improvement; and that it ought to be replaced by a principle of equality, admitting no power or privilege on the one side, nor disability on the other."

Many writers from Virginia Woolf onwards have believed that if women have money, they can become powerful. Is it a reality? Does the acquisition of wealth make the Nair women in the so-called matriarchal community powerful? The objective of this paper is to explore this paradoxical situation with reference to the works of a well-known writer of Malayalam literature.

M.T. Vasudevan Nair (henceforth, MT) is a prolific writer and has written a number of short stories, nine novels, few essays, travelogues and scripts for films. He has a unique style of writing and the stories are narrated in a very simple manner. The innumerable awards he had received include Gyanpith, 1996 and Padmabhushan, 2005.

MT's writing in general depicts the degeneration of Nair *tharawads*. The characters and situations are portrayed in a very realistic manner and that characteristic feature makes his works very valuable to the readers. Mostly, the character may be the writer himself or the people around him consisting of his friends and relatives. The background of his works is the Koodalloor village where he is born and brought up. In this sense, he can be considered as a regional writer. His Koodalloor can be compared to the Wessex of Thomas Hardy or Malgudi of R.K. Narayan. In the preface to his collection of short stories, he says:

> "In my literary life, I am indebted to Koodalloor more than anything else where Velayuthettan, Govindankutty, the gambler Konthunni uncle and Meenakshiedathi belong. My dear characters include father, mother, brothers, relatives, acquaintances and neighbours" (6).

Above all, most of the stories of MT revolve around life in Nair families to which he also belongs. The Nairs had a pride of place in the history of Kerala as they had a military tradition. They come under Shudras in the caste hierarchy. There are about sixty-four sub-castes and the most commonly among them are Menon, Pillai, Kurup, Nambiar etc.

The family unit of Nair community is called a *tharawad,* which is a joint family consisting of an ancestress and her descendants in the family line including sons and daughters. Their typical house consists of a quadri-lateral building known as *Nalukettu,* which encloses a central yard. On the basis of tradition, separate portions of the building are reserved for women, men and the *karanavan.* A special feature of their system is that the women continue to live in their respective houses even after marriage and the husband make visit to them.

The Nair community in Kerala is known to follow a unique system of property inheritance known as matriliny wherein the women inherit the family property and the family line is continued through female members. Though there is no satisfactory explanation, there are quite a few theories that throw light on the origin of matriliny. According to one theory, the Nairs adopted matriliny because of their respect for women inspired by the worship of Hindu Goddesses like Kali, Durga, Lakshmi and Saraswati. Another theory states that the Nairs being a martial race, the men were away from their homes most of the time and therefore the women had to assume control of their family affairs. This controlling position might have paved the way for matriliny.

Yet another theory states that it is the Nair-Namboodiri *sambandam* that gave rise to matriliny. In a *sambandam,* a Namboodiri man cohabits with a Nair woman without marriage. But, except for the sexual intimacy, the rules of castes and the differences thereof are strictly observed. History reveals that the system of sambandam originated as the Namboodiris wanted to maintain their supremacy in the society. As only the eldest son of a Namboodiri family can marry from the community to avoid problems of inheritance, the rest of the sons are allowed to have sambandam with Nair women. The Nairs were made to believe that the Namboodiris were Godly people and it was their duty to please them by offering them their women. The scriptures too came to their rescue. The Brahmins realized that they were free to have sexual relationship with Shudra women as they could not have the status of wife according to the sacred law. Pleasure without burden was their motive and the Nairs regarded it as a privilege. The Nair women used to have many such relationships and therefore it became imperative that they should remain in their respective houses. Moreover, the children too grow with their mothers, as the fathers do not have any obligations towards them. In this light, such relationships might have led to matrilineal system.

The influence of patriarchy is so much rooted in our culture that whether it is matriliny or patriliny, the women are always under the supremacy of man. In the case of Nair community, the only difference is that the power is in the hands of the woman's brother known as *karanavan* (uncle) instead of her husband and it is passed on to the *ananthiravans* (*marumakkal*) in the order of seniority. That is why, this system is also termed as *Marumakkathayam*.

It is observed that the female characters in general are powerless and lead a life of suffering in the joint family set-up of Nair *tharawads*. Still, they sacrifice everything for the well-being of the family members, especially children. Dr. Rati, in her article "MT's Female Characters" writes: "Most of the mother characters in MT's world are just toys in the hands of fate and society" (Thampan, 46). They are submissive in nature and do not question or resist the authority, but accept everything as fate. In the words of T.M. Premachandran,

> "... The men have destroyed the hopes and aspirations of women for their own selfishness and pleasure ..." (Basheer, 292).

Parukkutty, the heroine of "Nalukettu" is a victim of male supremacy. Her uncle's attempt in forcing her to marry a man of his choice is the beginning of her suffering. Though she has a lover and wishes to marry him, she does not open her mouth in front of her uncle. Her mother too stands powerless. When she realizes Parukkutty's dilemma, she can only say: "What can I do if Kunjeeshan decides?" (34). Uncle's decision becomes final in all matters of their lives and the women are supposed to follow them without any objection. After Parukkutty leaves her house with her lover, her uncle declares her dead and performs the last rites. Therefore, Parukkutty, who has lived in luxury, is then left with no choice but to work as a domestic servant to earn her livelihood. The male authority of her family pays no heed to her suffering and she suffers in silence like a typical Indian woman. These women do not even look at the face of men, but only at their feet.

In the novel "Kaalam" too the women characters are seen to lead a life performing their traditional roles. Sethu's mother's advice to her sister, "A woman should remain submissive to men" (2) reveals the inherent attitude among womenfolk in those families. The girl children are conditioned in that manner from the very beginning and therefore never attempts to question or resist the oppression of male power.

Malu, in "Kuttyedathi", opts for death as she realizes that it is not possible for her to marry the man she loves. In "Nurungunna Sringalakal", Sekharan's mother is a victim of male infidelity. She lives her whole life with tears in her eyes as her husband leaves her for another woman. When she argues, he simply tells her: "You mind your own business. All that will happen in the case of men" (SS, 74).

"Karkitakam" depicts the dilemma of women when they are forced to feast the guests even when there is hardly anything in the house. The helplessness of a mother when her child wishes to celebrate his birthday is presented in "Oru Pirannalinte Orma". When Kunhikrishnan's mother makes a request for some more rice to make pudding as an offering, to her brother, he beats her and shouts: "When do the women start arguing?" (SS, 102). The women neither have the power to take nor to ask for things. They are supposed to manage with whatever they get from their brothers.

My reading of MT's works has revealed the fact that the women characters are denied of any power and they are forced to remain tradition-bound. They are not given any power in decision-making processes and the whole system works according to the decisions of the male authority. Even, the acquisition of wealth does not help them to become powerful. Though regarded as matriarchal system, the women here too are as powerless as in the patriarchal society. What a paradox! It appears that their powerlessness is not natural but mainly the result of oppression by man. The socio-cultural conditions prevalent in the society too are against women and a hindrance to their freedom and progress. Besides, the women's attempt to maintain the image of Sita or Savitri who are ideal to the Indian mind is also responsible for their condition. Therefore, it becomes necessary that the women should be empowered and the men change their mindset so that a social change takes place. I conclude with the hope that we will be able to live in a world where there is no gender bias and the women too get power and respect as that of men.

Works Cited

Atrey, Mukta and Viney Kirpal, *Shashi Deshpande: A Feminist Study of her Fiction*, Delhi: BRPC, 1998.

Basheer, M.M. (ed.) *M.T. Story and Theme*, Trichur, Current Books, 1996.

Hiremath, R.C., *Women in a Changing World*, Jaipur, Pointer Publications, 2002.

Jain, Naresh K., "Tradition, Modernity and Change", in *Women in Indo-Anglian Fiction*, Manohar, 1998.

Menon, Sankara T.C., *Chandu Menon*, New Delhi: Sahitya Academy, 1974.

Nair, Vasudevan M.T., *Kaalam.* (K) Trichur, Current Books, 2003.

— *Nalukettu* (NK) Trichur, Current Books, 2003.

— Selected Stories (SS) Trichur, Current Books, 2002.

Noopur, Kulshresta Indira, *Women in Search of Identity,* Delhi: BRPC, 1999.

Parampil, K.T., "Matrilineal System Among Malayalis", *Caravan Reprints,* Set 1, New Delhi, pp. 79-86.

— "Matriliny Among Malayalis", *Caravan Reprints,* Set 1, New Delhi, pp. 87-100.

Showalter, Elaine, *Women's Liberation and Literature,* New York: Harcourt Brace Jovanovich, Inc., 1971.

Thampan, M.R., *M.T.yude Sargaprapancham,* Trivandrum: Kerala Bhasha Institute, 1997.

Valsala, "Oru kadalkshobhathinte Theerathu", *Mathrubhumi Weekly,* Kozhikode, July 27, 2003, pp. 12-17.

19

Staging Resistance: A Feminist Exploration of Women's Theatre in India

KAVITA PATEL

Faculty, Smt. Sadguna C.U. Arts College for Girls, Ahmedabad

Drama of life and the dramatic are matters close to women's hearts. One would assume that drama as an expressive mode would have close affinity with women. However, cultural history, both eastern and western, tells us otherwise. Drama and theatre, as cultural products, hold different places in the history of women's writing and cultural participation and a reason for that is to be found in the concept of 'genre'. In the history of women's writing, especially in the feminist critique, 'gender' and 'genre' are frequently paired as coming from the same root. That their connection to cultural history is almost as intimate as their etymology, is supported by the fact that women have had for their use fewer traditional genres than men always had and continue to have. The generic classification also institutionalizes the culture canon – the so-called classical tradition – the bulk of which comprises the work of men.

As playwrights, women scarcely figure on the literary map. They seem to have shied away from writing plays though they have excelled in all other genres. Women's voices have been heard in the dramatic space only in mimicry – repeating the words written for them by men and performing the roles envisioned for them by the male imagination. They have not sought to script their own lines. The first professional women playwright was Britian's Aphra Behn. Women playwrights in India contributed to the genre from the late 19th century though not in a significant way. The 1940s and 1950s recorded some noteworthy attempts. In the social history of Indian theatre, women have been closely and continuously associated with traditional theatrical and dramatic performances which never really lost touch with the genesis in rituals. The forms like *jatra, tamasha, chhau, lavni, bhavai, nautanki, ramleela, koodiyattam, pandavani* and *rasleela,* provide a kind of 'active culture'. The forces of change in terms of industrialization and resultant demographic shifts, the experience of imperialism and the freedom struggle – all prepared the way for the development of new kinds of cultural expression that marked a rupture from the past.

Modern Indian drama grew out of this milieu of conflict: between cultures and social hierarchies, between economic and political sectors, and among the ideological groups. Pervasive was the spirit of inquiry and of introspection. According to G.P. Deshpande, "Drama became, in a manner of speaking, the first art-form in modern India which was secular, it moved from the 'divine' imagination of the rishi… And the first democratic art-form of modern urban India" (2002: 5). The post-independence Indian drama has through the five decades grown more varied, rich and diverse in content and semiotics and draws upon myths, history, folklore, politics and society for material.

Literatures of the regions present a more varied spectrum. For my study, I have taken few Bhasha women playwrights whose plays are introduced first time in English. The playwrights choosen for the study are Usha Ganguli, Mamta

Sagar, Varsha Adalja, C.S. Lakshmi and Rasheed Jahan. Women's relationships, their struggles, and their journey towards emancipation constitute the thematic interest that all the playwrights share. These plays are written by women of diverse background and worldview. The title *Staging Resistance* plainly means to accept or to oppose. But, the underlying concern is with the creation of identities and a sense of self worth. The notion being highlighted in these plays is the way women are disempowered and negated at a profound level of their personal sense of being. The preoccupation of the playwrights is to expose the hidden aspects of past and exploring their consequences for contemporary experience; the re-interpretation of history, mythology and older texts; adaptations of folk themes; and the propagation as well as interrogation of ideology. The texts introduce various situations and issues, present women confronting difficult challenges down the years, within different social situations and changing contexts.

These plays dramatize women's resistance to social pressures, which push them to circumscribe their sphere of activity. They present a dialogic space, public and subversive, for the enactment of struggle of women against the human relationships that entangle them. The motivating spirit of resistance is manifest at various levels. We can look forward to these playwrights as assuming multiple points of view, new languages and new forms to articulate their experiences. Taken together as Women's Drama, they unfold as dramatization of narratives, interactions, recollections of female characters who refuse – or at least resist – falling into a silent consent of oppression.

This is what Usha Ganguli has tried to project in her play "Antaryatra: The Journey Within". Usha Ganguli is an established name in the world of Bengali theatre. Her solo performance, Antaryatra, is an intriguing experiment in the form of a rich narrative weaving autobiographical introspection, the voice of famous women theatrical characters and views on women's role in theatre. The whole play is in the form of interactions, between the narrator and her woman characters. The format of the play is rather non-linear, earthy, touching lives. The play tries to move the spectators with its realism towards identification with or recognition of emotional and psychological conflicts. To supplement this view, I quote the character of Munia in "Guria Ghar":

> *Muniu*: My first Identity is that I'm a human being. And I must strive to become a complete human being. I know that most people will accept what you say as the truth because these things are written in good books. But I must think of something to be able to live. I must think of the meaning of every word myself. I cannot use the words of others as my own. (73)

One more character named Mrinal in "Strir Patra" shares the same feeling but expresses it with a strong voice:

> I am not afraid of your narrow lanes any more... You kept me covered under the blanket of dark custom. But within a short time Bindu pierced through the darkness and discovered me...I am a free mind. Your Mejo Bou is dead. You think that I am planning to kill myself? Have no fear. I shall never use that old joke on me. I am not one to die easily. I have just started living...(84)

Mamta G. Sagar, a prominent writer in Kannada theatre, excels as an upcoming playwright and poet. She is deeply interested in theatre and has directed plays. Her play "Mayye Bhara Manave Bhara" [The Swing of Desire] is about Manasa – a wife and a mother – who overcomes all obstacles that get in the way of her becoming a successful dancer. The play highlights the emotional and psychological conflicts faced by Manasa. The conflict is in choosing, selecting the path, a voice within asserting to adhere or confirm to norms. Manasa's resistance leads her towards a resolution, a desired state. Here I quote Manasa's words which display her desires:

> *Manasa*: I want to be independent. I want to be a star... a butterfly dancing in the sun... I want to fly away, spreading my wings far and wide....I want to chase my dreams. (243)

Manasa, adamently carves to achieve her goal as a dancer. Pratap, her husband, finds her role as a dancer worthless. This conflict leads them towards a break-up. This point turns out to be the final resolution of Manasa's internal conflicts as she very plainly says:

> *Manasa*: I know that ! No matter what a man does, society is ready to support and defend him. But for a woman, the smallest mistakes become monstrous. She is insulted and thrown out of the society. She belongs nowhere, has nowhere to go, no place to live. Now, I am back to what I love most – my dancing. I dance for my satisfaction. I dance because I wish to. (246)

My third playwright is Varsha Adalja, a Gujarati woman. Her play "Mandodari" presents a woman's struggle with fate and the hovering clouds of war. The mythological character of Mandodari from the *Ramayana* becomes the mouthpiece of all wives and mothers suffering from the battles that men fight to satisfy their greed and their egoistic pursuits of love and lust. The character of Mandodari in the play gives way to a new shade of feminism. In the play we find her resistance at stake at three levels: as a woman, a wife and a mother. Her sole attempt is to prevent something by action or argument. As she argues with Kaaldevta:

> *Kaal*: I have come to destroy this golden Lanka.
>
> *Man*: Who can remain calm and undisturbed and watch the destruction of everything one holds dear? What woman can remain silent and watch the destruction of her beloved husband? I shall not allow this happen. (101)

Later, when she comes to know about the abduction of Seeta by Ravana, she addresses Lankesh and says:

> *Mand*: Lankesh, a woman is not an object to be used to settle enemity nor a victim of lust. Listen to me, my lord, please free Seeta....(105)

Not as a queen but as an ordinary woman Mandodari sympathises Seeta's state and talks to her:

> *Seeta*: Please help me, Mandodari, please persuade your husband to release me send me back to my Rama.
>
> *Mand*: That is impossible, now Janaki.
>
> *Seeta*: Your are a woman. Can't you understand the anguish of another woman?
>
> *Mand*: Here, woman is an object of pleasure... a mere plaything, to be used like a piece of linen that can be thrown away when it is soiled. To have power over woman is the right of man.
>
> *Seeta*: Do woman get no respect in asura culture? Among Aryans, the woman is worshipped as a goddess.
>
> *Mand*: O Seeta, the daughter-in-law of the Suryavamshis, don't you think there is ambiguity in the treatment of women as goddesses? (109)

Finally, when the news of Ravana's death is conveyed to her, she reveals to Kaaldevta:

> *Mand*: I was waiting for my lord's death. How would you understand the agony of being the wife of such a lustful yet blind man? The arrow that killed Ravana actually released his soul and gave the egoistic man his salvation though I am widowed now, I am a happy woman. (114)

The fourth playwright is C.S. Lakshmi or Ambai. Her play "Crossing The River" [Aatraik Kadaththal] presents a symbolical enactment of a woman's song of anguish and suffering and her desire for freedom from oppressive social norms. The play is about "a Sita and her appealing song". Whether she is Sita of *Ramayana* or Sita from contemporary society, the condition of her subjugation remains unaltered. But, still the quest is for the exploration of space. I quote from the text:

> *Sita*: I am Sita
> I am Sita
> Who
> Entered the forest

Got imprisoned
In the forest
And is now roaming
In the forest

Because of love,
Lust and politics.
I am Sita, the pawn
I am Sita, the cheated
I am Sita
Who has
Nothing.
What difference does it make?
Which Sita I am
Which is the real Sita and
Which the false?
I am Sita
That authority creates.
I am Sita brought up
With words,
Be this way
Stand this way
Sit this way
Lie this way
Think this way
I am you
All of you
All of you asking questions
I am the body of your questions

There is strengths left still.

I shall cross the river
I shall cross the river
I see the new world
To assume a new form
To create a new Rajya. (434)

The end of the play gives the feeling that the writer celebrates the great adventure women's lives can be. It offers new modes of perception, new lenses through which to view the past, respect the difference, and work towards an empowerment based on human possibilities that have been ignored.

My fifth playwright is Rasheed Jahan, a dedicated social reformer-activist and a prolific writer, although her life was cut short in 1952 and has left an indelible mark on the literature of the world. Her play "Aurat" [Woman] lay bare many of the cruelties imposed upon women with the sanction of society and religion. The play is about a woman named Fatima, whose husband Atiqullah – a Maulvi – desires to marry for the second time as none of their children lived:

> *Atiq*: One can at least try one's best to improve the situation. Look, I am nearly forty years old and I haven't a single child living. Children are the support of our old age. That is why Shariat has ordered that when a woman is found to be barren or if her children aren't alive then the man should marry again.
>
> *Fatima*: This is the first time I've heard the Shariat law about children not being alive. It is enough if you don't start making Shariat laws of your own. God forbid, I'm not barren. I've given birth to ten-twelve children, live or dead. What can I do if none of them lived? Is it my fault should I be punished for that? (518)

Here, we can see Fatima's resistance over, existence of something, a precondition that there is something against which she has to resist. At the end of the play, Fatima does not come out as a helpless woman. Throughout the play, we feel the power politics of patriarchy but Fatima resists and strongly expresses her rage:

> *Fatima*: What illness will I have but the one that you have infected me with? You have killed all my children. I'll do exactly what I want and go for treatment whenever and wherever I want. Nobody can stop me now. I've had enough of your orders. Be careful and sit down. If you want to keep your self respect intact, then take care. I warn you, if you try to hit me again, be ready to face the consequences. He pretends to be a man…wants to marry a second time! (536)

To sum up, I would like to say that each of the playwright try to explore the artistic and social territories of Indian life and are mesmerizing in their depth and detail and also in their covert and overt violence which after all, forms a part of woman's daily experience. They set out to make the audience review the past and present from a different perspective, to see that social or political order is not 'natural' but constructed in favour of men by men. But the plays also set out to celebrate women, to be positive, challenging us with ideas about the need to change society. These plays focus on sharing of experiences, to be able to strengthen, transform, and create new horizons of expectations.

Works Cited

Bassnett, Susan, "Towards a Theory of Women's Theatre", *Linguistic and Literary Studies*, 1984.

Deshpande, G.P., "Theatre of Modernity", A Celebration of Modernity, *Theatre India*, May 2002.

Gargi, Balwant, *Folk Theatre of India*, New Delhi: Asia Fine Books, 2000.

Mukherjee, Tutun, *Staging Resistance Plays by Women in Translation*, Oxford University Press, 2005.

Showalter, Elaine, *A Literature of Their Own*, London: Virago, 1978.

20

Psychodynamics of Female Creativity: Looking Back at Gangasati

DARSHANA TRIVEDI

Reader in English, School of Languages, Gujarat University, Ahmedabad

The present paper is divided into two sections. While the first section of the paper examines various aspects, which constitutes gynocentricism, the second section analyzes the life and writings of Gangasati – a medieval Gujarati poet in the light of gynocentricism. The conventional reading of Gangasati's poems consider her as a devotional poet, but it is interesting to note that Gangasati's poems have some significant traits of gynocentricism during the medieval period when Western feminist critics were not aware about any feminist theory.

I

Elaine Showalter distinguishes terms like *feminine*, *feminist* and *female* in her milestone work *A Literature of Their Own*. According to Showalter, the feminine or imitative phase covers the period of 1840-1880. Women writers of this period tried to fit themselves in patriarchal prescription of a 'good woman'. The female portrayed by women writers are happy to perform their domestic duties, aspiring for marriage and attempting to look beautiful to charm men. Women writers have imitated style, ideas, values and culture prescribed by men.

The second phase, which Showalter calls feminist phase or reactive phase, covers the period of 1880-1920. This is a phase of protest against the standards and values of established patriarchy. Women have become vocal about their rights and space. They have asserted freedom of mind and body from subjugation of men and have begun to expose the exploitation and oppression bore by them at the hands of men. They have questioned the standards and norms set for them by patriarchy and have ventured into the areas earlier prohibited for women.

The final phase, which Showalter calls female, is a phase of 'self-discovery' where in the women turn to concentrate on themselves without depending upon their opposite sex. There is no assertion of equality but acceptance of the "Poetics of Difference". The third phase has more or less the traits of gynocentricism.

The roots of gynocentric theory lies in Patricia Mayer Spacks' book *The Female Imagination*. Spacks has discussed a few feminist theories like that of propagated by Virginia Woolf, Simone de Beauvior, Mary Ellman and Kate Millet. *The Female Imagination* changed the course of literary history and criticism. It was the first attempt made by feminist critic to analyze how women's experiences shaped the women's creative expression. According to Showalter, "with the publication of this book, the premise of feminist thinking shifted from the 'equality' to the 'difference'. This is the first women-centred book, concerning women as a writer as well as readers. Elaine Showalter, who felt the need of a special term to name such a specialized discourse, noticed this. This shift of the centre of feminist criticism from revisionary readings to an investigation of literature created by women is the second mode of feminist criticism for which Showalter coined the term 'gynocentricism'. According to her, the second mode of feminist criticism is

> the history, style, themes, genres, and structures of writing by women; the psychodynamics of female creativity; the trajectory of the individual or collective female career; and the evolution and laws of a female literary tradition. No English term exists for such a specialized critical discourse, and so I have invented the 'gynocritics' (Showalter, 242).

The gynocritics have taken upon themselves the task to see women's writing as a distinct literary group. They work upon the characteristics, uniqueness and distinctiveness of the way women write. While discussing about 'gynocritics', K.K. Ruthven in *Feminist Literary Study* writes:

> It is commonly agreed that negative task of exposing androcentric bases against women in general and women in particular ought to be complemented by the more positive task of defining the specificity of women's writing (Ruthven, 63).

This 'positive task' is the orientation of the gynocritics. They are moving beyond the programme of dismantling of the androcentric culture towards a goal of rebuilding. The main endeavour of gynocritic is not to look for "equality but difference". According to Showalter, the main agenda of gynocritics includes the following:

The first task of gynocentric criticism is to plot the "precise cultural focus of female literary identity and to describe the forces that intersect an individual woman writer's cultural field" (Showalter, 200). Gynocritics map out the exact cultural and social determinants, which form the crux of a creative woman's identity. The second important agenda of a gynocritic is that writing is an activity well influenced by various economic, political and social factors. So, the gynocritics would work to situate women writers with respect to the variables of literary culture.

Gynocritics endeavour to retrieve old texts, written by women, lost with a passage of time, due to ignorance and disregard. They aspire to locate such texts and wish to place them in literary tradition. This would fill in the gaps in the female literary history and tradition and the author would be foregrounded in the literary tradition.

Promoting 'sisterhood' and a sense of 'community' among women writers is the main premise of gynocritics. The idea of 'sisterhood' stands as a symbol of rejection of the isolation and the powerlessness women felt because of the dominant and intensely oppressive patriarchal set-up. Gynocritics believe that women have a different world of experience, which they share as a community. Women need to come together to share and support each other's ideas and concerns.

"Poetics of Difference" is the foundation of gynocriticism. Gynocritics never desire for a 'sexless text'. As Showalter writes in *Feminist Criticism in the Wilderness*:

> ... a few years ago feminist critics thought we were on a pilgrimage to the promised land in which gender would lose its power, in which all texts would be sexless and equal, like angels. But the more precisely we understand the specificity of women's writing not as a transient by product of sexism but as a fundamental and continually determining reality, the more clearly we realize that we have misperceived our destination. We may never reached the promised land at all for when feminist critics see our task as the study of women's writing, we realize that the land promised to us is not the serenely undifferentiated universality of texts but the tumultuous and intriguing wilderness of difference itself (Showalter, 201).

Gynocritics desire "a promise land" where they can flourish independently as individuals.

II

Like her contemporaries Meerabai, Janabai and Krishnabai, Gangasati belongs to the Bhakti tradition. The Bhakti movement flourished as a revolt against the domination of the upper castes and the lifeless rituals of Hinduism, practised by the Brahmin priests. Bhakti poets were a group of lower caste people like washer men, leather workers, oil pressers, stone cutters, potters, weavers, silversmiths, artisans, women – who decided to challenge the prevalent power structure established by Brahmins. The Bhakti movement was an open challenge to the graphocentricity of Brahmins. The sole aim of Bhakti movement was based on the point of view that the path of devotion has no barriers of caste or sex. As Susie Tharu and K. Lalita observe:

> The women poets of the Bhakti Movement did not have to seek the institutionalized spaces religion provided to express themselves, the women's poetry moved from the court and the temple to the open spaces of the field, the work place and the common woman's hearth (Tharu and Lalita, 57).

Bhakti poets wrote in the regional languages, deliberately breaking the literary and religious hold of Sanskrit. They addressed their popular lyrics to people in languages the people spoke and could understand. As Kabir says: "Sanskrit is the stagnant water of the Lord's private well where as the spoken language is the rippling water of the running stream" (Tharu, 57). Most regional literatures locate their beginnings in the poetry of the Bhakti saints. The Bhaktas set their poetry in familiar contexts and found their imagery in the everyday lives of working people. As a result, they drew their symbolism primarily from non-Vedic sources. Their verses cultivate a rough-hewn directness.

It is surprising to note that a large number of Bhakti poets were women. Majority of Bhakti poets chafed at the strictures of the household and family. Lal Ded's songs describe her mother-in-law's taunts and the numbing triviality of domestic chores. Meerabai chafes at the restricted life in her husband's home. There is evidence that women had to struggle to find acceptance even within this movement. Women saints were often put to test in a major debate with the male leaders. Many women poets struggled hard to establish their identity within patriarchal set-up.

Gangasati, a medieval Gujarati poet, was born and grew up in this hostile atmosphere. The case of Gangasati was slightly different from her contemporaries like Meerabai, Janabai, Bahinabai, Ratanbai and Krishnabai. Though Meerabai is the best known of Gujarati saint poets, several other women like Gangasati and Ratanbai belonged to this devotional tradition and composed their lyrics in Gujarati.

Gangasati was the eldest daughter of Bhaijibhai Sarvaiya and Roopaliba. She was born in Rajpara, near Palitana in Bhavnagar district. Her original name was Hiraba or Hirba. Gangasati or Gangabai was not her original name. Looking at her bhakti, the devotees gave her a name Gangasati as per the convention of that society. Gangasati is only a form of address like Meerabai or Janabai given to her by patriarchy. The term Ganga or sati is not associated with the conventional meaning of the words. She had not chosen her name but only accepted the title given to her by her devotees as a mark of respect.

Gangasati belonged to a very cultured and religious family. She had observed all the Vedic/non-Vedic rituals like growing trees, looking after cows, and respecting and serving saints and guests. Thus, she was already deeply religious when she married Kahal Sangh or Kahalubha of Samthiyala. Gangasati brought Panki or Panbai, the daughter of Hamirbhai Khawas, as a companion to help her in household affairs. Later on, Panbai married to Ajay Singh or Ajubha, the son of Gangasati and Kahalsangh.

The married life of Gangasati and Kahalsangh was different from her contemporaries. Kahalsangh considered Gangasati as his *ardhangini* or *sahadharmacharini* almost an equal and took her advice in the family matters. Fortunately, Gangasati was not the victim of cruelty and torture of her in-laws. Both Kahalsangh and Gangasati progressed together on the path of bhakti. Their home became a centre for religious discourses and meditations and meeting place for the saints. When Kahalsangh had decided to take *samadhi,* he advised Gangasati:

> You can't join me; still you have to perform your duties towards Panbai. Give her the knowledge of Bhakti. First empower her through knowledge and then follow me if you wish.

These words of Kahalsangh are proof enough of patriarchy's rare and positive support for woman's empowerment. We have to keep in mind that Gangasati was born in a Rajput family where the birth of a girl child is considered as a curse even today. Listening to the words of her husband, Gangasati, a mother-in-law, decides to strengthen Panbai – a daughter-in-law through words. The relationship between Gangasati and Panbai is a rare and unique example of the relationship between mother-in-law and daughter-in-law in India. Gangasati is also an example of decentralization of power within the boundaries of the power structure. She decides to impart the wealth of knowledge to her daughter-in-law, which unlocks the complicated problems of life. Here, she becomes an example of Derrida's concept of non-logo centricity.

After her husband's *samadhi,* Gangasati wrote fifty-two *bhajans* (some scholars believe that they are forty in number) all of them addressed to Panbai. Critics consider her *bhajans* as "Gramopanishad", i.e., "the Upanishadas in colloquial language."

Here is a woman addressing another woman in woman's language. Thus, Gangasati has established the female tradition of writing in the medieval society. Her *bhajans* mark the stages by which the devotee advances in the religious experience, stages by which she seeks to lead Panbai. Gangasati relies on yogic exercises for the attainment of transcendental experience. In her famous *bhajan,* Gangasati asked Panbai to be firm minded and a woman of strong will. She says:

> Oh! The Meru Mountain may be swayed,
> But not the mind of the Harijan,
> Let the whole universe be shattered into fragments.
> But the mind uncorroded by misfortune.
> That is the true measure of the Harijan.
> (Tharu and Lalita, 88)

Gangasati's bhakti is different from her contemporaries Meerabai and Ratanbai. Meera worships Krishna in the form of a husband and accepts the feudal order, while Gangasati rejects the *saguna* bhakti and worships *Nirguna Nirakar.* Gangasati does not believe in the 'varnashrama' system. She and her husband challenged it openly and fearlessly. She writes:

> No division of caste and creed,
> High and Low
> In the Land of God, O Panbai I will show you
> That holy land.

Gangasati respected Panbai as a fellow human being. Not only that, she considers Panbai as an incarnation of 'vidya' in an age where women were considered as an incarnation of 'avidya' (ignorance). She advises Panbai to be consistent in learning: "Be consistent in learning and meditation."

Gangasati gradually teaches Panbai *Gyan Bhakti* and *Karmyoga*. She believes, "woman's emancipation is possible only through self-empowerment. Self-empowerment comes only through knowledge" (Jadeja, 25). She says to Panbai: "Only knowledge will lead you from darkness to light, from mortality to immortality" (Jadeja, 28). She advises Panbai to utilize every moment of life. While talking about the momentariness of life, Gangasati says:

> Momentary is the life O Panbai,
> Utilize every moment of life O Panbai.
> Suddenly life will come to an end O Panbai.

Gangasati preaches *Sayujya Mukti* to Panbai. At the end of her teaching, Panbai is empowered and starts composing poems by the grace of Gangasati. She writes:

> Eternal, immortal have I seen O devotee,
> He is the Lord of the Lord
> Blessed I am, looking at Him
> Tasted the bliss of Bhakti
> Says Panbai by the grace of Gangasati...

The last *bhajan* is an instance of female bonding between Gangasati and Panbai, who will continue and take further the tradition established by Gangasati.

Gangasati's life and works suggest how she carved her own space/identity within the patriarchy. She worked within the family structure and established her own female space. Her feminism is not anti-male or against patriarchy but she flourished as a poet by 'celebrating differences'. She enabled the empowerment of her daughter-in-law through literary communication. She has established a distinctly female literary tradition and developed a female literary response to male assertion, which makes her writings gynocentric.

- Some information about Gangasati's life based on the research, done by Shree Majbut Singh Jadeja, a retired IPS officer.
- Some scholars believe that Gangasati was a daughter of Vaghela or Zala family. But she was a daughter of Bhaijibhai Sarvaiya.
- Some scholars are of the opinion that the birthplace of Gangasati was Limdi but the research done by Jadeja says that it was Rajpara village in Palitana.
- Some studies say that Panbai was not related to Gangasati. She came as a companion to Samdhiyala. Panbai was a spinster and daughter of Hamirbhai Khawas.
- The time of Gangasati is between 1843-1894.
- Different versions of Gangasati's *bhajans* are available in different editions. Since she belongs to *Shruti Parampara* (oral tradition) we do not have any authentic edition of Gangasati's *bhajans*.

Works Cited

Buddha, Dhairyachandra, 2003. *Gangasati ni Bhajan Ganga.* Ahmedabad: R.R.Sheth & Co.

Jadeja, Majboot Singh, 1994. *Kahal Sangh Gangasati ane Panabi Ni Jivan Katha.* Bhavnagar: Pravin Press.

Meghani, Zaverchand (ed.) 1987. *Sorthi Sant Vani.* Bhavnagar: Prasar Press.

Rich, Adriene, 1997. *Of Woman Born: Motherhood as Experience and Institution.* New York: W. Norton & Co.

Ruthven, K.K., 1984. "The Gendering of Critical Discourse in Gynocritics." *Feminist Literary Studies.* Cambridge: University of Cambridge Press.

Sayalkar, Keshvlal, 1995. *Gangasati Akhyan.* Ahmedabad: Shree Pustak Mandir.

Showalter, Elaine, 1977. *A Literature of Their Own: British Women Novelists from Bronte to Lessing.* Princeton: Princeton University Press.

—, 1979. "Towards a Feminist Poetics". In Mary Jacobus (ed.), *Women Writing and Writing About Women*. London: OUP.

Spacks, Patricia Mayer, 1976. *Imagining A Self: Autobiography and Novel in Eighteenth Century England.* Cambridge: Harvard University Press.

Tharu, Susie, and K. Lalita (eds.), 1995. *Women Writing in India,* Vol. I. Bombay: OUP.

Vohra, Sunanda, 1995. *Gangasati Aem Boliya.* Ahmedabad: Ahmedabad Jilla Kalyan Sangh.

21

Looking Glass as a Metaphor for Self-Realization in Kamala Das' Poetry

JAVED KHAN

Professor of English, and Honorary Director, Centre for Training and Research in Language and Communication

Very few of Kamala Das' readers might contest the view that the woman in her poems is a rebel, a staunch feminist, rising in revolt against a phallocentric world order. Fewer still would make bold to challenge the charge of obscenity preferred against her. Even so, a majority of her readers would agree that the charge of nymphomania seems to hold but only on a facile reading of her poetry. The reason for this is that the female protagonist in her poems expresses her sheer contempt at the boorishness of vain glorious men. A close reading of her poems, however, would lead an alert reader to understand these as an attempt made to examine man-woman relationship quite systematically, even if a bit ruthlessly. Her's is a metaphoric quest for self-realization, which often betrays a sense of desperation with the existing scheme of things around her.

Metaphor, as a figure of speech, is an informal or implied simile. Myers and Simms (1989) explain that it is "a rhetorical figurative expression of similarity and dissimilarity in which a direct, non-literal substitution or identity is made between one thing or another". A looking glass reflects the image of a person stealing a look into it, or that of an object lying in front of or close to it. The nature of the reflection is dependent upon the make-up of the looking glass as well as a person admiring himself/herself in it, or an object it mirrors. A peep into the looking glass is likely to take one on an ego trip, presenting him/her with all those attributes he/she might have always craved for in life, or give him/her a rude jolt in exposing a persona minus the masks that he/she may be prone to wearing. Symbolically speaking, the looking glass has often been compared to *mãn* or mind in the Indian context in our various literatures including songs. The image mirrored in the looking glass is the real estimation of what we are if we were to accept the truths of life.

Myers and Simms (ibid) argue that one may apply (i) the genus/species classification of the variety of metaphors offered by Aristotle as analogical or proportional metaphors; or (ii) the Quintilian descriptive system, especially the first of the four classes: animate to inanimate as in case of person or object to its reflection; or (iii) the fourth of the classes: inanimate to inanimate as in case of the reflection to the self-realization it affords us. It is in a context of this kind that Kamala Das' poem "The Looking Glass" presents the readers with the image of Indian womanhood and the feminist sensibility.

The woman in Kamala Das' poems lays the blame for the collapse of the last link in man-woman relationship, i.e., the mutual desire for each other without any feeling of shame or remorse, squarely at the doorstep of man. Her verbal tirades against man puzzle me though the woman in her poems may feel justified in saying what she does as a representative of the womanhood, particularly so in the light of the fact that man-woman relationship which was clearly based on gender equality from the primeval times seems to her to have become unequal all of a sudden. Despite the fact that there are references to this in many poems by Kamala Das, I have tried to take a close look at "The Looking Glass". This is one poem, published for the first time in 1967 in one of her earlier collections *The Descendants*, seems to me to be a signature poem with Kamala Das because her fondness for it has made her choose it, close to 29 years thereafter, for inclusion in a collection of poetry titled *Only the Soul Knows How to Sing* published in 1996.

An old-fashioned word, the looking glass is used to refer to a mirror, or a piece of special flat glass that a person can look into and see himself/herself to decide what he/she looks/is like. In this context, the use of the phrase "a mirror of" something means whatever it may be that enables one to get a clear idea of what someone/something else looks like or is and, in the process, affording us the knowledge of what we look like or are. The intentions become clear from the title "The Looking Glass" with which the female protagonist signals to the readers her intention of enlightening them with the real nature of man in a man-woman relationship.

A superficial reading of the poem reveals the pain experienced by the woman in the poem. She begins by saying that it is easy for a woman to get a man to love her (make love), on condition that she be honest about his wants of a woman. The woman in the poem offers an extensive list of some free advice. She says that this is possible if and only if the following conditions are met:

- Standing nude before the glass with him to satisfy his ego with the knowledge that he is the stronger one of the two, much as she is softer, younger, lovelier than him, and begins to believe so.
- Admission that she adores him.
- Taking note of the perfection of his limbs, his eyes reddening under the shower, the shy walk across the bathroom floor, his stylish way of dropping towels to reveal his manhood, and the jerky way in which he urinated – every small, fond detail that makes him male and her only man in this universe.
- Gifting him everything that makes her a woman, including the scent of her long tresses, the musk of sweat

between the breasts, the warm shock of menstrual blood,
and all her endless female hungers.

There is a punch made explicit here with the expression "Oh yes." She seems to tell us that it is easy for a woman to get a man to love her. However, she needs to be prepared for the prospect of living without him afterwards. She calls it a living without life apparently as she moves around, meeting strangers, even as her forlorn eyes that had ceased searching for him, her ears that could only hear his last voice calling out her name, and her body which had gleamed at one like burnished brass under his touch, now drab and destitute, a pale shadow of the same.

One would not fail to notice that the rider is in the sense of "if and only if", which makes it a conditional sentence. Want is an extremely strong word, when used in English as a noun to mean a lack or something that one needs, but does not have. The context seems to suggest that the female protagonist in the poem is talking of needs when she uses the word wants. This seems to raise serious questions like: Why should a woman alone be honest about her wants? Is it that men do not have the same wants? Hasn't man made similar things dissimilar?

The female protagonist's outrage becomes clearer in the next few lines highlighting the humiliation that a woman must put up with in order to satisfy the male ego. It is here that the second meaning of the word 'mirror' (i.e., a mirror of something) comes into full play. One would not miss noting the irony there, and this apparently explains the use of that typically English expression, "Oh yes…" which contains within itself a strong emotion used to emphasize what one may be thinking, and polite disagreement with all or some of what has been said earlier. Thus, the protagonist seems to disagree emphatically with all that she had said earlier. Hence, the following statement: "…getting/A man to love is easy, but living/Without him afterwards may have to be/Faced" (lines 16-19). Thus, a poem like "The Looking Glass" apparently serves to warn women that they continue to face the distinct possibility of having to live without their men, who were their shadows as long as they had not given in to their overtures.

The female protagonists first love for a woman is her only real love. Her eyes search for the face of her first lover and her ears only hear his last purring voice calling out her name. She becomes oblivious to the rest of the world. All faces remind her of the face she adores and all voices sound a familiar ring in her ears. In short, forsaken by her lover, she is the dying image of what was once hunger and admiration. Quite evidently, she is spiteful of the fact that this is the painful reality of her existence, which man, proud and vainglorious that he is, cannot really appreciate. She also gives us the impression that it is indeed unfortunate on the part of man to treat his relationship with woman as one being merely limited to the duration of coitus, forgetting in the process that it represents an emotional unity for a woman. Implied in her complaints is the inequity of this relationship, which firmly repudiates the idea of unity and equality inherent in the Indian motif of Radha-Krishna.

Love and love-making, as represented in this motif, is an act of continual surrender and fusion into a single entity to form a wholesome unity. Thus, symbolic of unity and devotion, it is seen as a part of *līlā*. One does not have to stretch one's imagination to understand that Kamala Das takes it as something forming the basis of what she chooses to call *thapasya*, a phonetic corruption of *tapasya* in Hindi. *Tapasya* is a feminine form of the word *tap*, which is possibly derived from *tapas* meaning austerity, self-mortification, or self-restraint. *Tap* means penance or self-mortification undertaken with a view to attaining spiritual knowledge (*jnāna*) or salvation (*moksha*). It would be useful to bear in mind that sex in the sense of love-making is not a taboo in the Indian context, especially in view of the vital role it plays in creation. The worship of *shivling*, like the worship of the phallic symbol as a part of the Dionysian ritual at the time of harvesting season in the ancient Greek city-states, much celebrated in the Greek classics, provides one with sufficient evidence of how sex is not a taboo in the Indian tradition. *Shivling* is worshipped not only as a symbol of cosmogenic but also of progenitorial creation. Hence, the charge of obscenity preferred against Kamala Das appears to me to be a part of the standard male reaction, and let me make bold to draw attention to Das' reference to a standard male practice, where the shy walk across the bathroom floor, is used to buttress this point further.

The flamboyant, carefree, and even the-devil-take-you manner, if you please, in which Kamala Das gives expression to woman's response to male chauvinism in her poems through a candid discussion of the sense of frustration even in matters related to love-making is a healthy and welcome development in modern literature in Indian languages. It is true that the poems have been written in a typically confessional mode, but what can anyone have against that? Interestingly, the word 'confession' not only means an acknowledgement of a fact, sin, guilt etc., but also a statement of one's principles. Perhaps, that is what encourages Adil Jussawala (1973) to opine that Kamala Das' writing of love, sex and loneliness in the tone of an insistent confession "may be meant to touch some of the deepest points in the reader's subconscious" or be a "part of an elaborate private therapy" used to make the poet feel better. If this indeed be so, then, Kamala Das can be seen making an acknowledgement of fact and affirming her principles in life. One feels the need to examine the role such confessions play in touching the deepest points in the reader's subconscious, and how these may be a part of a private therapy.

The woman in the poems discards all masks and presents before the readers a picture of the suffering womanhood that has had enough and refuses to bear it any longer. She has been deprived of love that she had yearned for all along, and demands implicitly that her craving for equality in everything including love be accepted. Basically an Indian in terms of her sensibilities, she is a modern-day Radha seeking to resurrect her Krishna by whatever means it may be possible to do so. Her lament about the lack of devotion on the part of her man and the rough and callous treatment meted out to her as the object of his lustful longings must be understood in this context. What can she do other than rebel? She does so and quite effectively too!

It may be safe to assume that Kamala Das is a rebel much in the same way as the woman in her poems who is out to expose the parasitic nature of man in his relationship with his woman. The message she seeks to deliver through "The Looking Glass" is meant to shock womanhood rudely enough to awaken it to face up with the harsh realities of life vis-à-vis its relationship with men. There is another message too and that is one of warning to men to mend their ways and learn to behave sensibly toward their women, or face the prospect of their spurned women turning perforce to others for love.

The woman in Das' poems believes, perhaps, on the strength of her experience that it is not in man's nature to love. She berates the fact that whereas love for a woman is an act of giving, or surrender to the man in her life, her man takes it is his act of kindness towards her. Such an attitude seems to be born out of a false sense of superiority that man harbours. For a woman, love is a *tapasya,* and she seeks nothing except love and care. Thus, the woman in "A Losing Battle" concludes that "Men are worthless, to trap them/Use the cheapest bait of all, but never/Love" (lines 3-5; emphasis added). The readers get to learn subsequently that this cheapest bait is after all the "the wrappings of hairless skins," indeed a vulgar description of the female sexual anatomy. The contempt rings clearly in these words uttered by a woman who was slighted, or one who has lost all hope of her man ever being capable of love for her. Kindness, she seems to tell us, is his wont in matters of love and lovemaking because, being a man, he imagines himself to be superior to her. In other words, he refuses to accept the concept of gender equality. She recoils from the thought in disgust and, hence, the use of the word worthless, which makes it a classic case of pure lust.

A life without love, and love-making devoid of sincerity, sharing, caring, excitement, and attachment, which is an integral part of the process, is reduced to a mechanical ritual that robs it of all the feeling of satisfaction and the subsequent emotional equilibrium that it must invariably restore. The restlessness and pain arising out of such an unrequited love is simply shattering. While there is truth in the fact that men and women differ in terms of their physical make-up, there is also another truth that their needs are the same. Biological difference notwithstanding, the similarity of needs does not necessarily make one superior to the other, and this is what she seems to aver.

The Christian philosophy explains that Eve, the first woman caused to be created, was so created out of a rib from the left side of his body. This is also where the Indian philosophy related to the Radha-Krishna legend shares similarities because the divine Krishna caused Radha to be created by splitting his own body into two and Radha took shape out of the left side, giving rise to the concept of *ardhanāreshwar*.

The left portion of a human body contains the heart and thus a woman is ruled by her heart, which is why she is so loving and caring in nature. The painful implication of all this, I feel, is that man is left with all the cunning, scheming, selfishness etc., which is indeed an affront to those among the male species who cherish love and care.

Kamala Das seems to hint at this trait in man as the cause of his failure to accept the equality of the sexes. She states quite categorically in "An Introduction" that "he is every man/Who wants a woman, just as I am every/Woman who seeks love" (lines 44-46). In wanting a woman, a man only desires her body and not her love. Even so, the picture is different on the other side. In seeking love, a woman desires her man *in toto* – body and soul – something needed to requite love. Want and seek are words that beg a closer evaluation. Whereas want is a strong verb involving authority, power and a strong desire or need bordering on almost being an exclusive right, the verb seek is a meeker option meaning a search or an effort to find or obtain, something in all humility and submission. Kamala Das terms this act of seeking as *thapasya*.

Kamala Das uses the word *thapasya* for *tapasya*, which is but a corruption of the latter and means self-mortification or self-restraint. This is the other name for love in her philosophy of life. Self-mortification is seen as an act of hurting one's own feelings, thereby causing shame, anger, and loss of self-respect in some sort of a therapeutic effort to conquer the one's natural desires or those of the body through self-punishment or refusal of all comforts of life, causing their decay. Self-mortification is thus an attempt at the self-abnegation, and is useful for those who seek *moksha* or salvation, i.e., freedom from the never-ending cycle of births and deaths. An example of this is found in "The Conflagration" wherein the woman in the poem questions the idea of happiness and fulfilment of a woman in sex act. The poet seems to treat love as the source of salvation made possible through the comprehension of the ultimate truth of our existence. Actions of men and women are a cheat if caring and sharing involving both the partners as reflected in the concept of *ardhanāreshwar* is not restored.

A seeker is referred to in the Indian philosophy as a *sādhaka* and means someone who pursues spiritual discipline to attain the highest degree of realisation. Love can only be sought and not demanded. Philosophers and seers have used several epithets for love: caring for others, sharing with others, sacrifice, and the feeling of oneness and equality that knows no subjugation. Far from it. It is the sheer joy of the moment when all fuses into one – into a cosmic unity – something that Osho Rajneesh calls *sādhana* in his book *Sambhog se Sādhana Tak* (which I would roughly translate as *From Coitus to Meditation*). It becomes a source of pain when it is substituted by lust. Love-making, without the feeling of oneness and equality or of love, is an example of lust in action. Satiation of lust merely yields some sort of physical release but does not lead to the restoration of emotional equilibrium, which the fulfilment of love does. Kamala Das may not have stated so very explicitly, but she has implied it in several poems in lines like the one in "Jaisurya" in which she says, "Love is not important, that makes the blood/Carouse, nor the man who brands you with his/Lust" (lines 21-23). The woman in these poems experiences the same sort of fear as does an animal trapped by carnivores. The resultant effect is staggering and frightful. She reacts to the so-called sympathy and the mention of the physical aspect of love much in the same way as a bull does to a red rag. A situation of this kind reeks of slavery, thraldom: "It is a physical thing, he suddenly/End it, I cried, end it and let us be free" (lines 35-36 of "Substitute"). She finds it difficult to accept the fact that her man should give her a false feeling of being much loved in return for her love in coitus, and should shatter her pleasurable illusion by turning away after that. This is to her a complete rejection of the divine union. The passion, it turns out to be, was merely amorous and, therefore, the withdrawal is repulsive. One wonders if this has to do with the problem of ego in man who cannot accept the truth of even his momentary surrender to his woman. However, the woman in the poems takes this as man's brutal indifference to her need for love. Turning to rebellion, she experiments with promiscuity by surrendering in a fit of rage to young boys just stepping into adulthood.

She probably thought that she would get love from them but she meets with failure even with this crowd that she chooses to dub sarcastically as a band of cynics. This was only to be expected because, as she herself confesses, theirs was only a lustful longing for experience! The onset of adolescence leads to a certain hypersexual activity among the youth, whether male or female, for the sheer novelty of sexuality and experience, or an opportunity to prove their manliness/womanliness to the rest of their gang. Therefore, it should not surprise us that once their lusts were satiated, each one of the adolescent males parroted similar lines to what were obviously her cries for love: "I do not love, I cannot love, it is not/In my nature to love, but I can be kind to you" ("The Sunshine Cat", lines 9-10). The use of the negation not with the affirmative forms of auxiliaries, especially in do not and is not proves to be quite a revelation. Taking for example the first utterance, I do not love, we find on a close examination that it could imply (i) I do not love you, or (ii) I do not love you but I am only being friendly (assuming that do not has been used for emphasis), or (iii) I am simply doing what I am expected to do, or (iv) Love means nothing to me. The last one of the meanings fits in well with the following utterance: It is not in my nature to love. The revelation becomes more pronounced in the use of the contrasting subordinate clause, but I can be kind to you.

For the cynics, lovemaking was only an act of kindness – the idiomatic red rag! Juxtaposing this with the contempt of the mere physicality of the act, or what the woman in the poems contemptuously calls that kind of love in "An Introduction": "When/I asked for love, not knowing what else to ask/For, he drew a youth of sixteen into the/Bedroom and closed the door" (lines 25-20), we arrive at the meaning. What followed was supposed to be love as if "That was the only kind of love,/This hacking at each other's parts/Like convicts hacking" ("Convicts", lines 8-10). To hack at is a terrible phrase, which refers to the use of an axe for a rough cutting movement or blow, making the action here quite heartless. People may hack at wood but those who hack at the living things can only be called assassins, murderers. When proved guilty, they are convicted as murderers under the laws of the land. The implication is that violent lovemaking, devoid of love, leads to the death of that feeling because it is in no way a source of fulfilment.

The result, as we get to see it in "Convicts", is that after hacking at each other, "We lay/On bed, glassy-eyed, fatigued, just/The toys dead children leave behind" (lines 3-5). The spark of recognition, of fulfilment, of joy, when absent from the eyes of the so-called love birds after the event, makes them look like the lifeless toys left behind by dead children. The imagery in the phrase dead children is intriguing. Children, who are alive and kicking, are not likely to let go of their toys. Subsequently, the only natural reaction in "The Proud One" is that in spite of "loving him,/I found no courage then even to be kind" (lines 9-10). This is understandable. Such are the images one finds emerging from the looking glass, leading on to self-realization. One truth remains though: Love is not a *tapasya* any more as expected to be, thus violating the very concept of *ardhanāreshwar*!

The concept of *ardhanāreshwar* bears testimony to the fact that man and woman are the chips of the same block, a fact recognized in the Indian philosophy. Just like Lord Krishna, on his own admission, needs Radha for creation every Radha needs her Krishna. "The Looking Glass" presents the greatest irony of life wherein a man does not accept this reality, and it does so in a telling manner that characterises the poetry of Kamala Das. The woman in the poem accepts the inevitability of getting a man to love her but bewails the prospect of having to live her life without him afterwards – a frightening prospect Indeed! She laments the lack of understanding on the part of her man.

Kamala Das' poems deal with issues that are of common concern although the finer sensibility they bring with them may not be a part of our regular experience. The charge of exhibitionism hurled against her seems appealing but we need not allow ourselves to be carried away by it, for one would readily grant that her poems open newer vistas of awareness for her reader. We need to remind ourselves of the fact that all art conceals as much as it reveals and it is this inherent dichotomy that perhaps leads us to appreciate it. The artist has to fight a running battle with himself or herself to give adequate expression to 'self' in his or her artistic creation. It is a battle between the two selves within the artist: (a) that of the artist who desires to say it all, and (b) that of the private person in him or her who shies away from any revelation.

Overtly, Kamala Das stands exposed to the charge of being obscene but a foray into the inner recesses of the artist's mind through her poems is a revealing experience. Therein lies the saga of anguish and agony of the entire womanhood, which may not necessarily be of their own making. The façade easily shatters and the tautness of a carefree attitude gives way to a despair that "few of her poems have, in fact, escaped," notes Parthasarathy cautiously. The frank liberal-mindedness undoubtedly looks unusual in the Indian context, and more so, because the private person, the other self of the creative artist, seems to hold most of the traditions of the Indian society close to her heart.

The resultant resentment makes the woman generalize about men. She implies that they are beasts, lustful, licentious and heartless brutes! Love can never be replaced by lust because they are two contradictory things. Lust is a word that means a strong sexual desire, especially when uncontrolled or considered wrong. Love, on the other hand, is a strong feeling of fondness for another person, especially between members of a family or between people belonging to opposite sexes. To have a feeling of fondness is to be loving in a kind, gentle, or tender way. Love loses its sheen when the moment of intimacy lacks kind, gentle, or even tender handling of the loved one. Only strong and uncontrolled sexual desire is then left and this, in turn, becomes the motive of action. Certainly, this is an abomination for those who consider love as the greatest gift of God to humankind!

We neither know nor do we need to what impelled Kamala Das to write poetry of this kind. The subject matter of her poetry may not necessarily be the outcome of her personal experiences. After all, she is a highly respected citizen of this free country who has everything a woman would want to have. Our concern should not be the personal life of the artist, as T. S. Eliot rightly points out, while theorizing on 'depersonalisation' in art, but the focus of our inquiry should be the product. We must rest content to concentrate on the product of the artistic endeavour and the aesthetic value inherent in it. Never mind the sheer cynicism of the woman in the poems who turns the world of human relations and experiences into a kindergarten out of a deep sense of frustration. The irony is quite marked here. The girl child in the poem can be seen deriding the conservatives who do not understand that the world has changed. Incidentally, "Punishment in Kindergarten" shares a lot of similarities in terms of the experiential universe with Stephen Spender's poem "My Parents kept Me from Children Who were Rough", although the source of the trauma suffered by the protagonists in their childhood is different.

The subject of attack in that symbolism apparently seems to be on the lack of understanding and inexperience that informs the behaviour of the kids in the age group of two to five years. Kamala Das appears to suggest that the irresponsible and indifferent behaviour of adults is akin to the world of the kindergarten with all its disorderliness. The world we live in is full of categorizers, the tradition-bound conservatives, who want and expect everyone to fall into the slots meant for him or her. For example, they would like a girl to "Be wife.... Be embroiderer, be cook,/Be a quarreller with servants. Fit in. Oh,/Belong" ("An Introduction", lines 34-36). Their demand that a girl needs to 'fit in', 'belong', and thus be a part of the system evolved by the categorizers is not acceptable to the woman in the poem. The word 'belong' means to be suitable or advantageous or to be in the right place. The right place for a female, according to the conservatives, is the hearth and home because they feel that woman was created to be so. She is required to keep her man happy, and to do that successfully, she must satisfy his two hungers: one for food and the other for cohabitation. Clearly, this is abhorrent to the feminists of the radical kind and their sympathisers who believe in the equality of the sexes.

Categorizers are the main cause of inequity of the system they perpetuate. The flirting teacher in "Punishment in Kindergarten" wanted the girl-child to 'join the others' and, because she failed to do that, says angrily, "Why don't you join the others, what/A peculiar child you are!" (lines 6-7). She seemed oblivious of the fact that the little girl was trying to seek shelter in the arms of the cruel teacher. The teacher was so busy romancing with her boy-friend, whom she had brought along with her on picnic, that she had no time for her. The phrase, 'Join the others' – i.e., doing what is thought to be normal, usual – is the battle cry of the conservatives. One who fails to fall in line, fit in, and join the others is dubbed as queer, not in the derogatory sense, but in the sense of strange. However, one does not really know what they really mean after all. The use of the word peculiar as an adjective relates the child to what is strange or unusual, especially in a troubling or displeasing way. It would indeed be very unpleasant if people were to seek to perform the roles not assigned to them and insist on taking on other roles. Hence, the aversion of an average male to women taking on a militancy that is unusual in them and his reaction to their demands for the restoration of equality. I believe this to be the reason for the gender conflict and I am convinced that, like all revolutions, this struggle will herald the dawn of a new world order. Needless to say, the process has already begun.

Indian philosophy holds that the soul or the *ātmān* mingles with the *jīva* to make the *jīvātmān,* which binds the five elements called the *panchmahābūt*: ether, fire, air, earth and water. The body disintegrates, when the corpse is cremated, and the elements so released merge into their respective sources. A fact of this kind also supports the idea of equality. Identity of some kind is necessary for a being (*jīva*) and seems to be important in this world of *mithya* and *maya*. When a person learns to identify himself or herself, he is either hetero-sexual or homosexual/lesbian, and potent or impotent in his or her sexual orientation. A male who lacks sexual drive is usually considered to be impotent because the natural instinct is dead in him for whatever reasons. The woman in Kamala Das' poem, "Composition", asks herself whether she was indeed a normal human being, i.e., a heterosexual. If she were not to be so, then she can only be a lesbian (supposedly deviant in sexual behaviour) or else just plain frigid.

Kamala Das' poems can easily be taken to be the product of an exercise of both 'self-expression' and 'self-realization'. The spontaneity of expression may make them appear obscene because she does not mince her words. The simultaneity of the attempts to cling to the tradition and the yearning to help affect a change gives the poems a sharper edge. The ambivalence reflected in them, although at the superficial level, makes them all the more attractive. The 'I' in "An Introduction" represents all of us and the acceptance of this fact enables us to appreciate better our desire for change despite the fear of deviation. The Indian psyche accepts sex as an integral part of a categorical relationship that has social sanction. Any free public debate about it is a taboo even now as we watch the early years of the 21st century unfold a new dawn. Of course, we understand that this is sheer hypocrisy because sex is not only the means of creation but also a source of spiritual fulfilment bordering divinity. The erotic art in the Ajanta and Ellora caves provides evidence of how love was an art for our ancestors. The looking glass, which is a symbol of introspection, allows us the opportunity of making an honest reassessment of what we are because art mirrors life.

We expect intellectual honesty from an artist. True, the artist must work within the bounds of decency to define and redefine reality as well as human sensibilities. Honest expressions of truth are seldom obscene if they were to be seen entirely as fair. Or else, the cave paintings, the sculpture on the pillars and domes in our heritage sites, caves etc., which are but the symbols of our national legacy and pride, would also fall in the category of the obscene. Open expressions of love, of what love stands for, and of how love is different from lust are issues that make Kamala Das' poems what they are.

Love, says the reflection in the looking glass, is *tapasya* and not a cheap example of the lustful longings of the lovers in "The Freaks" whose minds "are willed to race towards love" but the race degenerates into an idle "tripping... over puddles of desire" (lines 6-9). It is not surprising that only "skin's lazy hungers" are unleashed as a result of the so-called race. Another ugly truth brought home by the reflection in the looking glass is the never-ending trauma of a woman doing everything possible to keep her hold on her man. The animal in him threatens to stray away the moment the eternal "other woman" flaunts "a gaudy lust" and is a "lioness to his beast" (lines 2-3 from "A Losing Battle"). Juxtaposing this with the complaints of the protagonist in "The Freaks" who has no other alternative but to master the art of flaunting "a grand flamboyant lust" as a "face-saving" device, perhaps, to keep her man from straying (lines 19-20), we discover how the age-old institution called marriage tames a woman to "fit in" and "belong" as per the dictates of the categorizers and their world, i.e., the metaphoric kindergarten! It is this that creates the crises of identity of all kinds, even the sexual identity.

The poem "The Looking Glass" has been used both as a poem to buttress home the point that the looking glass is Kamala Das' metaphor for self-realization.

Kamala Das must be credited with the fact that she accepts sex to be as ordinary a need for a woman as are food, shelter, security etc. The looking glass helps blow up several myths. Firstly, the myth that a woman is only a passive recipient as the society takes her to be. She gives expression to her disgust at the very thought that a woman needs to master the art of retaining her man using all her coyish styles. Secondly, the myth that woman is the silent sufferer of all humiliations because a man is also made to undergo these trials. She seems justified in demanding fairplay and equality in status on the ground that the soul knows no difference of sex, which is but only a biological fact. Lastly, the myth that the male is superior of the two is exploded in the light of the fact that nature did not make man superior though he was the first to be created because this could have been accidental. Woman is the creative principle as she sustains the foetus, and all religions recognize this truth.

She observes that love is life-giving and invigorating, for it is thought to act as a restorative. The looking glass confirms this to be so. The woman in Kamala Das' poems remarks that sex is not only the union of bodies but also of souls, and the looking glass helps us understand this truth in "The Doubt" wherein the protagonist, recovering from a long illness, realises that it was her soul which yearned for her man and not her emaciated body. This fact debunks the myth of deviant sexual behaviour, for sex does not always become the focal point of human relations. Kamala Das nods in agreement. She confronts us with the question of morality. The looking glass reflects the frowning face of the protagonist who seems to chide us by affirming how, like everything else in life, including truth, morality is also relative in nature, for each epoch in the life of a nation must seek to redefine it in keeping with the changing needs of the changing times.

Kamala Das observes that relationships need to be put on an even keel in tune with the rights of the individual in the drama of life. The looking glass presents us with the picture of ruined relationships, the series of events contributing to this sorry state of affairs, and helps restore a semblance of sanity by jolting us out of our slumber. Kamala Das confirms the view that the institution of marriage had been created for subjugation of the fairer sex. The image in the looking glass confirms this stand, positing it with the experiences taken from "The Sunshine Cat" and "Composition." Hence, the statement that the assignment of roles in marriage was "arranged in (the) most humorous heaven," though sarcastic, is indeed plausible.

Kamala Das confesses of women's failure in bringing about a change in the male psyche. Here the looking glass reflects a blurred image. Wait and watch is the name of the game after one comes to terms with the facts of life as does Kamala Das. The looking glass seems to assure the woman that changes are bound to come with the passage of time. She has by now attained self-realization and prepares for the promise of change to be fulfilled.

References

Myers, Jack and Michael Simms (eds.), *The Longman Dictionary of Poetic Terms* (New York and London: Longman, 1989).

Rao, B. Sridhar, *Sex Problems and Their Management* (Bombay: Jaico Publishers, 1977).

Walsh, William (ed.), *Readings in Commonwealth Literature* (Oxford: Oxford University Press, 1973).

Index